Amazing Facts II
Tons of Trivia

Thomas F. Shubnell, Ph.D.

ISBN-10: 1518752616

ISBN-13: 978-1518752612

Cover and interior design by TFS

Please ask your local library to carry my books.

We live in an interconnected world. Many are used to reading quickly, then going back and reading more background information later. I have included links within the text of this book.

Links are easy enough to overlook while reading, but available for further in depth reading online. For eBook readers, the links are live for easy clicking.

Autohagiography

If you enjoy this, you will also love, "Gracious Me . . . Is Nothing Sacred." A non-sectarian and hilarious look at all religions from the beginning of time. It truly proves that laughter is good for the soul.

Medical humor abounds in the best selling "Medical Humor - medical nonsense to tickle your funnybone. A great collection of medical funny stuff, including stories, jokes, and hilarious pictures and cartoons.

"Bacon Orgazmia" is a pandect of porcineology and a homage to the goodness and gallimaufry of all things bacon, including history, types, recipes, events, and more.

"Unelectum All" is a reader's digest of politics. It makes the case for change using politicians own words. It begins with early campaign promises and follows with political absurdities that unfold after elections.

A wacky book, "Men vs. Women, a Book of Lists" examines life from a different perspective and tells it all - the differences between the sexes are real and funny.

Even more fun can be found in "The Best of Terrible Tommy and Yucky Chucky," a collection of the best Terrible Tommy and Yucky Chucky jokes of all time.

More hilarious reading can be found in "Giggles, Gags, and Quips, Special Picks" a collection of the best jokes, pictures, billboards, stories, and cartoons.

Relationships can be funny, as shown in "Flowers, Foreplay, Facelifts, and Flatulence" a humorous romp through the four stages of relationships.

Also collect all the "Greatest Jokes of the Century" series of books. 25 wildly funny and hilarious compendiums of the greatest jokes, tidbits, stories, and trivia that are all sure to induce uncontrollable laughter.

"The Art of Installation and the Science of Implementation" is a serious project management primer, including tools and techniques for successful software implementation projects.

Don't forget to collect my Profound Thoughts, a 5 book series of great wisdom, aphorisms, and quotes from great minds.

Amazing Facts and Bite Sized Brain Food is a collection of thousands of amazing facts about the things you don't know, but want to know, and facts you think you know, but don't. Nestled in among the facts are bite sized tidbits of knowledge you can use to spice up any conversation.

All written by Thomas F. Shubnell and available online, your favorite bookstore, or as eBooks.

Table of Contents

Technology Facts

Interesting Technology

Artificial Singing Star - Singer Aimi Eguchi is Japan's latest artificial star. She is a member of the Japanese pop band AKB 48. Eguchi's character is entirely computer generated, using features from six other band members. She is the second computer generated singer in Japan.

Hatsune Miku, a computer generated cartoon, was the first. Miku regularly sells out 'live' concerts featuring 3-D holographic images of the singer performing on stage. *The statement to, 'not believe everything you see' is becoming more real every day.*

Video Glasses - Finally this technology is getting closer. I have been waiting for this since they first were developed a number of years ago. It was the same old story, high prices and low quality. Now, we are so close. The only thing missing is that most do not yet support wireless technology. Wouldn't it be nice to eliminate that monitor or TV screen and just wear cool glasses?

Vuzix has updated its line of video eye-wear and is compatible with both 2D and 3D content, the glasses display an equivalent of up to 75-inch screen as seen from a distance of 10 feet and feature separate focus adjustment for each eye as well as adjustable eye distance and viewing angles.

Weighing approximately 3oz with twin 1280 x 720 LCD, 16 million color displays with 35 degree diagonal field of view and 16:9 / 4:3 aspect ratio. Brightness, contrast, hue, and color saturation are adjustable via on-screen controls. It even has an adjustable nose bridge for folks that have a nose like mine.

Connectivity options include composite AV cable, component video cable, and AV cable for most videophones, portable DVDs, and camcorders, but no HDMI input or wireless connectivity. These can connect to PCs and laptops for game playing with VR head tracking.

Two rechargeable AA batteries for up to three hours of video playback or lithium ion batteries for up to seven hours. *I love technology.*
http://www.vuzix.com/home/

Moverio is an alternative $770 pair of glasses that is an 80 inch 3D experience and has a slot for a picture card and plays music. Not quite HD quality, but close.

Unwanted Calls - I have begun receiving calls on my cell and it is irksome. Some texts have also been coming through. Seems the scammers are losing too many home phone numbers as so many people are eliminating them to save money. Now the spammers are attacking cell phones.

There is a web site you can use to look up numbers at 800notes.com. It asks for a name, but no email address and you can type in your first name as many folks seem to do. Type in the number and you can see if anyone else has been called, plus details. I have used this before and it has very interesting information. The home page shows examples of comments.

There is also the government national do-not-call registry, donotcall.gov which I signed up for, but it seems many scammers ignore it. I just registered again.

PS - Some scammers call and claim to be from the registry and want to help you sign up. Do not fall for it. Go to the site and sign up for free directly.

Elementary my Dear Watson - IBM's Watson supercomputer, like the one that was used on the TV Show Jeopardy, is now used to evaluate cancer treatment options for Wellpoint, the Blue Cross and Blue Shield Association's largest health plan. It is also used as an adviser for oncologists at Cedars-Sinai's Samuel Oschin Comprehensive Cancer Institute in Los Angeles.

Cedars-Sinai's historical data about cancer, as well as its current clinical records, are being fed into a version of Watson that will reside at WellPoint's headquarters in Indianapolis. WellPoint will work with Cedars-Sinai physicians to design and develop applications that will help doctors prescribe specific treatments for patients.

IBM and Memorial Sloan-Kettering Cancer Center are adding the latest in oncology research, and the hospital's accumulated experience to Watson's vast knowledge base, and keep updating it. They said the result should help the hospital diagnose and treat cancer more quickly, accurately, and personally. "The capabilities are enormous," said Dr. Larry Norton, deputy chief for breast cancer programs at Sloan-Kettering. "And unlike my medical students, Watson doesn't forget anything."

If successful, the finished product could be used anywhere in the world to aid cancer treatment.

What's in a Name, TWAIN - TWAIN is a standard for communication between imaging devices (usually scanners) and computers. Because it is always written in upper case, it is often assumed that TWAIN is an acronym – with the "AIN" coming from 'acquired image network'.

It is not. According to the twain.org website, the word "twain" was chosen from Kipling's the Ballad of East and West, which coined the phrase "and never the twain shall meet..." to symbolize how hard it was to connect a scanner to a computer. It was changed to upper case to make it more distinctive.

That TWAIN has no relation to Samuel Clemens (Mark Twain), whose pseudonym was taken from the steamboat practice of calling out the depth of the water to make sure it was deep enough for the boat to safely pass. Mark twain meant the depth of the water to be two fathoms. *A fathom is about 6 feet. Twain is an archaic word for two.*

3D Printing First - Have written before how 3D printing is becoming more and more mainstream, but the following is amazing.

A 83-year-old female patient had developed a chronic bone infection and doctors believed reconstructive surgery would have been risky because of her age and so opted for the new technology.

A transplant jaw made by 3D printer claimed as first time a 3D printed object has been used in an operation. The implant was made out of titanium powder - heated and fused together by a laser, one layer at a time. Once completed, the part was given a bio-ceramic coating.

The lower jaw was fitted to the woman's face June 2011 in the Netherlands. Shortly after waking up from the anesthetics the patient spoke a few words, and the day after was able to swallow again. She went home after only four days.

ENIAC Facts - In February 1946, the first ever general purpose digital electronic computer was dedicated at the University of Pennsylvania. The machine was called the ENIAC (Electronic Numerical Integrator and Computer). It cost over $500,000 ($6 million today), weighed about 57,000 pounds and took up 1,800 square feet. It had 17,468 vacuum tubes, 70,000 resistors, 7,200 diodes, 10,000 capacitors, and 5 million hand soldered joints. It used enough electricity to power 114 homes. The longest time between vacuum tube failures was 4 days and 20 hours.

The first task it was to perform calculations pertaining to the development of the hydrogen bomb. It stayed in service for nine years.

Erasable Ink From Printers - Toshiba Tec has developed a revolutionary copier system that can erase printed text from regular copy paper.

The printer uses a special erasable toner, and when the printed page is passed through the color erasing device, the printing disappears and the paper can be used again. This toner can only be used with compatible copiers, but any regular copy paper can be used. The initial ink color was blue, but the company is working on other colors.

"This is a special kind of toner that loses its color when heated, so this technology makes it look as if the printing has disappeared. With this system, one sheet of photocopy paper can be used at least five times, so this product combines economy with ecology."

In addition, the FriXion Ball line of erasable ball-point pens and highlighters from Pilot, are based on the same principals as used in this system. The imprint from the printing process is slightly visible, so recycling sensitive documents is not recommended.

Hard Drive Capacity - Seagate has demonstrated hard drive technology that squeezes a trillion bits into a single square inch, claiming it is the first hard drive manufacturer to do so.

During the next 10 years, the company says, this will lead to standard 3.5-inch drives that can store 60 terabytes of information. Today's 3.5-inch drives (like the one in your current PC) give you three terabytes of storage, stuffing about 620 billion bits into each square inch.

To give you an idea of how much that is, the hard disk contains more bits in a single square inch than the Milky Way has stars.

Magnify Small Print - If you can't read that small text on cans, boxes, or anything and you have your phone or digital camera available, use the macro focus feature to snap a photo. You should be able to zoom in and magnify the text enough to read.

Reading and Viewing Tip - When you are looking at any page on your computer screen, including email, there is an option to hold down the CTRL key and move the scroll wheel on a mouse forward or back to make the size larger or smaller. If you do not use a mouse, you can hold down the CTRL key and click on the + (plus sign) or - (minus sign) to make what you see larger or smaller.

Finding Stuff - When you are reading a long page and just looking for a name, you can hold down the CTRL key and hit the letter F. A box will open on the bottom of the screen and you can begin typing the word. It will find and highlight that word on the page. This also works in Microsoft Word documents. If the word is not found, the box will turn pink to let you the word is not on the page.

Weird Tracks - NASA's Mars Curiosity rover does not have built-in GPS. The only way to track Curiosity's whereabouts and how far it has traveled is by following the six explorer's wheel marks.

For this reason, engineers put holes in Curiosity's treads so that every time the wheels turn, they leave a unique imprint on Mars. Orbiters photograph the print and scientists can determine how far the rover has moved.

The track pattern spells out "JPL" in Morse code through a series of "dots" and "dashes." JPL is an acronym for NASA's Jet Propulsion Laboratory, the agency arm in charge of Curiosity.

Ink Jet Printer Origin - A Canon engineer discovered this one when he set a hot soldering iron a bit too close to his pen. The pen reacted by spitting out ink just moments later, and the principle behind a new piece of tech was born.

Microsoft Suit - Microsoft threatened to sue a high school student named Mike Rowe for registering MikeRoweSoft.com. It claimed that it was copyright infringement, because it sounded phonetically the same as Microsoft. The student was a part-time web designer and thought it would be funny to add Soft at the end of his name.

When Microsoft found out about the domain, it asked him to give up the domain and offered to give him $10 to cover the registration expenses. He counter offered with $10,000, because he was upset at Microsoft's offer. Microsoft accused him of being a cybersquatter.

The case resulted in a PR loss for Microsoft, as the media portrayed it negatively. In the end, Microsoft flew Mike to its headquarters, gave him training as a developer, and an Xbox in exchange for the domain.

Ten Ideas for Your Smartphone - Your phone is a great place to keep information that you may need to access quickly. Here is a list of things to consider.

• A picture of where you parked your car.

• Printer cartridges showing refill numbers

• Any replaceable items around the house, like battery sizes, light bulb watts, air filter sizes, etc.

• Travel confirmation numbers. It may be quicker than sorting through a few hundred emails. Another trick is to forward the confirmation email to yourself just before you leave, so it is on the top of the stack.

• Pictures of current medications including prescription names and dosages.

• Pictures of furniture or wall paint cans to remember colors.

• Recipes or ideas from a magazine that you find while waiting for your doctor or dentist.

• Things that you might want to buy, like the brand of perfume or shampoo you saw.

Another smartphone trick is to add one or more phone contacts or notes with phone numbers to call in the event your wallet, passport, credit cards, etc., are stolen. You do not need to keep the actual credit card number (in case your phone is stolen), the company can look it up when you call.

Take a video of the inside of your home, including valuables and save it in the cloud. This is what an insurance company would love to see, in case of fire, flood, robbery, or other disaster.

Bonus Idea - Add an ICEmergency contact to your contact list for the person to be notified in case of an accident or medical emergency. You can also add an ICEmergency note with doctor names and numbers, allergies, medications, etc. There are also free applications (Apps) for this on iPhone and Android. If you are a caretaker for others, keep their info on your phone, also.

Quantum Computing Explained - Today's computers rely on electrons to deliver information in binary bits, or yes/no, 1/0, on/off. Laws of quantum physics allow bits to be in multiple states simultaneously so it has the potential to be millions of times more powerful than today's most powerful supercomputers.

Quantum bits, or Qubits are more versatile than standard bits because they can exist in three states instead of two. Current computers represent things as a one or zero, but a quantum computer can render a qubit as representing a one, a zero, or every fraction between one and zero at the same time.

An interesting thing about qubits is that by just looking at one, it changes its state, so scientists had to devise a way to look without the qubit knowing it was being looked at. (*Long story, but fascinating.*)

A 30-qubit quantum computer is approximately as powerful as a 10 teraflop computer. It can solve <u>10 trillion floating point operations every second</u> vs. an average computer, which performs about seven gigaflops (seven billion) per second. Quantum computers process multiple calculations at once vs. current computers, which process one at a time.

Google and NASA have a 512-qubit quantum computer housed in a 10 foot black cabinet, but do not expect to buy one for your home in the near future. The NASA Ames machine may be upgraded to a 2,048 qubit chip in the next year or two. *There are 25.4 million nanometers in one inch and fingernails grow one nanometer every second.*

Gorilla Glass Uses - Most of us know that Gorilla Glass is used as part of a touch-screen for hand-held phones and tablet computers. It was chosen because it is lightweight, durable, resistant to scratches, and tends to crack, rather than shatter when stressed, as Annie Davenport, a friend of mine recently found out.

Gorilla Glass, which is made by Corning is currently estimated to be in use by over a billion and a half devices and still growing. Corning makes the glass using a propriety chemical process that causes more than the normal number of ions to be introduced into the glass.

Now Corning has a deal with at least one car manufacturer to begin using the glass for windshields. The beauty of this glass is that it would cut down on the weight of the vehicle. It would also promote better gas mileage and better noise suppression.

Corning is working on another glass with unique properties, microbiological glass, which can kill bacteria on contact. Another exciting glass it is also working on is called Willow Glass, which is a bendable type of glass that is about as thin as a dollar bill. Bendable screens have been touted for use in foldable tablets for the past few years. *Samsung has one in the lab now, but I do not know if the screen is glass or plastic.*

Battery Facts - A major site compared 40 batteries using fast drain and slow drain technology. Its findings mimicked other findings from a number of other tests.

The data yielded some interesting results. First, highest price is not highest value, and second, zinc batteries, although usually the cheapest are poor value as they drain faster than alkaline and lithium batteries. Brand name has no relation to quality, but are usually higher priced.

Bottom line is that buying the cheapest non-brand-name alkaline battery is almost always the best value. Lithium batteries last the longest, but are almost always not the cheapest. In the tests, Ikea alkaline batteries blew away the competition for best value.

Think about how often you change batteries for everyday use items, such as TV remote, computer mouse, clock, smoke detectors, flashlights, etc., it is usually once every year or two, or even longer.

My advice - if you need long stable battery life (such as for a good camera), pay more and buy lithium. If you want the best value and do not mind changing batteries a bit more often, buy the cheapest alkaline you can find.

More New Types of Glass - At a recent industry show, Nippon showed off some new glass that is amazing. It first seemed like a joke as a sign said "Invisible glass" with arrows pointing into thin air. Visitors were asked if they could see the glass and many could not. There really was glass, but it didn't become apparent until viewed from the side. The glass reflects just 0.08 percent of the light that travels through it. A normal sheet of glass reflects about 4 percent of light. Nippon Electric Glass said it is targeted at museums where items need to be displayed, but protected.

It also showed off G-Leaf glass, which is so thin and flexible that it is supplied on a roll to customers.

It looks exactly like a roll of plastic film, but the 35-micron thick sheet is actually glass. It has been used in flexible display panels and can be gently curved around corners.

Nippon also showed the impact resistance of its chemically strengthened glass that is already used in smartphones and tablet PCs.

A sheet of Zero glass was on display and every thirty seconds a one pound steel ball dropped from a height of three feet onto a sheet of the glass the size of a small TV screen. Every time the ball fell, it bounced off the glass with no damage to the glass. *Sorry, no picture available for the invisible glass.*

Laser Headlights are Coming - Audi and BMW have been working on laser (Light Amplification by Stimulated Emission of Radiation) headlights available in for LeMans, Europe and to be introduced in the US on selected models as soon as approved by the

US FDA. They promise to be much better than the relatively recent LED headlights. The laser lights will put out more light and use two-thirds the power of LEDs, which use one fourth the power of ordinary headlights. They are also much more efficient and brighter than the current Xenon headlights used on some cars. In addition, they are just 10 square micrometers and 1/10,000th the size of a 1-square-millimeter LED.

The inventor of the headlights says Laser lighting may even do away with household LED and CFL lighting before either takes off. These new Laser lights are also ideal for businesses, signage, and projectors used in movie theaters, as well as smartphone projectors. The Laser lights are different than you might think of a laser beam. These lights are diffused blue beams and reconstituted to a white specific width for use. There is no danger of an accident creating a beam that could be harmful to the naked eye.

Einstein came up with the theoretical foundation for lasers in 1917 and they were first demonstrated in 1947. They have been in use since then for various applications, but almost always as a concentrated beam.

It took from 1879, when the incandescent light began until a few years ago for radical change, now we have another whole new generation of lighting in a few years. *In spite of the hype from manufacturers, it will likely be a few more years before we can buy one for our homes.*

Google Package Track - Here is a Google feature that may come in handy around the holidays. Track your packages by entering any tracking number into Google search and it will show you where your mail is. No need to login to USPS or FedEx.

Google Flight Info - Enter your airline name, flight number, and city of departure or arrival (separated by commas) into the Google search box and it will give you current information, including gate information. As mentioned in another post, you can enter your shipment number into the search box for status of your package from UPS and Fedex. *I love this.*

X-Ray Vision Glasses - Another of those inventions, which started out in comic books has just been announced. Evena Medical just unveiled its new Eyes-On Glasses System that helps clinicians see vasculature below the skin and deliver needles safely on the first try. Hard to locate veins are easier to see and access.

The glasses are based on Epson's technology like Google Glass, that can display graphics for the wearer to see, and has a pair of forward facing cameras for 3D imaging along with illumination to brighten the target. It uses multi-spectral lighting and the infrared and near-infrared frequencies the cameras uses are tuned for looking at vasculature.

In addition, the glasses include digital storage to enable verification, documentation, and telemedicine capability to share images remotely. The glasses also interface with hospital electronic medical records systems for documentation.

Television

TV Types - LG announced a new TV that has a 55 inch screen, is a bit less than one quarter inch thick (less than the width of a pencil) and weighs about 16 pounds. OLED means Organic Light Emitting Diode. It is the newest technology for TVs. It produces a picture far brighter than anything on the market. OLED emits light as opposed to LCD TVs which reflect light. This means that they are not good for outdoor viewing, but the picture is truly eye-popping good. Watch for much bigger screens with OLED displays in malls and other places.

At the Consumer electronics show (CES), Samsung introduced an LED TV, which is .3 inch thick. LED is newer than many of the current flat screen TVs and is brighter. Think of it as better than LCD, but not as good as OLED.

Am sure there will be many more goodies at the show and I will let you know if there is any wizbang technology ready to hit the street. In the meantime, do not buy a new tablet, like the iPad until the new models come out, because it always drives the price of the old ones down. That is not always true for TVs, because dealers are already marking down last year's models to make room for the new ones. TVs are not susceptible to new features every few months like other technology and we usually keep them longer than a few years.

A while back, I got rid of a 30-year-old TV and it cost me ten dollars to have it recycled. None of the new TVs will last a third of that time, but each new one will be more exciting to watch. Already in the labs is the next generation AMOLED (Active Matrix Organic Light Emitting Diode) which claims to be viewable in direct sunlight.

3D TV is still a technology in search of an audience. It will not be ready for prime time until the producers make 3D content, we do not need to wear dorky glasses, and the quality gets better. Watch for sports to be among the first to adopt the technology. *I am still waiting for glasses to replace the screen. They are almost ready for prime time and I hope to be first on my block to own a pair.*

PC TV - Google's Android operating system version 4.0, better known by as "Ice Cream Sandwich" (an alternative to Microsoft Windows), is used in a smart television, a 55-inch 3-D (240Hz refresh rate) LED.

The TV lets you switch among video on demand, Internet apps, and regular TV. You can share music, videos, pictures, etc., from tablets and phones and computers. It has a dual core processor, 1 gig of RAM, a hard drive and 2GB SD card. There is also a built-in 5 megapixel camera for video chats. The remote control features a touchpad, 5-way keys and a motion sensor. It can also respond to voice commands.

4K TV - Television manufacturers are always eager to shore up their business with new technology and are gearing up to roll out sets with what's known as 4K screen resolution. These TVs have about four times the resolution of 1080p screens, the current standard for high-definition sets.

Regardless of the size of its screen, a 1080p TV has about 2 million pixels arrayed across 1,920 vertical columns and 1,080 horizontal rows. Although electronics manufacturers haven't yet settled on a standard, 4K resolutions generally have at least 7 million pixels - and sometimes many more - arranged across about 4,000 columns and 2,000 rows. All those extra pixels allow 4K televisions to display images in much finer detail than HDTVs.

On bigger screen sizes at close distances, the difference between 1080p and 4K is stunning. At a close viewing range, HD video on a big screen can look pixilated, and colors and images can blur into the background. By contrast, 4K video looks super sharp and almost lifelike. At a further distance the difference tends to be less noticeable.

You might want to wait for 4K. The first 4K TVs will likely be outrageously expensive. Toshiba's 55-inch 4K television has been available in Japan for $10,000 or so. Another reason to wait is that no shows are being produced in 4K yet. In fact very few are produced in 3D so far, but ESPN is betting that many will love the 3D sports events it will be producing.

The 4K video processor should only add about $10 to the cost of a TV, but the big cost issue is the display technology. The ability to cram that many pixels into a relatively small space is on the cutting edge of display manufacturers' capabilities.

Manufacturers sold about 3 million 4K TVs during April, 2015 worldwide, but they are still very expensive and lack much 4K content.

See Through TV Screens - Samsung's new transparent LCD screen, is a breakthrough that could one day make any window into a display or touchscreen. The transparent screen is available to showrooms for display cases, but Samsung has been testing its invention on vending machines.

The clear glass on the machines' windows can advertise a particular product or display nutrition information. It has been a success, with sales in vending machines equipped with the transparent LCDs up 600% over others.

Normal TV screens require back or side lighting to display an image, but Samsung's transparent screen uses ambient light like sunlight or room lighting. That makes the product relatively cheap. New ideas for use might be bathroom mirrors, department store windows, and more.

Closed Captions Updated - Ever since closed video captioning was developed in the 1970s, it hasn't changed much. The words spoken by the characters or narrators scroll along at the bottom of the screen.

A team of researchers from China and Singapore has developed a new closed captioning approach in which the text appears in translucent talk bubbles next to the speaker. The new approach improves the viewing experience for over 66 million people around the world who have hearing impairments.

They put scripts around the speaker's face and synchronously highlight the scripts. The new technique shows the text appears in different locations and styles to better reflect the speaker's identity and vocal dynamics.

Using a technique called visual saliency analysis, it automatically finds an optimal position for the talk bubble so that it interferes minimally with the visual scene. Professionals can also further adjust the generated captions, such as moving the talk bubbles. When the speaker is off-screen, or a narrator is speaking, the words appear at the bottom of the screen as in static closed captioning.

Facts about Television - The first time color TV sets outsold B&W was in 1972. That was also the first year that broadcast satellite TV began, although cable had been around for years before that. Only 20% of U.S. households had two or more sets at the time, and almost all portable TVs (usually the choice for a second set) were still black and white due to the technology involved for color. By 1979 no more black and white consoles were made. About six channels were available for watching and the average screen size was 22 inches.

During the 90s the average screen size was 27 inches and the 'giant size screens' were 40 inches. The average TV screen size was about 47 inches in 2010 and averages 63 inches in 2015.

Robots

More Robots in Our Future - Hon Hai, the world's largest contract electronics manufacturer and owner of Foxconn, announced that it intends to build a robot-making factory and replace 500,000 workers with robots during the next few years.

Not long ago, Terry Gou and Masayoshi Son, the founder of Softbank from Japan, unveiled Pepper the robot in Tokyo. Masayoshi Son defined it as the first ever humanoid robot in human history. Pepper is able to read emotions from its human users through sensors, voice detection and cloud computing technologies. For instance, Pepper will have a different mood when its owner seems happy.

Hon Hai now has about over a million employees. The company signed a letter of intent to invest $3.3 billion in robots for its Taiwan factories. He said the robots will increase the production value of Foxconn by about $4 billion over the next three to five years and create about 2,000 new jobs. It plans to build most of the robots itself, due to lack of production speed from some suppliers. *Seems like some of the science fiction stories of robots making robots are coming true. The word Singularity leaps to mind.*

Dental Robot - Robots have come a long way in the past few years and it seems like their usefulness is growing every month. The new lifelike dental robot is used to teach dental students.

Technology is useful in so many ways. Better to let those students make their first mistakes on a robot, before getting into real mouths.

Robots in Healthcare - Toyota has developed robots for care support, in response to society's aging demographics. These robots have been co-developed with Fujita Health University. They utilize advanced technologies from Toyota, including motor control technology developed for automobiles, as well as walking control and sensor technology used in bipedal robots.

"The first feature I would like to show you is the independent walking assistance. Even people with one leg paralyzed, due to a stroke or the like, retain the use of their groin muscles. So they can swing the leg forward. The amount of swinging motion depends on the wearer's intention. If the person wants to walk quickly, there's a lot of swinging, and if they want to walk slowly, there is less, and this is detected by a sensor on the thigh. There is also a load sensor on the sole of the foot, to detect when it touches the ground. The wearer's intention can be detected using just these two sensors."

The brace and backpack each weigh 3.5kg, with the backpack containing a battery and controller. When a commercial version is released, the weight of the backpack will be halved, so this part will fit into a waist pouch.

The automatic walking assist robot has also been used in tests to help with walking practice. By changing the support force as the patient recovers, this system can help people to practice walking naturally from the start.

In addition, Toyota is developing a balance training assist robot using its Winglet technology for personal mobility, and a robot that helps move people out of a bed and into a wheelchair.

"Moving someone onto the toilet used to require two people, but it can now be done by one person. We think this could reduce the burden on caregivers' backs, and also help patients feel more at ease."

Internet and WWW

Web and Internet Defined - Internet technically began to exist in the form we know it on January 1, 1983 when its predecessor, Arpanet began using TCP/IP – the system of network communication still used today.

The web was invented by Englishman Tim Berners-Lee in 1989. The World Wide Web is made up of servers (which serve the pages) and clients (browsers like Firefox, Safari, IE, and Edge) which display the page.

The Internet is the set of technologies beneath the web which enable the web to exist. If the Internet did not exist, the web would not function. If the web did not exist, the Internet would still function.

Other programs that use the Internet and have nothing to do with the web are email, IRC (Internet Relay Chat), most internet messaging programs, newsgroups, BitTorrent, telnet, FTP, etc.

How Big is the Internet - Some experts say that the Internet is growing by an exabyte of data every day. To put that in perspective, an exabyte equals 250 million DVDs.

After an exabyte comes a zettabyte, which equals 1,000 exabytes. In 2011, no single data center could hold a zettabyte of information. Cisco predicts annual global IP traffic will surpass the zettabyte threshold in 2016, and the two zettabyte threshold in 2019.

The Internet will have up to 50 billion things (or devices) connected to the it by 2020; or, the equivalent of 6 devices for every person on the planet.

The National Security Agency is building a $2 billion data center in Utah that will be the world's first to store a store a yottabyte of data. That's 1,000 zettabytes or 1 million exabytes (or 1 million billion gigabytes).

Over half of Americans have watched TV streamed from the Internet.

Reminder Phone Calls - Is it me or is this just strange? Here is a site that you can use to type in a message and have it call you at some specific time to remind you with the message. There is one free try, then there is a charge by the minute. http://wakerupper.com/

Old Movies Online - If you are interested in old movies from the thirties and forties, including the famous Reefer Madness, Tarzan, Sherlock Holmes, Lamont Cranston, Inner Sanctum, etc., YouTube is the site to watch.

All the movies are in the public domain and free to watch. It also has current news programs from around the world and comedy, sports etc. Not much in the way of details, but the titles and descriptions provide some info.

Future Me - Received this goodie from my 'way much older' brother, who just had yet another birthday and who is likely planning something with this I do not want to know about. The site futureme.org allows you to send a free email message to yourself in the future. You can also send an email to others, but have to set up a free account to do so.

You can post-date it for anytime in the future, weeks, months, years. Might be fun to get something back that you were thinking now or planning for the future to remind yourself of the plan. . . and answer for it. It cautions to not use work email addresses, lest you change jobs.

The site has many copies of emails that others have sent and allowed the site to post. It has also made a book of some of the emails. Great fun and might honestly answer the question, "How did that work out for you?"

Free Google Calendar - Free online calendar application called Google Calendar. If you have a Google account, you can create a Google Calendar. If you don't have one, you can register for a free account.

You can use Google Calendar to schedule events and invite people to participate. By sharing folders, you can compare your schedule with other users. If everyone keeps his or her calendar up to date, it's easy to avoid conflicts. A single user can open multiple calendars and view all the scheduled events in a single window. Google displays each calendar's events in a different color.

Google includes its search feature within the Google Calendar system. You can search for specific calendars. Calendar owners can choose to keep a calendar private or share it openly with everyone. you can also set it up to send you an email to remind you of events in the calendar.

New Internet - June 6, 2012 marked the beginning of the new internet. The good news is that it happened with little fanfare and almost no one noticed. The old Internet is almost out of room. The new Internet is vastly bigger. It's ready for trillions and trillions more computers, devices, web sites, etc.

In order to be on the Internet, a device or Web site needs an address. The old Internet had about 4.3 billion IP (Internet protocol) addresses. The original inventors never thought they would run out of numbers, but today, there are more mobile phones in use than that. The new Internet allows for about 40 trillion trillion trillion (or, 340,000,000,000, 000,000,000,000,000, 000,000,000,000) addresses.

This new Internet is known as Internet Protocol version 6 (IPv6) and the old Internet is IPv4. (IPv5 was scrapped).

Here's an example of what an old Internet address looked like: 192.0.2.1. Here is an example of a new IPv6 address: 2001:0db8: 85a3:0000:0000: 8a2e:0370:7334.

Network engineers have been working on this for years and you shouldn't notice anything different as they completely switch everything from the old Internet to the new Internet, which will take a few more years. As of mid 2015 the majority oc countries are less than one percent IPv6 compliant.

If you are going to sign up for a new ISP (service provider) or buy a new home router or launch a new Web-based business, make sure it works with IPv6.

Even though the new Internet is totally turned on, not every network provider has become IPv6 compliant. Many businesses have been spending millions of dollars and years to upgrade their networks.

Over time, the new Internet will have all kinds of devices (things we can't even imagine) connected to the Internet, like every appliance in your home, medical sensors, and much more.

Social Site Facts - Facebook has 901 million users, Twitter has 555 million users, Google+ has 170 million users, and Linkedin has 150 million users. The average user spends 405 minutes on Facebook, 89 minutes on Twitter, 3 minutes on Google+, and 21 minutes on Linkedin.

English and the Internet - According to the translation firm Smartling, native English speakers only represented 3% of the total Internet population in 2011. Yet, 56% of online pages are English-only.

Many would not spend time on a Japanese website without understanding Japanese if Google Translate didn't exist. Conversely, many would not spend time on an English website without an online translator.

Download vs. Upload - These words seems to confuse many people when discussing computer usage.

Download is taking something on the Web/Internet or a main company computer and putting it on your personal computer, such as programs or updates. Think of the Web/Internet as the big computer in the sky that drops stuff down to your device.

Upload is taking something on your computer and putting it up on the Web/Internet or company computer, such as photos or files.

Internet and Devices - During 2012, there were more mobile devices in the world than people, according to Cisco's annual report. At the same time, many of the world's population do not yet have Internet access. Analysts are predicting 25 billion smart devices in circulation during 2020.

Interesting Internet Tidbits - According to Massachusetts Institute of Technology, more information now crosses the Internet every second than the entire Internet stored 20 years ago. It says, every hour Wal-Mart Stores Inc. collects 50 million filing cabinets' worth of information from its transactions with customers.

Cloud computing is the practice of using a network of remote servers hosted on the Internet to store, manage, process data, and run applications, rather than a local device. The services usually charge monthly fees.

Microsoft has unveiled a system that can translate what you say into Mandarin and play it back in your voice.

The Google Now personal assistant can tell you if there's a traffic jam on your regular route home and suggest an alternative.

Apple's Siri can reschedule an appointment.

IBM's Watson supercomputer can field an awkwardly worded question, figure out what you are trying to ask, and retrieve the answer for you.

Top Ten Web Facts - There are 14.3 trillion web pages on the World Wide Web.

68.8% of all email traffic is spam. (back in 2008, 53.8 trillion spam emails were sent).

51% of all spam is about pharmaceuticals, the top category of all spam.

30.8% used Internet Explorer in 2012 (in 2008 it was 70%).

43% of the top 1 million websites are hosted in the U.S.

44.8 % of internet users live in Asia.

11.4% of internet users live in North America.

68.4% of smart phones use Android operating system (introduced Sept 2008) vs. iPhone (introduced June 2007) 19.4%.

4 billion hours of video are watched on YouTube each month.

In 2012, there were 2.7 billion likes on Facebook each day and 5 billion Google's +1 button each day.

Internet Usage - Iceland (96%), Norway (95%), and Sweden (94%) have the highest percent of populations using the Internet. The Netherlands, Denmark, Luxembourg, Bermuda, and Finland all have over 90% of their respective populations using the net.

Canada is 16th with 86% of its population using the Internet. The US ranks 28th, with 78% (244 million people) online.

China has 591 million people using the Internet, but that is just 44% of the country's 1.3 billion population.

Future of the Internet - Cisco does annual predictions about the internet and here are few interesting predictions for the year 2017.

In the year 2017 more data will move on the internet than the beginning of the internet.

The Asia pacific region will generate 36% of all internet traffic by 2017.

There will be 3.6 billion internet users.

There will be over 19 billion connection.

Internet speeds will be 3.5 times faster than 2012.

Almost half of the world's population will have internet access.

Personal tablet access will increase from 27 million 2012 to 190 million.

Overall tablets will be about 425 million.

More than 827 million TVs will have internet access.

Average household internet traffic will increase from equivalent 13 hours of HDTV to 30.

Smartphones and tablets will increase to 29% of all usage and PCs will slip from 88% to 57%.

Cisco has proven to be very accurate in its past predictions about the net.

National Telephone WEA

The federal government implemented a centralized system of control over all communications, with the announcement that all new cell phones are required to comply with the program, which will broadcast emergency alert messages directly to all Americans' cell phones and other connected devices.

WEA (formerly PLAN) was established pursuant to the Warning, Alert and Response Network (WARN) Act. Participating wireless carriers were required to deploy WEA by April 7, 2012.

Although users can opt out of receiving the alerts from FEMA and the Amber Alert program, messages direct from the president will be mandatory.

The thought of cell phone users being forcibly targeted with text messages from Barack Obama during the election season has obviously caused concerns that the emergency alert system could be exploited for political reasons.

The system went live in the New York and Washington Metro areas in December, 2011 and caused panic in New Jersey after Verizon customers received text messages warning them that a "civil emergency" was in progress and to take shelter. This prompted alarmed citizens to flood 911 lines with anxious calls.

Verizon Wireless later apologized to its customers for causing alarm, admitting that the confusion was caused by a "test" of the emergency alert system.

The emergency alerts are designed to be incorporated into the Intellistreets system which turns all street lights into surveillance hubs that can record conversations and broadcast messages.

The alerts are geographically targeted to cell towers in the location of an emergency. Phones that are using the cell towers in the alert zone will receive the WEA. This means that if an alert is sent to an area in New York, all WEA-capable phones in the alert area can receive the WEA, even if they are phones that are roaming or visiting from another state.

Consumers will receive only three types of alerts:

- Alerts issued by the President,

- Alerts involving imminent threats to safety or life,

 -Amber Alerts.

Participating carriers may allow subscribers to block all but Presidential alerts.

For the first time ever the government will have a direct line to millions of Americans who use cell phones. *Between this and the GPS required on all cell phones, we no longer need worry about being alone.*

Moravec's Paradox

Hans Moravec, adjunct faculty member at the Robotics Institute of Carnegie Mellon University, pointed out that machine technology mimicked a savant infant. Machines can do long math equations instantly and beat humans in chess, but they cannot answer a simple question or walk up a flight of stairs (until recently). He, along with many others has been working to solve that paradox and help computers evolve on their own.

Early artificial intelligence (AI) researchers believed intelligence was characterized as the things that highly educated scientists found challenging, such as chess, symbolic integration, and solving complicated word algebra problems. They thought, if those could be done so easily by computers, things that children of four or five years could do effortlessly, such as visually distinguishing between a coffee cup and a chair, or walking around on two legs, or responding to words would be infinitely easier for computers to learn.

Computers/robots are finally beginning to move and think like people. Narrative Science can write earnings summaries that are indistinguishable from wire reports. We can ask our phones, 'I'm lost, help.' and our phones can tell us how to get home. (The smartphone was introduced in 2007.)

Computers that can drive cars were never supposed to happen and ten years ago, many engineers said it was impossible. Navigating a crowded street requires a combination of spacial awareness, soft focus, and constant anticipation. Yet, today we have Google's and other self-driving cars and they have been approved by some states as allowable on city streets. *Ten years from impossible to common.*

IBM, working with Memorial Sloan-Kettering cancer information is using its computers to diagnose diseases and the Cleveland Clinic, among others to help train aspiring physicians. It just invested a billion dollars to set up 'Watson' into a separate business unit for medical and other complex decision making activities.

Bottom line, we are experiencing solutions to the paradox and it is very exciting, although I am not sure machines will ever replace human emotions or that we will ever want to.

Wordology

FUN WITH WORDS

When looking up a particularly complex topic on Wikipedia, you might try replacing the "en" (for English) with "simple" in a Wikipedia URL. You will then get information written using simple English words and grammar that should make the most complex topics easy to understand.

Aluminum vs. Aluminium - Aluminum is the older term, while aluminium was created later by the British to make it sound more like the other elements.

In 1807 Sir Humphrey Davy isolates the metal for the first time and called it alumium.

During 1812, he changed the spelling of his element to aluminum (adopted in the United States)

That same year, British scientists disliked the new name and changed it to aluminium to match the other classic sounding elements, such as Magnesium, Helium, Potassium, etc.

Most countries use the ending "-ium" for "aluminium". In the United States and Canada, the ending "-um" predominates.

That's my symposium on aluminium. - Incidentally, the Greek symposium was originally a drinking party and forum for men of good family to debate, plot, boast, or simply to revel with others.

Get Off the Dime - "Get off the dime" dates back to the days of dance halls and "taxi dancers," women employed by the halls to dance with strangers, usually for ten cents per dance (immortalized in the 1930 Rodgers and Hart song "Ten Cents a Dance").

A contemporary account, published in 1925, explains the phrase: "Sometimes a ... [dancing] couple would ... scarcely move from one spot. Then the floor manager would cry 'Git off dat dime!'" Similarly, "dancing on the dime" meant to dance very closely with very little movement, behavior that might well attract the attention of the Vice Squad and get the hall closed. Thus "get off the dime" referred both to the the customer as the "dime" he had paid and to the small spot ("dime") on the floor where the couple seemed frozen.

Paint the Town Red - This colorful saying means to spend a wild night out, usually involving drinking. It probably originated on the frontier. In the nineteenth century the section of town where brothels and saloons were located was known as the 'red light district'. A group of lusty drunken cowhands out for a night on the town might see the whole town as red. The saying is still use around the world to mean the same thing, a bawdy area of town. Many foreign city sections got the same name from visiting GIs during their tour of duty.

Stump Someone - Stumping someone now means ask someone a question they can't answer.

Pioneers built their houses and barns out of logs and frequently swapped work with neighbors when clearing new ground. Some frontiersmen would brag about their ability to pull up big stumps, but it was not unusual for the boaster to suffer defeat with a stubborn stump and he bacame stumped.

Grawlix - It is the term for a string of typographical symbols, especially "@#$%&!", used to represent an obscenity or swearword. Also, a series of violence related images in a speech bubble to represent obscenity or swearwords. It was likely coined by cartoonist Mort Walker in the 1960s. He penned Beetle Bailey and Hi and Lois comic strips.

Jumbo - Jumbo was a large African bush elephant, born 1861 in the French Sudan, imported to a Paris zoo, transferred to the London Zoo in 1865, and sold in 1882 to P. T. Barnum, for the circus. The giant elephant's name is now a common word 'jumbo', meaning large in size.

Top of The Morning to You - This phrase appears to not be originally Irish, although some have said it has been Irish and out of use for hundreds of years. Hollywood keeps it alive, along with the response, "and the rest of the day to yourself."

It was used in Theodore Cyphon, a novel by George Walker, published in 1796. The protagonist is greeted not long after landing on the shore of Essex, "Halloo! you teney" cried one, "The top of the morning to you. Have you seen pass a tall chap, in a light blue coat, with striped trowsers."

Put on Your Thinking Cap - To put one's thinking cap on means to take time to think something over. It likely has its origins in the 17th century when jurists and other scholars commonly wore tight-fitting, square caps. An English judge of this era would put on his 'considering cap' (white wig) before passing sentence in all cases.

Follow up - A new paper in the Journal of Experimental Social Psychology finds that "wearing a white lab coat, a piece of clothing associated with care and attentiveness, improved performance on tests requiring close and sustained attention." The researchers found no effects when the coat was identified as a painter's coat. "The main conclusion that we can draw from the studies is that the influence of wearing a piece of clothing depends on both its symbolic meaning and the physical experience of wearing the clothes. There seems to be something special about the physical experience of wearing a piece of clothing."

Hoisted by His Own Petard - Many have heard this statement. Here is the background. Shakespeare, in Hamlet, act III, scene 4, lines 206 and 207: "For 'tis sport to have the engineer/ Hoist with his own petar ..."

The Dane is chuckling over the fate he has in store for his childhood comrades, Rosencrantz and Guildenstern, who are plotting to have him killed. Deferring his existential crisis for a moment, Hamlet turns the plot on the plotters, substituting their names for his in the death warrant they carry from King Claudius.

He continues: "But I will delve one yard below their mines/ And blow them at the moon." The key word is "mines," as in land mines. A small explosive device designed to blow open barricaded doors and gates, the petard (or "petar," as Shakespeare wrote) was a favorite weapon in Elizabethan times.

Hamlet was saying, figuratively, that he would bury his bomb beneath Rosencrantz and Guildenstern's bomb.

The word "petard," comes the Latin peditum, to break wind. So, a small explosion.

Wenis - It is pronounced wee nis. The skin on the end of your elbow. It is also the name of an Egyptian pharaoh of the fifth dynasty.

Hagiography - Hagiography is the study of saints and refers literally to writings on the subject of such holy people, and specifically to the biographies of saints and ecclesiastical leaders.

Christian hagiographies focus on the lives, and notably the miracles of men and women canonized by the Roman Catholic Church, the Anglican Communion, the Eastern Orthodox Church, the Oriental Orthodox Church, and the Church of the East. Other religions such as Buddhism and Islam also create and maintain hagiographical texts concerning saints and other individuals believed to be imbued with the sacred.

The term "hagiographic" has also been used as a pejorative reference to the works of biographers and historians perceived to be uncritical or reverential to their subject. *Almost all my books begin with an autohagiography.*

Knock Off Work - The phrase, which means to quit work for the day, originated in the days of ships propelled by oarsmen. To keep the oarsmen rowing in unison, a man with the gift of perfect rhythm would beat time on a block of wood; when it was time to rest or change shifts; he would give a special knock. The term to knock off became popular in the late 1800s and early 1900s.

Blond vs. Blonde - You see the words used interchangeably, but there actually is a difference. The difference is gender. When referring to a woman with yellow hair, you should use the feminine spelling 'blonde'. When referring to a male with yellow hair, you should use the spelling 'blond'.

Gymnasium - The word gymnasium comes from the Greek gymnazein, which means 'to exercise naked'.

Glass Slippers - Cinderella's slippers were originally made out of fur. The story was changed in the 1600's. The glass slipper is likely to have arisen from a confusion between the French, "une pantoufle en vair" (a fur slipper) and, "une pantoufle en verre" (a glass slipper.)

Dog Days of Summer - The earliest reference to some aspect of this expression goes way back to the Ancient Egyptians. They noted that the heliacal rising of the star Sirius heralded the hottest part of the summer. The star's hieroglyph is a dog. Sirius would appear in Egypt just before the season where the Nile typically floods. So it is thought the star's hieroglyphic symbol being a dog symbolized a 'watchdog'.

It is the brightest star in what is now known as the Canis Major (Latin for Greater Dog) constellation. It's rising marked the start of the hottest part of the year, which then became the 'Dog Days'.

The Roman's and Greeks had expressions for Dog Days. They both believed that, when Sirius rose around the same time as the Sun, this contributed to that time of year becoming hotter. As such, they would often make sacrifices to Sirius, including sacrificing dogs, to appease Sirius with the hope that this would result in a mild summer and would protect their crops from scorching. *Seems to me that offering dead dogs to a dog might not please him as much as they thought.*

Stuffed Shirt - Someone who is pompous and conceited is called a 'stuffed shirt'. The description goes back to American women's fashion in the early 1900's. At that time, women wore 'shirtwaists'. These were dresses or blouses tailored like shirts.

As dummies were not yet in existence, stores displayed the garments in their show windows stuffed with tissue paper. They may have looked good from afar, but on closer inspection they were flimsy, without substance.

Petrichor - This word describes the scent of rain on dry earth. The word is constructed from Greek, *petra*, meaning *stone* + ichor, the fluid that flows in the veins of the gods in Greek mythology.

The term was coined in 1964 by two Australian researchers, Bear and Thomas, for an article in the journal *Nature*, where the authors describe how the smell derives from an oil exuded by certain plants during dry periods and is absorbed by clay-based soils and rocks. During rain, the oil is released into the air along with another compound, geosmin, producing the distinctive scent. *Now you have a name for that great aroma.*

Going Dutch - Some pejorative expressions using Dutch were created through cultural enmity between the English and the Dutch during their fight for naval supremacy in the seventeenth century. Some included: Dutch reckoning (a bill presented without any details and which gets bigger if you argue), Dutch widow (a prostitute), and Dutch feast (an alcohol-fueled event in which the host gets drunk ahead of his guests).

Others, including *Dutch courage* and *Dutch uncle*, *Going Dutch*, *Dutch lunch*, *Dutch treat*, *Dutch party*, and *Dutch supper*, all with closely similar meanings, are American creations from the nineteenth century. They were used in the literal sense of a meal reflecting a particular culture.

The evidence shows they were more correctly German, as in Pennsylvania Dutch. A newspaper report in 1894 mentions that for a Dutch supper to be successful everything must be "consistently expressive of the fatherland" and mentions rye bread, cabbage salad, Wienerwursts (hot dogs), and beer. Americans invented the terms based on their observations of the habits of the immigrants. Early users applied them as straightforward descriptions and not as derogatory terms. *So, let's do lunch, Dutch treat.*

Six Types of Collectors - *Deltiologists* study and collect postcards.

Phillumenists collect matchbooks and other match-related items. The world's top phillumenist has a collection of over 700,000 different labels.

Pannapictagraphists collect comic books and probably can't even spell what they are.

Vexillophiles collect and display flags.

Plangonologists are collectors of dolls.

Arctophiles collect teddy bears.

Moot - This definition from the Oxford Dictionary may surprise you. Definition of moot: adjective
1 subject to debate, dispute, or uncertainty: whether the temperature rise was mainly due to the greenhouse effect was a moot point
2 North American having little or no practical relevance: the whole matter is becoming increasingly moot
- verb, raise (a question or topic) for discussion; suggest (an idea or possibility): the scheme was first mooted last October. *This whole thing is becoming moot.*

Third Degree - To get the third degree means to be thoroughly questioned. The third degree of something has been regarded as the upper limit, or extreme since before the time of Shakespeare when he wrote, "For he's in the thirde degree of drinke, he's drown'd." He was referring to a very drunk man. It is a natural progression when referring to the most extreme type of questioning, it would be referred to as the third degree. It has come to also mean inflicting of pain, physical or mental, to extract confessions or statements.

In Masonic Lodges there is also the rituals involved before reaching the third, or highest level, which includes intense questioning. The Knights of Columbus have the third degree as the highest to be obtained, before reaching Sir Knight.

Taser - Few people, including police know that Taser stands for Thomas A. Swift's Electric Rifle.

"Tom Swift and His Electric Rifle; or, Daring Adventures in Elephant Land" was a young adult novel published in 1911. It was one of a series of more than a hundred books about Tom Swift, with the most recent series in 2007.

In the novel, Swift's invention of the electric rifle, which fires bolts of electricity can be calibrated to different levels of range, intensity, and lethality. It can shoot through solid walls without leaving a hole, and is powerful enough to kill a rampaging whale. With the electric rifle, Tom and friends bring down elephants, rhinoceroses, and buffalo, while he saves their lives several times in battle with the red pygmies.

In one book, written in 1912, Tom develops a telephone that can actually send pictures.

The Taser was really invented by Jack Cover, completed in 1974, and marketed by Taser International.

Called on the Carpet - To be called 'on the carpet', i.e. for reprimand by superior, is likely an early 1900's, American colloquial, from one's uncarpeted work area to carpeted offices of one's superior.

During the early 1700s it also referred to a cloth (carpet) covering a conference table and therefore came to mean "under consideration or discussion." In 19th-century America, however, carpet meant "floor covering," and the expression, first recorded in 1902, alluded to being called before or reprimanded by a person rich or powerful enough to have a carpet.

Grand Slam - The immediate origin was from the card game, Bridge. Grand slam means to take all 13 tricks in a hand.

It has since come to take on other meanings, such as in tennis to win all four major singles titles; the Australian Open, the French Open, Wimbledon, and the US Open in one year. A grand slam in golf is to win; Masters Tournament, U.S. Open, British Open, and PGA Championship in one year. It is used in baseball to signify hitting a home run with all bases loaded.

Chess, Curling, Rugby, and other sports each have a grand slam definition of their own.

Denny's restaurant chain is famous for its Grand Slam breakfasts consisting of various combinations of meat, eggs, bread, and pancakes. We also cannot forget Grand Slam Pizza in Dripping Springs, Texas.

Ten-Four, Roger That -The ten-codes or ten-signals are code words used as stand-ins for common phrases in radio communication, such as *ten-four*, meaning message received.

Charles Hopper, a communications director with the Illinois State Police, developed them in 1937 to combat the problem of the first syllables or words of a transmission being cut off or misunderstood. Preceding every code with "ten" gave the sometimes slow equipment time to warm up and improved the likelihood that a listener would understand the important part of a message. The codes also allowed for brevity and standardization in radio message traffic.

The codes were expanded by the Association of Public-Safety Communications Officials-International (APCO) in 1974 and were used by both law enforcement agencies and civilian CB radio users. Over time, differing meanings for the codes came about in different agencies and jurisdictions, undoing the codes' usefulness as a concise and standardized system. The problem came to a head in 2005 during rescue operations after Hurricane Katrina. After several instances of inter-agency communication problems, the United States Federal Emergency Management Agency (FEMA) discouraged the use of ten-codes and today the federal government recommends they be replaced with plain, everyday language.

In the days of the telegraph, the Morse code letter *R* (dot-dash-dot) was sometimes used to indicate "received" or "message received/understood." When radio voice communication began to replace telegraphs, *Roger*, the code word assigned to the letter *R* in the radio alphabet used by all branches of the United States military from 1941 to 1956, took on the same role.

Roger means "last transmission received/understood." *Wilco* (**Will Co**mply) is the code used if the speaker intends to convey "message received and will comply." The phrase *Roger Wilco*, often heard in the movies, is redundant and not really used since *Wilco* alone acknowledges receipt of message and states intent to comply.

    Skid Row - The term Skid Road or Skid Row, a slang term for a run-down or dilapidated urban area, was an actual road in Seattle, Washington during the late 1800's. The real name of the road was Yesler Way (now better known as Pioneer Square), and it was the main street along which logs were transported. It soon became a rather sketchy street that loggers began to call 'Skid Road'. It also became the dividing line between the affluent people of Seattle and the mill workers along with the more impoverished population of the city.

    Stock, Broth, Soup - These terms are often used interchangeably, but they are different. Stock is water or other liquid in which vegetables, meat, bones or all of them are simmered over a long period to extract flavors, then the solids are removed. It normally contains no salt and is not soup. Stock is not meant to be eaten until it is combined with seasonings. Dried stock cubes are called bouillon cubes.

Broth differs in that it is a basic soup where the solid pieces of flavoring meat or fish, along with some vegetables remain. It is often made more substantial by adding starches.

Soup is a liquid savory food which can be thin, as in broth, or thick with other ingredients added.

Racking - Rack likely comes from the Middle Dutch 'rec', meaning 'framework', and the Old English 'recken', meaning 'to stretch out'. Usage became the word used for a frame that you put things on to dry or to stretch something out on.

Later the word also came to mean a frame for putting people on for torture. This expanded the meaning to include causing mental or physical harm, or suffering, or to stretch, or strain. So, when someone says they are racking their brain, it means they are straining their brain.

Tridge - If a bridge is two, then a tridge must be three. These are usually called tri-bridges. There are twelve in the world.

A Tridge is the formal name of a three-way wood footbridge above the confluence of the Chippewa and Tittabawassee Rivers near downtown Midland, Michigan. It opened in 1981 and consists of one 31-foot tall central pillar supporting three spokes. Each spoke is 180 feet long by 8 feet wide. *BTW tridge also refers to three player Bridge (cards).*

Hysteria - From the Greek 'hystera' or uterus. For a few thousand years until the late nineteenth century, hysteria referred to a medical condition thought to be particular to women and caused by disturbances of the uterus.

Definitions include: uncontrollably emotional; irrational from fear, emotion, or an emotional shock; very funny as from hysterical or uncontrollable fits of laughter.

In psychology they say it is a disorder in which a psychological conflict is converted into a bodily disturbance.

During the 1800s it was decided that men could also be hysterical. In time it could be applied to anyone as the definition expanded to be an emotional state, rather than a physical state.

Incidentally, the Oxford English Dictionary says the colloquial term 'hissy fit' for someone would go into hysterics and throw a tantrum if they did not get their way comes from hysteria.

College – University - In the US a college and university are essentially the same thing. They are both institutions which give degrees. In commonwealth nations the terms are more distinct. A college can be a school affiliated with a university. The college prepares the student for the degree and the university with which it is affiliated gives the degree.

Another way to describe the difference in the US is a college offers a collection of degrees in one specific area while a university is a collection of colleges. When you go to a university you are going to be graduating from one of their colleges, such as the business college. A Community College is different from both in that it cannot grant a bachelor's degree.

Some "colleges" in the UK are really secondary schools. One famous example is Eton College, where students typically enter at age 13. In Australia and New Zealand, college means high school.

Give the Cold Shoulder - This is a rude way of telling someone they are not welcome. In medieval England, it was regarded as a polite gesture. After a feast, the host would let his guests know it was time to leave by giving them a cold piece of meat from the shoulder of beef, mutton, or pork. Even though it now seems rude, the meaning lingers that it is time to go.

Discreet vs. Discrete - Discreet describes showing reserve, prudence, or cautiousness in one's behavior or speech. The noun form of discreet is discretion. Both discreet and discrete derive from the Latin "discretus", meaning separate, situated, put apart, which derives from the Late Latin discernere (where the word "discern" came from).

Discrete means "distinct, separate, or unrelated." The noun form of discrete is discreteness.

These two items are discrete.

The politician was not discreet.

Discrete and discreet are homophones; words that sound alike, but differ in meaning or spelling or both.

Canuck - The term "Canuck" originated in 1869 from Johnny Canuck, a nationalistic symbol billed as a younger, simpler cousin to America's Uncle Sam or Britain's John Bull. During World War II, Johnny Canuck was used as a mascot in pro-Canadian propaganda as Canada's personal defender against the Axis Powers.

A Canuck is also a small or medium-sized hardy horse, common in Canada. In addition, it is the name of the NHL hockey team in Vancouver, Canada.

41

Capitonyms - These are words that change their meaning based on whether the first letter is capitalized or not. Capitonyms are particularly troublesome when they appear at the beginning of a sentence, as there is no way, based on the single word alone to tell which meaning is being referred to.

Examples of these include: August vs. august (month vs majestic or venerable); Calorie vs. calorie (1000 calories (food) vs. 1 calorie); Divine vs. divine (related to God vs. to discover by intuition or insight); etc.

Dead as a Doornail - Many years ago, doors were built using only wood boards and hand forged nails, the nails were long enough to nail the vertical wooden panels and horizontal stretcher boards securely together and protrude out the back.

By pounding the protruding point of the nail over and down back into the wood it was almost impossible to pull out and said to be dead. It was called dead, because it could not be used again. This technique was called clinching the nail.

So the saying dead as a doornail became to mean cannot be undone. Also clinching something means finishing it.

Idiot - This word has its origins in the ancient Greek word idiōtēs, meaning a private person, a person who is not actively interested in politics. The word is now commonly used to mean someone of relatively low intelligence.

It seems to have come full circle from its original meaning. Because of the word's negative connotations, 'idiot' slowly changed how it is used today. *Ironically, many people now use that word to describe politicians, who are always interested in politics.*

Ossicone - Ossicones are the nubs that stick out on the heads of Giraffes and male Okapi. They remain covered in skin and fur and are never shed, unlike other antlers and horns. Ossicones consist of cartilage that has turned to bone. In a young animal, ossicones are porous, with clusters of bony tissue interrupted by blood vessels and folded skin. As the animal ages its ossicones grow denser and more compact.

Both male and female giraffes have a pair of these hair-covered horns, but males use these to roughhouse with each other as they are growing up. As males mature, other calcium deposits can form near these horns, making it appear they have up to five horns.

Paladin - Someone who fights for a cause. *Some of you might remember the old TV western series 'Have Gun, Will Travel' with Richard Boone.*

Third World Countries - They are not primitive, underdeveloped, or poor, as many believe. A third world country is just a country that is not considered a capitalist country (first world) or a communist country (2nd world). The terms "first world" and "second world" virtually disappeared from usage after the fall of the Soviet Union.

The terminology came about just after WWII with the first world countries that were aligned with the United States common political and economic structure (capitalists). Second world countries were those that aligned with the Soviet Union in terms of their political and economic structure (communists and socialists). Third world countries were the rest that were not aligned with either, whether poor or not. The politically correct term to refer to poor or underdeveloped countries is "Developing World."

Junkie - Early heroin users supported their habits by collecting and selling scrap metal, hence the name junkie.

Meme - The internet makes communication around the world immediate, and with it copying and sharing of interesting and not so interesting information. The neologism (a new word or phrase) 'meme' (rhymes with team) has reached widespread use to describe the viral spread of jokes, ideas, and more via the internet.

"Meme" was coined by evolutionary biologist Richard Dawkins before the web was in use, in his 1976 book, The Selfish Gene. He stated, "We need a name for the new replicator, a noun that conveys the idea of a unit of cultural transmission, or a unit of imitation. 'Mimeme' comes from a suitable Greek root, but I want a monosyllable that sounds a bit like 'gene'. I hope my classicist friends will forgive me if I abbreviate mimeme to meme. If it is any consolation, it could alternatively be thought of as being related to 'memory', or to the French word même."

The French word même means "same" or "alike." The Greek word "mimeme" he takes "meme" from comes from the Ancient Greek meaning "that which is imitated" "something imitated" "something copied".

Dawkins was hoping that the word would be used as a unit of human cultural transmission, such as a melody, fashion, or catch-phrase. People refine memes as they sometimes alter the information when they transmit it to another human. *Bacon, while being still being delicious has also become a meme.*

Breaking the Ice - Originally this phrase literally meant to break ice, like ice breaker ships that would make a path for other ships to follow.

During the late 17th century, the phrase took on the current meaning of forging a path through an awkward silence or awkward social situation.

About this time, ice-breaker also became common. It is a mechanism, such as a party game to break up socially awkward situations and to get people talking.

Buttload - A buttload is a real unit of measurement or unit of volume that is used for wines, ales, ciders, and other alcoholic beverages.

A butt is defined to be 2 hogsheads, which in the US is 63 gallons, so a butt is 126 gallons. A hogshead (corruption of the word oxhead) traditionally was two barrels and a hogshead of beer or ale is 54 gallons.

This has no relation to boatload, which is "the cargo that a vessel carries or is capable of carrying". A boatload might be about 54,107,280 gallons. *It should also not be confused with butt that is a target for practicing archery, a part of the anatomy, or any other of the many definitions for butt.*

Mondegreen - Mistakes due to mishearing or misunderstanding are called mondegreens. Most people have at one time or another inadvertently made a mondegreen when singing songs without knowing the correct lyrics.

American writer Sylvia Wright coined the term in her essay "The Death of Lady Mondegreen," published in Harper's Magazine in 1954. She got the idea from a poem she misquoted when a child.
"Ye Highlands and ye Lowlands,
 Oh, where hae ye been?
 They hae slain the Earl O' Moray,
 And Lady Mondegreen."
(The actual fourth line is "And laid him on the green".)

Here is an example: 'Scuse me while I kiss this guy" (from a lyric in the song "Purple Haze" by Jimi Hendrix: "'Scuse me while I kiss the sky"). The title of the animated Christmas show "Olive, the Other

Reindeer", is a mondegreen on "all of the other reindeer", a line from the classic Christmas song "Rudolph the Red-Nosed Reindeer".

Sport - The word sport was formed as an abbreviated form of disport. It first appears in a Middle English romance called Ipomadon in about 1440, 150 years before Shakespeare.

Disport derives from Anglo Norman desporter "to carry away" or, metaphorically "to divert, entertain", formed from des 'apart' and porter 'carry'. The word originally referred to 'amusement'. It did not gain its modern use until the 19th century. *We are still amused.*

Hurricanes and Storms - Umbrellas do not provide protection from hurricanes and storms. During the rainy season we also have many types of storms. The word 'hurricane' is thought to have come from the Mayan name for the god of storms 'Hurukan'.

When a storm has wind speeds of 38 mph it is called a tropical depression. It is called a tropical storm if it has wind speeds between 39-73 mph. Above 74 mph it is called a hurricane. Anything above 111 mph is known as a major hurricane.

Hurricanes are classified differently depending on what country you live in. In the United States, typically the Saffir-Simpson Hurricane Wind Scale is used, classifying the hurricanes from Category 1 through Category 5, based on their sustained wind speeds. This scale was developed by Herbert Saffir and Bob Simpson, in 1971.

Saffir developed the scale trying to estimate the amount of property damage a specific hurricane would do, primarily looking at damage the wind would do to structures. Simpson added flood damage. What they came up with is the following table:
Category 1: 74-95 mph
Category 2: 96-110 mph
Category 3: 111-129 mph
Category 4: 130-156 mph
Category 5: 157 mph and up.

Calories and calories - Deserts do not have Calories, but desserts do. Of course, getting your just deserts means getting what you deserve. So getting your deserts and getting your desserts might be the same thing. No wonder there is such confusion about the words.

Calories share the same type of confusion. A calorie is a unit of measure required to increase the temperature of one kilogram of water one degree Celsius. A food Calorie is actually 1,000 calories compared to calories in chemistry. Usually calories are spelled with a small 'c' and food Calories spelled with capital 'C'.

Food Calories are counted, according to the National Data Lab, based on an indirect calorie estimation made using the Atwater system. The total caloric value is calculated by adding up the calories provided by the energy-containing nutrients: protein, carbohydrate, fat, and alcohol. Because carbohydrates contain some fiber that is not digested and utilized by the body, the fiber component is usually subtracted from the total carbohydrate before calculating calories. The label on a food item that contains 10 g of protein, 20 g of carbohydrate and 9 g of fat would read 201 kcals or 201 Calories.

Arcuate - The back pocket of Levi jeans has a double arch design called the Arcuate for which the company holds a trademark. Arcuate means 'curved like a bow'.

During World War II, the US government ruled that the design served no practical purpose, was only decorative, and due to wartime rations involving cotton, did not allow the company to use extra thread to create the arcuate. To maintain the trademark during those years, the company painted the design on the jeans.

Ullage - The space in a bottle of wine that is not occupied by wine. In other words, the amount the bottle lacks in being full. Pronounced ull ij.

Eggcorn - An eggcorn is a change in pronunciation and/or spelling which results in a new word or phrase that still makes a certain amount of sense, but deviates from the original. That is the difference between an eggcorn and a malapropism, which is an error in speech that results in something similar, but nonsensical.

"That is mind-bottling."
"That man has old-timer's disease."
"I'll have a glass of skimp milk?

Eggcorns are completely or or nearly equal, from a phonetic standpoint. The listener may not even realize that an eggcorn has even been uttered.

Say, 'Texas has a lot of electrical votes'. This is not an eggcorn. Although it sounds almost the same, any connection to the original meaning of "electoral" is gone.

The term "eggcorn" was coined by linguist Geoffrey Pullum in 2003. He used the example of a woman who said "egg corn" rather than "acorn" which sound almost identical, depending on pronunciation.

Paraprosdokian - This is a figure of speech similar to garden-path sentences in that both feature a sort of linguistic "twist" partway through. Paraprosdokians differ in that the grammar is not usually confusing; rather, the end of the sentence ends up being surprising or disorienting. Henny Youngman's famous line, "Take my wife—please!" is a prime example of a sentence whose final word ramps up the tension of the previous phrase, and provides unexpected humor to the listener.

Comedians use paraprosdokians all the time as a means of keeping an audience off-guard. A few more examples:
"I've had a perfectly wonderful evening, but this wasn't it." (Groucho Marx)
"Your argument is sound, lots of sound."

"I haven't slept for ten days, because that would be too long." (Mitch Hedberg)
"I don't belong to an organized political party. I'm a Democrat." (Will Rogers)
"If I'm reading this graph correctly, I'd be surprised." (Stephen Colbert)
"You can always count on Americans to do the right thing . . . after they have tried everything else." (Winston Churchill)

Take a Raincheck - This phrase usually means, "I won't do it now, but I will later." This is the commonly accepted meaning and is now considered to be correct. It is included here merely out of interest, because the original meaning was slightly different. Initially, a raincheck was offered to people who had tickets to a baseball game that was rained out. They would offered a raincheck, which was a ticket for a game at a later date to make up for the missed game.

This eventually found its way into shopping jargon in general where a raincheck was an offer to sell an out-of-stock good when it arrived back in stock. The meaning has eventually broadened to a point that it is not an offer any longer, just a response.

Galocher - The term French kiss is commonly attributed to American soldiers returning from World War I, who apparently picked up the technique from the adventurous French maidens.

France has never had a word for 'French kiss' until now. The verb "galocher" meaning to kiss with tongues had just been added to the Petit Robert 2014 French dictionary. It is pronounced ga luh shay.

It comes from 'La galoche' an ice-skating boot, so the new term plays on the idea of sliding around the ice. Also, "galosh" or "overshoe" was used for hundreds of years before that, giving galocher a sort of onomatopoeic connection between the sound that galoshes make on a wet street and the sound that tongues make during a French kiss.

Ironic - Often the word 'ironic' is much misused to remark on a coincidence, such as, "This is the third time today we have run into each other. How ironic." It is also mistakenly used to describe something out of the ordinary or unusual, "Yesterday was a beautiful, warm day in November. Truly ironic." It is also wrongly used to emphasize something interesting. For example, "Ironically, it was the best movie I have seen all year."

A true ironic remark conveys a meaning that is the opposite of its literal meaning, so in an ironic statement one thing is said, while another thing is meant. For example, it would be irony on a nasty stormy to say, "What wonderful weather." If you were suffering from a bad cold you might say, "I feel lwonderful." These are both examples of verbal irony.

Irony is also often confused with sarcasm. The two are similar, but in sarcasm there is an intent to ridicule or mock, often harshly or crudely.

Dramatic irony is inherent in speeches or a drama and is understood by the audience, but not grasped by the characters in the play.

Eavesdrop - Eavesdropping originally came from Anglo-Saxon laws against building too close to the border of your land, so the rain running off your roof would run on to your neighbor's property. The eaves drip is the width of ground around a house or building which receives the rain water dropping from the eaves.

The primary function of the eaves is to throw rain water off the walls, prevent erosion of the footings, and reduce splatter on the wall from rain as it hits the ground.

Eavesdropper became the word for a person who stands within range of the eaves drip in order to listen to what is said inside the house. Now it has evolved to the act of secretly listening to the private conversations or reading online records of others without their consent. *The word eaves is both singular and plural.*

Decimate - The original meaning of the word had nothing to do with large-scale destruction. Ancient Roman "decimatio," from which "decimate" derives, meant "the removal of a tenth."

Decimation used to be a punishment for cities or armies where one in ten people was picked out in a draw and had to be beaten to death by the remaining nine.

Silicon vs. Silicone - Silicon is a naturally occurring chemical element, and silicone is synthetic.

Silicon has properties of both metals and nonmetals and is the second most abundant element in the Earth's crust, after oxygen. It is rarely found in nature in its pure form. We usually find silicon dioxide or silica, better known as quartz, the most common component of sand.

As silica, silicon is a key ingredient in bricks, concrete, and glass. As silicate, it is used to make enamels, pottery and ceramics. It is also used widely in modern electronics, because it is an ideal semiconductor of electricity. When heated into a molten state, silicon is formed into semi-conductive wafers, which serve as the base for integrated circuits. Silicon Valley, California was named due to the high concentration of computer and electronics companies in the area producing silicon-based semiconductors and chips.

Silicone is a synthetic polymer made up of silicon, oxygen, and other elements, typically carbon and hydrogen. Silicone is generally a liquid or flexible plastic. It's useful properties are low toxicity and high heat resistance. It also provides good electrical insulation.

In the medical field, silicone can be found in implants, catheters, contact lenses, bandages, and more. It is also contained in items, such as shampoos, shaving cream, non-stick kitchenware, personal and automotive lubricants, sealants, and sex toys. Silicone is heat resistant and slippery. It is also used in electronics to make casings that can shield sensitive devices from electrical shocks and other hazards.

Apron - An apron is an outer protective garment that covers primarily the front of the body. It may be worn for hygienic reasons as well as to protect clothes from wear and tear. The apron was traditionally viewed as an essential garment for anyone doing housework until the mid-1960s in the United States. Wearing aprons remains strong in many places.

A pinafore is a full apron with two holes for the arms that is tied or buttoned in the back, usually just below the neck. Pinafores have complete front shaped over shoulder while other aprons usually have no bib, or only a smaller one.

Cobbler aprons are a type of apron that covers both the front and back of the body. It is fastened with side ties or with waist bands that tie in the back. It covers most of the upper part of the body and is often made of leather.

The Salon Apron protects clothing from hair color stains and hair clippings while serving as a place to keep tools quickly accessible. A Salon Apron is typically water repellent.

Barbecue aprons are fashionable for the back yard chef (with at least one pocket to hold a beer), while white half aprons are still used by serious chefs.

Apron is a corruption of the original old French word "naperon," a change that likely occurred when people misheard "a naperon" as "an apron."

Atoms, Particles, Elements, and Molecules - Atoms are the smallest pieces of matter; they are made of particles (protons and electrons). When atoms are grouped together, the groups are called molecules, which are the smallest bits of compounds.

By way of example, within the element copper, a copper atom is the smallest piece of copper that exists. Hydrogen is an element; two hydrogen atoms and one oxygen atom combine to form a molecule of water, which is a compound.

Element - a basic substance that can't be simplified, such as copper
Atom - the smallest amount of an element, such as copper atom
Molecule - two or more atoms that are chemically joined together, such as hydrogen or oxygen
Compound - a molecule that contains more than one element, such as water.

Socks and Sox - The Red Sox and White Sox baseball teams have the "Sox" spelled that way, because they were named during the time when there was a movement to simplify the spelling of many English words. Socks became sox, but tradition won and the spelling of sox did not catch on as part of the language.

Jail and Prison - These two words do not mean the same thing. In the US, jails are run by county sheriff's office and prisons are run by the state. In Canada, jails are run by the provincial government and prisons are run by the federal government.

Piggyback - Back in the 16th century, goods were transported in packs that people carried on their own back or animals backs. The term used to describe this was "pick pack" because you would pick up a pack in order to carry it on your back.

"Pick pack" eventually became "pick-a-pack" as in pick a pack and carry it on your back. Eventually, because an individual was picking a pack to carry on his back, the term "pick-a-pack" became "pick-a-back".

The insertion of the "a" caused a problem and ultimately paved the way for the original phrase "pick pack" to become 'piggyback'. Due to the pronunciation of the term as a whole, "pick-a-pack" often sounded like "pick-i-back" which sounded like "picky back". This ultimately gave rise to the term "piggyback" around this time for people carrying a pack on their back. By the 1930s, the definition further progressed to describe riding on someone's back and shoulders. The pig was the only animal that sounded like "picky" and "pickyback" became piggyback.

I.E. and E.G. – Specifically, "i.e." is an abbreviation for the Latin "id est", more or less meaning "that is". "E.g." is an abbreviation for the Latin "exempli gratia", meaning "for the sake of example", or the short version, "for example".

As a general rule, if you can substitute in "for example" where you have used "e.g.", you are probably using it correctly. Likewise, if you can substitute "that is" where you are using "i.e.", you are also probably using it correctly.

The key distinction, with "e.g." is you are stating one or more examples, with "i.e." you are not talking about anything, but what you specifically say.

It is a mistake to include an "etc." after an "e.g." list, because "et cetera" is implied, so it should not be included at the end.

Naked and Nude - Naked implies that a person is unprotected or vulnerable. It also describes something that is unadorned or without embellishment, as in the naked truth. Nude means one thing, not clothed.

Aptronym - Have you noticed that some people seem to have very appropriate and entirely coincidental names? Names such Usain Bolt (Jamaican sprinter), Lord Brain (brain surgeon), or Alto Reed (saxophonist). This is called an aptronym, as in 'aptly named'.

Some people believe that the name can influence life decisions leading a person to work in a field relating to their name. This is called 'nominative determinism'.

Close, but No Cigar - This means to fall short of a successful outcome. It was first used in the United States in the early 1900s and

51

is likely the phrase originated at fairgrounds. Much like fairs today, booths would be set up and fair workers would host difficult to win games for fair goers to try. Games of strength, accuracy, and skill were played by men and women.

Back then, prizes were for mom and dad, and cigars were a very common prize given out to winners. The phrase apparently originated when someone came close to winning one of the games, but ultimately lost and so did not win a cigar. Workers yelled it out when people lost, trying to draw crowds and encourage the person to try again. As the fairs traveled, the phrase spread rapidly and it began to be used any time someone did not meet expectations.

Jaywalking - Jaywalking in the Untied States means a pedestrian crosses a street without regard to traffic regulations.

For instance, depending on where one lives, it may be against the law to cross a street where there is a crosswalk nearby, but the person chooses not to use it. Alternatively even at a crosswalk, it is often illegal to cross if there is a 'Don't Walk' signal flashing.

Contrary to popular belief, the term jaywalking does not derive from the shape of the letter J. It comes from the fact that "Jay" used to be a generic term for someone who was dull, rube, unsophisticated, poor, or a simpleton.

To Jaywalk was to be stupid by crossing the street in an unsafe place or way, or some person visiting the city who was not familiar with the rules of the road for pedestrians in an urban environment. As stated in the January 25, 1937 New York Times, "In many streets like Oxford Street, for instance, the jaywalker wanders complacently in the very middle of the roadway as if it was a country lane."

Cogitate - It means to take careful thought or think carefully about. Also, to think earnestly or studiously; reflect; ponder; meditate: as, to cogitate a means of escape. In addition, to revolve in the mind; think about attentively; hence, devise or plan: as, he is cogitating mischief (*something I never did as a child*).

Orchestra, Symphony, and Philharmonic - Orchestra is a broad term for any ensemble featuring a large proportion of string instruments. There are two basic orchestras; chamber orchestras (small) and symphony orchestras (big)

A symphony orchestra and a philharmonic are almost the same thing. They are the relatively same size and they play the same kind of music. The two terms help us tell different orchestras apart, especially in cities that have multiple groups, as Brooklyn Symphony and Brooklyn Philharmonic. Symphony orchestra is a generic term and philharmonic orchestra is mostly used as part of a proper name.

Every philharmonic is a symphony, but not every symphony is a philharmonic. *Also, 'Pops' is an orchestra that usually also plays (popular) show tunes.*

Turtle, Terrapin, and Tortoise - All three animals come under the class of reptiles, in the taxonomic order of Testudines or Chelonia. They all have the major characteristics of reptiles as they are cold-blooded, have scales, breathe air, and lay eggs on land.

The distinction between them comes mainly from what living habitat they are adapted for, though the terminology differs slightly in certain countries. In Australia, other than sea turtles, they are all called tortoises. In the United States, the term 'turtles' is given to chelonians that live in or near water.

In general there are a few commonly accepted distinctions between turtles, tortoises, and terrapins. Turtles may be completely aquatic, like sea turtles, which rarely come up onto land, except to lay eggs. Other types of turtles are semi-aquatic and live by fresh water ponds or lakes. They tend to swim, but also spend a lot of time on land, basking in the sun and occasionally burrowing in the mud. Turtles have adapted to an aquatic life and are streamlined for swimming with webbed feet, or in the case of sea turtles, long flippers. Turtles are omnivores. Depending on the type of turtle, they may eat jelly-fish, small invertebrates, sea sponges, and sea-vegetation. In the case of fresh water turtles, they may eat plants, insects, and small fish.

Tortoises are almost exclusively land-dwelling, usually with stubby feet, and are not good swimmers. They occasionally enter water to clean themselves off or drink, but can easily drown in the deep water or in strong currents. Their bodies are adapted to living on land and have high domed shells and column shaped feet much like elephants. They also sometimes have sharp claws for digging. Tortoises are mostly herbivorous and primarily eat low-lying shrubs, cacti, grasses, weeds, fruit, and other vegetation.

The term terrapins is sometimes used for turtles that are semi-aquatic and live near brackish waters or swampy regions. They are sort of like a mix between a turtle and tortoise, as they spend most of their time divided between water and land. They are also usually small and have a hard-shell that is shaped somewhere between a turtle's streamlined one and a tortoise's rounded dome shaped one.

Caught Red Handed - Caught red handed, has its origins in Scotland around the 15th century. Given the context it was often used in the earliest references, the phrase "red hand" or "redhand" likely came about referring to people caught with blood on their hands.

The first known documented instance of "red hand" is in the Scottish Acts of Parliament of James I, written in 1432. It subsequently came up in various legal proceedings in Scotland, usually referring to someone caught in the act of committing some crime, such as "apprehended redhand", "taken with redhand", etc.

The first documented instance of the expression morphing from "red hand" to "red handed" was in the early 19th century work Ivanhoe, written by Sir Walter Scott.

Getting off Scot Free - Many think these words have some vague reference to Scottish people. It actually does not. In the thirteenth century, scot was the word for money a person would pay at a tavern for food and drinks. It was also used when passing the hat to pay an entertainer.

Later, it came to mean a local tax that paid the sheriff's expenses. To go scot free literally meant to be exempted from paying the tax.

Nitpicking, Bigwigs, and Perukes - By 1580, syphilis had become the worst epidemic to strike Europe since the Black Death. Without antibiotics, victims developed open sores, nasty rashes, blindness, dementia, and patchy hair loss.

Powdered wigs, called perukes came in to fashion. Victims hid their baldness, as well as the bloody sores that scored their faces, with wigs made of horse, goat, or human hair and coated with powder scented with lavender or orange, to hide the odor.

When Louis XIV was seventeen his hair began thinning. He hired 48 wig makers to save his image. Five years later, the King of England, Louis' cousin, Charles II, did the same thing when his hair started to gray. Other aristocrats immediately copied the two kings. They sported ostentatious wigs, and the style trickled down to the upper-middle class.

The cost of wigs increased, and perukes became a scheme for flaunting wealth. An everyday wig cost about 25 shillings, a week's pay for a commoner. The bill for large, elaborate perukes could cost as much as 800 shillings. The word 'bigwig' was coined to describe snobs who could afford big, flowing wigs.

At the same time, head lice were everywhere and nitpicking was a painful and time-consuming chore. Wigs curbed the problem. Lice stopped infesting people's hair, which had to be shaved for the wig to fit, and moved to the wigs. Delousing a wig was much easier than delousing a head of hair. A wig-maker would simply boil the wig to remove the nits.

Poll, Polled, Polling, Polls - The word comes from the German Poller, meaning head. Modern use seems to have evolved from counting heads. Poll has many definitions:

Noun,

1. The casting and registering of votes in an election.

2. The number of votes cast or recorded.

3. The place where votes are cast and registered. Often used in the plural *polls*.

4. A survey of the public or of a sample of public opinion to acquire information.

5. The head, especially the top or back of the head where hair grows.

6. The blunt or broad end of a tool such as a hammer or ax.

polled, **polling**, **polls** Verb,
1. To receive a given number of votes.

2. To receive or record the votes of: polling a jury.

3. To cast a vote or ballot.

4. To question in a survey; canvass.

5. To trim or cut off the hair, wool, branches, or horns of: polled the sheep; polled the trees.

Sometimes, when the polls do not go their way, people feel like they have been clipped.

Crash Blossoms - Crash Blossoms are ambiguous headlines that usually convey more than one meaning and make you want to scratch your head. Here are a few examples.

"Chinese cooking fat heads for Holland"
"Analysis: China currency move nails hard landing risk coffin"
"Doctor Testifies in Horse Suit"
"American Ships Head to Libya"

"Don't help old, blind council tells parking officers"
"McDonald's fries the holy grail for potato farmers"
"Dog helps lightning strike Redruth mayor."
"Virginia Beach man accused of decapitating son to stay in hospital"
"Kids Make Nutritious Snacks"
"Miners Refuse to Work After Death"
"Teacher Strikes Idle Kids"
"US President Wins on Budget, but More Lies Ahead"

Pleased as Punch - This phrase came from an English puppet show, Punch and Judy begging in the 1600s. No two performances of the show were totally alike, but they all usually involved the same events:
1. Punch kills his infant child
2. Punch punches Judy until she dies
3. Punch goes to prison and escapes using a golden key
4. He then kills doctors, lawyers, and a hangman
5. He kills Death, as in the Grim Reaper
6. Then it all ends spectacularly as he kills the Devil.

Languages are Fading Away - There are an estimated 6,500 languages in the world and half or more of them could cease to exist by 2100.

Languages are dying out around the globe through globalization, social change, and a shift in populations from rural areas to cities. Of the 6,500 languages estimated to be still in use, only 11 are spoken by half the world's population, and 95 percent of the languages are spoken by less than five percent of the global population.

Same and Opposite - Clip can mean "to bind together" or "to separate." You clip sheets of paper to together or separate part of a page by clipping something out.

Continue usually means to persist in doing something, but as a legal term it means stop a proceeding temporarily.

Fight with can be interpreted three ways. "He fought with his mother-in-law" could mean "They argued," "They served together in the war," or "He used her as a weapon."
Hold up can mean "to support" or "to hinder."
Out can mean "visible" or "invisible." For example, "It's a good thing the full moon was out when the lights went out."

Masculine and Feminine Words - Fiancé vs. fiancée. The former is a male engaged to be married; the latter is a woman engaged to be married.

Brunet refers to a man's hair color and brunette refers to a woman's hair color.

In education, female is professor emerita and male is professor emeritus.

Latinizing Words - For a while, it was popular to change the spelling of ordinary words to make them appear more Latin to increase their stature. Receipt is a victim of the Latinizing craze. When the word came into English from French it had no 'p', and no one pronounced it as if it did. Enthusiastic Latinizers later added the 'p' on analogy with the Latin receptus. This is also how debt and doubt got their 'b's, salmon and solder got their 'l's, and indict got its 'c.'

Most of the words that were Latinized did have some distant connection, through French, with the ancient Latin words that dictated their new spellings. However, sometimes a Latin-inspired letter got stuck into a word that had not come through Latin. "Island" came from the Old English íglund, and was spelled illond, ylonde, or ilande until someone picked up the 's' from Latin insula and stuck it where it was never been meant to be.

Four Kinds of Irony - *Verbal irony*: This manifests when the speaker says one thing, but means another (often contrary) thing. The most well known type of verbal irony is sarcasm. For example, "He is as funny as a heart attack".

Tragic irony: Tragic irony occurs only in fiction. It manifests when the words or actions of a character contradict the real situation with the full knowledge of the spectators. For example: In Romeo and Juliet, Romeo mistakenly believes that Juliet has killed herself, so he poisons himself. Juliet awakens to find Romeo dead so she kills herself with his knife.

Dramatic Irony: In drama, this type of irony manifests when the spectator is given a piece of information that one or more of the characters are unaware of. For example: in Pygmalion, we know that Eliza is a prostitute, but the Higgins family does not.

Situational Irony: Situational irony manifests when there is a difference between the expected result and the actual result. Take for example this account of the attempted assassination of Ronald Reagan: As aides rushed to push Reagan into his car, the bullet ricocheted off the bullet-proof car, then hit the President in the chest. The bullet proof car was intended to protect the president, but nearly caused his death by deflecting the bullet toward him.

18 Common Related Words - What do all these words have in common? - Boredom, flummox, rampage, butter-fingers, tousled, sawbones, confusingly, casualty ward, allotment garden, kibosh, footlights, dustbin, fingerless, fairy story, messiness, natural-looking, squashed, spectacularly - They were all invented or first used in print by Charles Dickens.

Vowel-less Words - English is a funny language with many interesting words.

BRR – The way you tell people it is very chilly.

HMM – Accepted (in addition to "hm") as a sound of contemplation. When you are thinking more, it is "hmm" instead of "hm."

NTH – Having the quality of being the last in a series of infinitely increasing or decreasing values. (As in, "the nth degree.")

PHT – An interjection used to signify mild annoyance or disagreement.

SHH – A way to urge someone to be quiet.

TSK – An interjection often used in quick repetition like "tsktsk" to express contempt or disdain.

PFFT – A way to express that something is dying or fizzling out.

PSST – Used to attract someone's attention.

More Interesting Words - *Dysania* means having difficulty getting out of bed in the morning. *Griffonage* means illegible handwriting. *Acnestis* is the area between your shoulder blades. *Semordnilap* is a word or phrase that reads one way forward and another backward (parts/strap). *Scroop* is the sound produced by the movement of silk, as in long dresses. *Penthera* phobia is fear of your mother-in-law. *Karate* means empty hand. *Lunule* the white crescent shaped part at the top of a finger nail.

Punt is the indent on the bottom of a wine bottle. *Agraffe* is the wire that keeps the cork on a bottle of champagne. *Barm* is the foam on the top of a glass of beer.

Box Tent is the little plastic piece used in pizza boxes to keep the top from smashing the pizza. *Kemmerspeck* is the weight gained from emotional overeating (literally grease bacon).

String is a group of ponies. *Business* is an assembly of ferrets. *Smack* is a group of jellyfish. *Gam* is a group of whales. *Murder* is a group of crows. *Trip* is a group of goats. *Parliament* is a group of owls. *Pass* is a group of donkeys. *Prickle* is a group of porcupines.

The only word that consists of two letters, each used three times is the word "deeded."

A hamlet is a village without a church and a town is not a city until it has a cathedral.

The 'v' in the name of a court case does not stand for 'versus', but for 'and' (in civil proceedings) or 'against' (in criminal proceedings).

Defining Itself - I find it fascinating how some words can be a definition of themselves, such as 'word' is a word that tells us it is a word. Here are a few more self explanatory words:
English - Not German
Erudite - Scholarly word that means scholarly.
Noun - Is a noun
Used - This word has been used
Polysyllabic - This word has multiple syllables
Common - This word is
Unhyphenated - This word is
Floccinaucinihilipilificatious - A worthless word meaning to estimate worthless
Obfuscatory - Is and means not easy to understand
Suffixed - Has a suffix
Hyphen-bearing - Contains a hyphen
Monepic - Describes a one-word sentence
Cacophony - Sounds like and describes disagreeable sounds.

Spelling Bee

The "bee" in spelling bee means a gathering or get together. The earliest documented case of this word appearing with this meaning was in 1769, referring to a spinning bee, where people would gather to protest purchasing goods from Britain due to the high taxes on those items.

Any sort of major competition or work gathering, with a specific task in mind, was a 'bee'. Gatherings that were commonly labeled with 'bee' were: apple bee, quilting bee, barn bee, hanging bee, sewing bee, and corn husking bee, among others.

The popular theory among etymologists today is that it is likely that the actual origin of bee, in the sense of gathering, derives from the Old English bēn (prayer / favor), or the Middle English 'bene'. This resulted in "bean" meaning "help given by neighbors".

The first US National Spelling Bee was in 1925, sponsored by the Louisville Courier-Journal. Nine finalists competed in the first spelling bee in Washington D.C. The winning word that year was "gladiolus", spelled by Frank Neuhauser.

In 1941, E.W. Scripps Company began sponsoring the National Spelling Bee and changed the name to Scripps National Spelling Bee.

It offers a study booklet to prospective contestants that contains between 1,000 and 4,000 words. It also currently offers a list of over 24,000 words that include all words used in the National Spelling Bee since 1950, sorted by frequency of use in the contest. The word that has been used the most in the National Spelling Bee is connoisseur.

The winner of the National Spelling Bee receives several prizes including: $30,000 cash prize from the National Spelling Bee; $5,000 cash prize from Sigma Phi Epsilon Educational Foundation; $2,500 savings bond; a complete reference library from Merriam-Webster; a lifetime membership to Britannica Online Premium Encyclopedia; $2,600 worth of reference works; and a trophy. The second place contestant receives $12,500.

To date, 45 girls have won the spelling bee vs. 41 boys. *That is sure to create a buzz.*

Eight Regional Slang Words

English is bad enough without more words, but it seems some parts of our great country have come up with some words of their own.

whoopensocker (n.), Wisconsin - Whoopensocker can refer to anything extraordinary of its kind, from a smooth dance move to a knee-melting kiss.

wapatuli, (n.), Wisconsin - Nearly everyone who has been to college in America has either concocted a homemade alcoholic drink with any combination of hard liquors or other beverages. A wapatuli can also refer to the occasion at which it is consumed. In Kentucky, the word for terrible liquor is splo and in the mid-Atlantic, moonshine is ratgut or rotgut.

jabble (v.), Virginia - When you are standing at your front door rifling through your purse for fifteen minutes, because you can't find your keys it is because all the stuff in your purse is all jabbled up. It means 'to shake up or mix', but can also be used as 'to confuse'.

sneetered (v.), Kentucky - If you've ever been hoodwinked, duped, swindled, fleeced, or scammed, you have been sneetered. The noun version, sniter, refers to that person responsible for your sneetering.

chinchy (adj.), South, Midwest - This useful word perfectly describes your stingy friend who is too cheap to split the bill or pay his fair share.

mizzle-witted (adj.), South - This word means 'mentally dull', but depending on where you are in the country, mizzle can also be used as a verb meaning 'to confuse', 'to depart in haste' or 'to abscond'.

mug-up (n.), Alaska - When Alaskans take a break from work to grab a cup of coffee, they are enjoying a mug-up or coffee break.

bufflehead or bufflebrain (n.), Pennsylvania - This word means a fool or idiot. *I guess calling someone a mizzle-witted bufflehead would be doubly unkind.*

Words from Comics

Many words we use came from newspaper comics. Here are a few:
Goon - The word "goon" to describe a simpleton or stupid person dates back to the 16th century, when sailors sometimes compared folks to the albatross, often colloquially referred to as a "gooney bird." However, "goon," when used to describe a muscular, not-so-bright, hired thug, comes from the Popeye comic strip, notably Alice the Goon, an eight-foot tall giantess with hairy forearms.

Wimpy - J. Wellington Wimpy was a hamburger loving soul and also a character in the Popeye comics. While the word "wimp" is from World War I, the soft-spoken, intelligent, cowardly Wimpy gave us a way to describe being a wimp.

Dagwood Sandwich - A Dagwood is any stacked sandwich that consists of a variety of meats, cheeses, and other condiments. Dagwood Bumstead, husband in the Blondie comics built the piled-high wonders out of anything and everything he could find in the refrigerator.

Milquetoast - Someone who is even wimpier than Wimpy is a total milquetoast, as in Caspar Milquetoast, a character from a one-panel comic strip by H.T. Webster called The Timid Soul. Caspar's surname was a play on the bland dish called milk toast that was often served to invalids or folks with "nervous" stomachs. Caspar Milquetoast was a guy who would buy a new hat rather than trespass when his blew off his head and onto a lawn with a "Keep Off the Grass" sign.

Mutt and Jeff - Mutt and Jeff were two comic strip characters created by Bud Fisher in 1907. Augustus Mutt was a tall, lanky ne'er-do-well who liked to bet on the ponies, while his pal Othello Jeff was short, rotund, and shared Mutt's passion for "get rich quick" schemes. The strip became so popular that "Mutt and Jeff" is used to describe any duo displaying opposite physical characteristics.

Keeping up with the Joneses - In the comic strip of their origin, they were never seen. Keeping Up with the Joneses was written and drawn by Arthur Momand and was first published in the New York Globe in 1913. The strip followed the daily life of the Aloysius P. McGinnis family, and Mrs. McGinnis' envy of their wealthy neighbors, the Joneses. Al endured his wife outfitting him in "trendy" clothing like lime-green spats and lemon-colored gloves, because that is how Mr. Jones dressed.

Dinty Moore - Both the Hormel canned stew and the triple-decker corned beef/lettuce/tomato/Russian dressing sandwich that bear this name were inspired by the tavern owner in the popular George McManus comic strip Bringing Up Father. Maggie and Jiggs were Irish-American immigrants who won a million dollars in a sweepstakes. Maggie eagerly adapted to their new lifestyle, but former bricklayer Jiggs missed his boisterous pals and frequently went to hang with them at Dinty Moore's, where they would feast on corned beef and cabbage and Irish stew while enjoying a few toddies.

Whammy and Double Whammy - According to the comic strip Li'l Abner, Evil-Eye Fleagle was a zoot-suited hood who came from Brooklyn, New York. He could shoot beams of destruction from his eyes. A regular whammy could knock a dozen men unconscious and the double whammy could collapse a building. *I trust these provided a 'Linus blanket' for your curiosity.*

Holiday Wordology

Between Thanksgiving and Christmas holidays there are many words we do not tend to use so much during the rest of the year, so thought I might add some of these words and their origins.

Mirth and Merry - Both mirth and merry come from an Old English word meaning "joy" or "pleasure." These words are themselves derived from an older German root meaning "short-lasting." Thus, something merry is short-lived, although the consequences may not be. In the 17th century, the word "merry" could include decidedly earthier connotations, such as a merry-bout of sexual intercourse. Sometimes a merry-bout resulted in a "merry-begot," an illegitimate child.

The word merry also gave us the merrythought, which we now call the wishbone. The custom of pulling apart the wishbone dates back at least to Roman times and may have evolved from the Etruscan practice of alectryomancy, the practice of divining the future using rooster clavicles. According to Roman legend, the Etruscans selected the wishbone because its "V" shape resembled a human groin, the repository of life. Thus, the wishbone was seen as an appropriate way to unravel life's mysteries.

In the 17th century, it was sometimes thought that whoever ended up with the longer piece of the merrythought would marry first. Some believed the person with the longer piece would get whatever wish he chose. English settlers brought the practice with them to the New World, and we still pull the wishbone apart today. The proper term for the bone we pull apart is "furcula." It comes from the Latin furca, meaning "pitchfork."

Fork - It is not particularly a holiday word, but used more often during the holidays. Before becoming the word for what was then a two-pronged utensil, the term was used in England to refer to a forked instrument used by torturers. Although the fork seems like an obvious tool, it was not used for eating until the eighth or ninth century, and then only by the nobility in parts of what is now the Middle East. Popular legend has it that Catherine de Medici brought the fork to France from Italy when she married King Henry I of France in the 16th century. However, the use of the word to mean a table fork came a hundred years earlier.

Sage - The herb sage is associated with Thanksgiving, but historically, sage's primary use has been medicinal. This is reflected in its botanical name, Salvia officinalis. In Latin, salvus meant "healthy," a word that also gave us the English "safe." Sage has been used to treat inflamed gums, excessive perspiration, memory loss, depression, sore throat, swollen sinuses, acne, toenail fungus, hot flashes, and painful menstruation, among others. Because sage is also used to combat diarrhea, gas, and bloating, it is the perfect herb for a holiday that often results in overindulgence.

Tofurky - This relatively new holiday word makes many cringe. It is a turkey substitute created in 2000 by Turtle Island Foods. Tofurky is made from tofu, wheat gluten, oil, and natural flavors, which include certain yeasts that lend Tofurky a "meaty" taste. Tofu is fermented soy bean curd valued for its high protein content, as well as its ability to absorb flavors from other foods. Tofu is probably best enjoyed without thinking of the origins of the word, literally "rotten beans," which come from Chinese dou ("beans") and fu ("rotten").

Christmas - This word comes from the Old English words Cristes moesse, 'the mass or festival of Christ'. The first celebration took place in Rome about the middle of the fourth century. The exact date of the Nativity is not known, but even in pre-Christian times the period from December 25 to January 6, "The Twelve Days of Christmas" was considered a special time of year. The abbreviation Xmas, thought as sacrilegious by some, is entirely appropriate. The letter X (chi) is the first letter in the Greek word for Christ.

Reindeer - Did you know this word is actually redundant. Rein is Scandinavian for 'reindeer', so reindeer translates to 'reindeer deer'. It came to English from Old Norse hreindyri.

Mistletoe is thought to be based on a German word for bird excrement from the fact that the plant is propagated in it. Some think it is derived from another German word (mash) which refers to the stickiness of the berries. It is combined with an Old English word (toe) meaning 'twig'. This shrub usually grows on broad-leaved trees like apple, lime, and poplar.

Christmas Carol is a term which originally referred to a non-religious ring dance accompanied by singing. Eventually it came to mean a merry song with a tune that could be danced to. The Italian friars who lived with St. Francis of Assisi were the first to compose these songs in the early 1400s. Since the nineteenth century, carols have been sung in place of hymns in many churches on Christmas Eve and Christmas Day.

Saint Nicholas was not only wealthy but modest, and he liked to help people in need without drawing attention to himself. Poor families would often find a gold piece or well-filled purse without knowing where it had come from. His American successor, Santa Claus, carried on the tradition.

Poinsettias have been a symbol of Christmas in the United States since the 1820s when it was first shipped to North America by Joel Poinsett, the American minister to Mexico.

Wassail - It comes from the Middle English waes haeil, which means 'be in good health' or 'be fortunate'. Wassailing was the Old English custom of toasting the holiday and each other's health. Wassail is also the name of the spiced apple beverage used in such toasting and has been drunk since around 1300.

WHAT'S IN A NAME

Belsnickel - German for "fur-Nicholas," is a fur-clad Christmas gift-bringer figure in the folklore of southwestern Germany, where my family is originally from. The figure is also preserved in Pennsylvania Dutch communities.

Belsnickel's fur covers his entire body, and he sometimes wears a mask with a long tongue. He is a companion of Saint Nickolas, a bit scary, and visits children at Christmas time to deliver socks or shoes full of candy, cakes, nuts, and fruit, but if the children are not good, they will find coal and/or switches (stick) in their stockings instead. Other traditions had him strewing those goodies on the floor and if an adult bent down to pick up something they were hit on the back from Belsnickel with a switch.

In many places, Belsnickel was a precursor to Santa Claus or St. Nickolas and the popularity in the US faded in the early 1900s. Many of the old traditional Santa equivalents always had coal and a switch for bad kids along with the goodies. *Alas, many good life lessons have been replaced with the current - everyone gets everything attitude.*

FICO - This is the scoring that is used for credit reporting. FICO is a public company that provides analytics and decision making services, including credit scoring intended to help financial services companies make complex, high-volume decisions.

FICO was founded in 1956 as Fair, Isaac and Company by Bill Fair and Earl Isaac. It went public in 1987 and was originally called Fair, Isaac and Company, it was renamed Fair Isaac Corporation in 2003, then changed its name and ticker symbol to FICO. It also sells other financial related products.

The big three credit reporting companies use this scoring to determine your creditworthiness. Each has its own name, but all use the FICO calculations methodology. Score is calculated on the following. Payment history 35%, amounts owed 30%, length of history 15%, new credit 10%, and types of credit used 10%. It includes only information on your credit report, and nothing else, like race, age, employment, income, etc. It is a snapshot in time and changes as your circumstances change, so you can influence the number for better or worse. Scores range from 300 to 850 with 60% of people falling between 650 and 799.

FICO score is used for home and auto loans, calculating interest rates, and buying insurance, etc. Some states allow employers to use the score to determine potential hiring.

Pop Rocks - Pop Rocks were invented by Chemist William A. Mitchell, who worked for General Foods. He also invented Tang, Cool Whip, quick-setting Jell-O, a tapioca substitute, and powdered egg whites, among other things. He received over 70 patents in his lifetime.

Easter Island - Those famous heads that we have all seen pictures of turn out to have bodies. Many of the 887 moai known to date have been excavated and found to have bodies. The island's real name is Rapa Nui.

These statues ring the island and have been a source of fascination and conjecture for centuries. Contrary to some stories, the majority of the statues face inward, not looking out to the ocean.

Wilhelm Scream - The Wilhelm scream is a frequently-used film and television stock sound effect first used in 1951 for the film Distant Drums.

The effect gained new popularity (its use often becoming an in-joke) after it was used in Star Wars and many other blockbuster films as well as television programs and video games. The scream is often used when someone is falling to his death from great height.

Two minutes of fun. You will recognize it the first time you hear it. LINK

EPSON - One of the innovations for the Tokyo Olympics was the development of the electronic printer which was used to print the times of results.

The printer was developed by Seiko and the printer was called the "Electronic Printer" or "EP." The printer module was successful and became incorporated into early calculators.

Years later, Seiko launched a range of dot matrix printers into the US market and the US distributor was named EPSON, or "son" of "EP."

The brand became so established that Seiko renamed itself the Epson Corporation a few years later.

Boy Scouts - In February 1910 William D. Boyce incorporated the Boy Scouts of America. Scouts were originated by Englishman, Sir Robert S.S. Baden-Powell.

Boyce was visiting England and one foggy day in London town, he lost his way. A young boy guided him, but refused any monetary reward. A surprised Mr. Boyce asked why. The boy replied that he was a Scout and Scouts did not accept a reward for doing a good turn. This gesture of good will so inspired Boyce that he searched out Baden-Powell to learn more about the British Scouts. Upon his return to the United States, he formed the Boy Scouts of America.

St. Anthony The Great - He is also referred to as 'the Abbott' was an Egyptian Christian in the pre-Islamic period, who lived in the desert as an anchorite (religious hermit) for part of his life.

His relationship with pigs and patronage of swineherds stems from his work to treat skin diseases. Skin diseases were sometimes treated with applications of pork fat, which reduced inflammation and itching.

Swineherds took Anthony as their patron, and he thus became the patron saint of charcutiers (pork butchers) and also the patron saint of bacon. St Anthony is normally portrayed in pictures with a pig nearby.

Listerine - Listerine was invented 133 years ago, first as a surgical antiseptic, but also as a cure for gonorrhea. An article from 1888 recommends Listerine "for sweaty feet and soft corns, developing between the toes."

During the next century, it was marketed as a refreshing additive to cigarettes, a cure for the common cold, and as a dandruff treatment. In the 1920s the powerful, germ-killing liquid finally landed on its most lucrative use as a cure for bad breath.

Quilling - Most of us know what quilting is, but quilling is a bit different. Quilling, or paper filigree, is an art form using strips of paper that are rolled, shaped, and glued together to create decorative designs.

The name originates from winding the paper around a quill to create a basic coil shape. The paper is glued at the tip and the coiled shapes are arranged to form flowers, leaves, and various ornamental patterns similar to ironwork.

During the Renaissance, French and Italian nuns and monks used quilling to decorate book covers and religious items. The paper most commonly used was strips of paper trimmed from the gilded edges of books. These gilded paper strips were then rolled to create the quilled shapes. Quilling can be as simple or as complex as your imagination allows. It is making a comeback and is great fun for children and adults.

Bisquick - Bisquick mix was reportedly invented in 1930 by a General Mills executive who, while on a journey by train, complimented the chef in the dining car on his fresh biscuits. The chef showed him how he pre-mixed shortening with the dry ingredients of flour, salt and baking powder and kept the mixture on ice in the train kitchen so he could prepare the biscuits very quickly.

When they mass-marketed the idea, General Mills replaced the shortening with hydrogenated oil so that the product would not need to be refrigerated. At first they marketed it solely as a fast way to make biscuits, but soon, in an effort to increase sales, they started suggesting that consumers use it to make a variety of other foods, including pizza dough, pancakes, dumplings, cookies, and pies.

M&Ms - Forrest Mars, Sr., the founder of the Mars Company, got the idea for the confection in the 1930s during the Spanish Civil War when he saw soldiers eating chocolate pellets with a hard shell of tempered chocolate surrounding the inside, preventing the candies from melting.

Mars received a patent for his own process on March 3, 1941. One M was for Forrest E. Mars Sr., and one for Bruce Murrie, the son of Hershey's Chocolate president William F. R. Murrie. Murrie had 20 percent interest in the product. The arrangement allowed the candies to be made with Hershey chocolate which had control of the rationed chocolate. During the war, the candies were exclusively sold to the military. Mars bought out Murrie after the war, but kept the name. Murrie was also the guy who came up with the Mr. Goodbar (chocolate with peanuts) idea.

You can special order M&Ms with a saying or name on them from its web site. I did this for a birthday present. It is a bit pricey, but much fun, especially for children to see their own name on the little goodies.

Stanley Cup - March 1894 play-off competition for the coveted hockey award known as Lord Stanley's Cup began. Montreal and Ottawa played for the first championship honors. Montreal took home the trophy.

The original trophy was purchased by Sir Frederick Arthur Stanley, Lord Stanley of Preston. He then donated it to the Canadian Amateur Hockey Association.

In 1926, the playoff format took the order that remains in place today and the National Hockey League has been the permanent forum.

The teams with the most Stanley Cup titles since 1927 include the Detroit Red Wings (9) and Toronto Maple Leafs (11), with the Montreal Canadiens (24). Larry Robinson holds the record for playing in the most Stanley Cup games (203 for Montreal and 24 for the LA Kings).

The Stanley Cup competition remains the oldest in professional sports in North America.

Beverly Hills - The area we now call Beverly Hills was a series of ranches until it was purchased in the 1880s by two men named Charles Denker and Henry Hammel. Their ultimate ambition was to turn the area into a "North-African themed subdivision called Morocco." Severe drought and an economic collapse forced them to sell the land in 1900 to the Amalgamated Oil Company. After the company failed to find oil under the land, they changed its name to Rodeo Land and Water Company and called the area Beverly Hills, after Beverly Farms in Massachusetts.

Beverly Farms itself is named after the town of Beverly, which it skirts. The town was once a popular tourist resort; President Taft had a summer house there. It also claims to be the birthplace of the U.S. Navy, although this is debated. In 1668, English settlers named the town after the village of Beverley in Yorkshire, England.

During the 700s, a bishop founded a monastery in the town of Inderawuda and called it Beverlac, possibly after a colony of beavers in a nearby river. Eventually a slightly altered version of the name came to stand for the whole town, and Bishop John became known as St. John of Beverley after his canonization in 1037. *So, beautiful and ritzy Beverly Hills is actually named after some medieval English beavers.*

Kindergarten - Friedrich Froebel, German, invented kindergarten. He was a teacher, author and toy maker. His experience as an educator led him to the conclusion that playtime can be very instructive; an essential part of a child's education. He founded the first kindergarten for this purpose in 1837 in Blankenburg, Germany.

Froebel also invented of a series of toys designed to stimulate learning. He called them gifts. Architect Frank Lloyd Wright's mother gave her son some of these, maple wood blocks. Wright often spoke of the value the gifts had brought him throughout his life.

The first public kindergarten in the U.S. was started by Conrad Poppenhusen in College Point, Queens, New York in 1870.

Hamptons - According to legend, The Hamptons area of Long Island is named after the Earl of Southampton. Thomas Wriothesley, the 4th Earl when Southampton was founded in 1640, was a Cambridge-educated aristocrat. He eventually rose to one of the most powerful political offices in Britain, Lord High Treasurer.

Since the town of Southampton was the first to be settled in that area, and since the other Hamptons (Bridgehampton, East Hampton, etc.) take their names from that town, all of them can claim to owe their name to the Earl.

However, according to the Easthampton Historical Society, "19th century snobbishness" may have resulted in locals spreading that story, since being connected, however tangentially, to aristocracy was a big deal in early America. According to their records, Southampton was more likely named because it resembled the town of Southampton in England with no connection to the Earl.

The word hamp means pasture. The Native Americans had deforested much of Long Island and farmed it, so the open flat land bordered by a coarse, brown sandy beach likely evoked memories of the south coast of England. *So the Hamptons are either posh or pasture, your choice.*

Adidas - Adolph 'Adi' Dassler and his brother Rudolph owned their own shoe company in Germany during the 1920s and 30s. Their products were so popular, many of the German competitors in the 1928 Olympics wore Dassler Brothers shoes.

During WWII the brothers had a falling out. Both joined the Nazi party, but Rudolph was more fanatical and went off to fight, leaving Adolph to make shoes for the military. After the war ended, Rudolph formed his own company, Puma. Adi then renamed the original company after himself, and Adidas was born.

Reno - In 1868 a little town in Northwestern Nevada was officially named, Reno (after General Jesse Lee Reno, a Union officer of the Civil War).

It was first settled by the Washoe Indians who used the area for festivals and ceremonies. As settlers moved in, it was known as Fuller's Ferry, and later, as Lake's Crossing.

In the mid 1800s, Reno was just another settlement of silver miners. When the Comstock Lode was discovered in the Virginia City area, fortune hunters throughout the world came to the area to strike it rich. Today, they still come to strike it rich at Reno's glitzy gambling casinos.

Reno is also a haven for quickie divorces (six-week residency is required), is known as the biggest little city in the world, the winning slogan from a contest held in 1929. *If you look on a map you will find that Reno is actually west of Los Angeles.*

Sports Names - In the four major US professional sports, (Baseball, Basketball, Football, and Hockey) there are only seven teams whose nicknames do not end with an "S."

Basketball: Miami Heat, Utah Jazz, Orlando Magic.

Baseball: Boston Red Sox, Chicago White Sox.

Hockey: Colorado Avalanche, Tampa Bay Lightning.

Football: None.

The only reason I find this interesting is because my name starts with an S.

Duffel Bags - Duffel bag now stands for a particular style of bag. They were originally named for the thick Duffel cloth they were made out of, which was produced in the town of Duffel, Belgium. Duffel coats are named for the same cloth.

National Basketball Association - The 1949–50 NBA season was the inaugural season of the National Basketball Association. Commonly 1949–50 is counted the fourth NBA season. The league was created in 1949 by merger of the 3-year-old BAA and 12-year-old NBL. It recognizes the three BAA seasons as part of its own history.

The top-paid player in the first year of the NBA was the Detroit Falcon's Tom King who made $16,500. He managed this salary by not only playing for the team (salary $8,000 plus a $500 signing bonus) but also by convincing the team owner to hire him to be the publicity manager and business director for which he was paid an additional $8,000. Photos exist of King, still in his uniform with a typewriter on the bleachers, hammering out a press release after a game.

Chuck Conners, best known as 'The Rifleman' on TV, played for the Boston Celtics in the first year of the NBA.

The silhouette on the NBA logo is Jerry West. He is also the silhouette for the Mountaineer which stands outside the Mountainlair (student center) at West Virginia University.

Bloomers - Amelia Jenks Bloomer was born in 1818. She was a women's rights advocate, social reformer and temperance advocate. She married Dexter Bloomer, who encouraged her to write for his newspaper. Later she wrote for her own periodical about women's rights.

Among other things, she worked for more sensible dress for women and recommended what was called the Bloomer Costume in 1849. Bloomer believed that "pantalettes" were appropriate clothing for women. These were baggy pants that narrowed at the ankles and were meant to be worn under dresses. Bloomer advocated them because they both preserved a woman's decency and allowed her to participate in more activities without having to worry about indecency. Elizabeth Smith Miller introduced the clothing, but it was Amelia that gave bloomers the name we still use today.

Later she established churches, helped pass suffrage legislation, and founded the Soldier's Age Society. In 1871, she became the president of the Iowa Women Suffrage Society and helped pass a law that put an end to the distinction between male and female property rights. She petitioned congress to either end her taxation or end the "political disabilities" that did not allow her an active role in the government.

Moxie - This word takes its name from a soft drink, rather than the other way. The word is no longer used much. It means 'the ability to face difficulty with spirit and courage'.

The soft drink was invented by Dr. Augustin Thompson, a Maine native and Civil War veteran who worked in Lowell, MA. He patented a nostrum called Moxie Nerve Food in 1876. He eventually reformulated his drink and shortened the name to Moxie, in 1884.

An aggressive marketing campaign helped the brand grow into one of the first mass-produced soft drinks in the United States. One early advertisement for the drink read, "It nourishes the nervous system, cools the blood, tones up the stomach, and causes healthful, restful sleep. The family who orders a case from their grocer feels better and happier; the man who buys it in town at the druggists by the glass can accomplish more work."

Maine declared Moxie its state soft drink in 2005 and the beverage is celebrated with a festival in Lisbon Falls, ME, every year.

BVD - This men's underwear maker was originally founded by a group of New Yorkers named Bradley, Voorhees, and Day to make women's bustles. Eventually the trio branched out into knitted union suits for men, and their wares became so popular that "BVDs" has become a generic term for any underwear.

Sooner - The name refers to an Oklahoma resident and also the OU football team. Many settlers entered Oklahoma before the legal time for settlement in April 1889, thereby beating out law-abiding folks who followed the rules and moved in on time. Sooner came to mean both an Oklahoman and anyone who begins too soon.

Pumpernickel - Pumpernickel is one of those words that rolls off the tongue and sounds almost playful. It is a dark coarse sourdough bread made of rye flour and rye berries. The name comes from the German pumpern, meaning to break wind and Nickel meaning goblin or satan.

The name stems from its reputed indigestibility and is crudely referred to as 'the devil's fart' by some dictionaries. The long cooking time is what gives it its dark color.

The stories about the name coming from the French and Napoleon, but they have been debunked.

Pumpernickel is commonly found on hors d'oeuvres trays, topped with caviar, smoked salmon, or other goodies. It is referred to as an 'upscale bread'. In the US some add molasses to get the dark color without the long cooking time. It is great eaten in small doses and is also wonderful with strong cold cuts and cheeses.

Diomedes - There are two islands known as the Diomedes, about two and a half miles apart in the middle of the Bering Strait, between Siberia, Russia and Alaska. One of them, Little Diomede, belongs to the US, and has a population of about 150. The other island, Big Diomede belongs to Russia and is uninhabited, except for Russian border guards.

The space between these two islands marks not only an international border, but the International Date Line as well, making it possible for the folks on Little Diomede to wake up on a Sunday and look across the water to Big Diomede, where it's already Monday. *I guess this means the Russians are ahead of the US, at least by a day.*

Chantilly Lace - Some of you might remember the Big Bopper's hit of the same name in 1958. LINK

Some will remember what it looks like. This style of lace-making dates to the 1600s. While the majority of the lace was actually produced elsewhere, it gets its name from the town of Chantilly, France.

Slut - This unpleasant term is used these days to refer to an immoral or sexually promiscuous woman, but the origin of the term had a more innocuous meaning. It actually meant a woman who did not keep her room tidy. Another early meaning was kitchen maid or drudge. Only later did it begin to mean immorality of a sexual type. In Thomas Hoccleve's 1402 Letter to Cupid, "The foulest slutte of al a toune." In Victorian English, sluts wool referred to the little piles of dust that gather on the floor if it was not swept

----

Balaclava - It has been a favorite headgear of skiers and robbers and before that was worn by British troops unaccustomed to the bitter cold Russian weather during the Crimean War. They were also used as helmet liners as they could be rolled up to just cover the head.

It started being called Balaclava almost 30 years later and the name comes from the town of Balaclava in present-day Ukraine where an important battle in the Crimean War was fought.

Nanker Phledge - Mick Jagger and the Rollin' Stones were paid 30 guineas (about 30 Pounds or about $50) and played to a crowd of a bit more than 100 people. The pseudonym Nanker Phelge was used between 1963 and 1965 for several Rolling Stones group compositions.

Union Station - Many towns have a Union Station. Some larger ones are in Chicago, Chattanooga, Cincinnati, Denver, El Paso, Indianapolis, Kansas City, Los Angeles, Nashville, New York, St. Louis, Washington, D.C., and more.

Union stations or depots were constructed to consolidate rail traffic into a single terminal instead of having each railroad build a separate station and approach-track system. They formed a 'union', or coming together of railroad companies, facilities, and tracks.

The intent was to save money and hundreds of acres of valuable downtown real estate. It was and remains a success for achieving those goals. In addition, it is handy for travelers to have one place to go, regardless of final destination.

A railroad operating only a handful of trains per day through a town could not afford to build a fancy station, but several railroads sharing one facility could. Many Union Stations were impressive works of architecture and were preserved long after the trains that used them disappeared.

Scotch Tape - According to legend, Scotch tape earned its name when a frustrated customer told a 3M scientist to "take it back to your Scotch bosses and tell them to put more adhesive on it." Today, Scotch "Magic Tape" is manufactured in one place in the world: Hutchinson, Minn.

Fiddle and Violin - The violin (fiddle) was invented a thousand years after the Great Fire of Rome. It belongs to a family of stringed instruments, which includes the cello and viola. Among these three, it is the highest-pitched and smallest.

Renowned violin maker Andrea Amati constructed the very first violin sometime in 1555. Before that, there was a violin-like instrument called violetta, which only had three strings instead of the four strings that are found in modern-day violins.

Many archive documents relate that from about 1585 Brescia, Italy was the cradle of a magnificent school of string players and makers, all with the title of 'maestro' of all the different sort of multi-string instruments of the Renaissance: viola da gamba, violone, lyra, lyrone, violetta, and viola da brazzo.

A Persian geographer, Ibn Khurradadhbih of the 9th century was the first to cite the bowed Byzantine lira, which is held upright as a typical instrument of the Byzantines and equivalent to the rabāb used in the Islamic Empires of that time. The Byzantine lira spread through Europe westward and in the 11th and 12th centuries European writers use the terms fiddle and lira interchangeably when referring to bowed instruments.

The rabāb was introduced to Western Europe and both bowed instruments spread widely throughout Europe giving birth to various bowed instruments.

Lutherie - This is the practice of crafting stringed instruments, such as a violin or guitar. Lutherie is commonly divided into two main categories: makers of plucked or strummed string instruments or makers of stringed instruments that are bowed, which may require the additional help of an archetier. An archetier is someone skilled in the crafting of bows.

Experimental luthiers are craftsman who design string instruments with altered parts, or who create new and original instruments as are commonly used in the rock and jazz genres. Most instruments are never replicated or mass produced on a scale like the guitar or violin. However, additions to major instruments, such as the original vibrato bar become a vital part of the instrument.

Denny's - Richard Jezak and Harold Butler founded Denny's as Danny's Donuts in Lakewood, California in 1953. It expanded to twenty restaurants by 1959, when the chain was renamed Denny's to avoid confusion with another chain, Coffee Dan's.

KKR bought 47% of Denny's among others from owner TW corporation. Eventually, Denny's operations dominated the parent company so much that the Flagstar Companies changed its name to Denny's Corporation.

Five Famous Name Origins - *Wendy's* was opened on November 15, 1969. It was named after the fourth child, Melinda Lou Thomas, of founder Dave Thomas, who also helped stop Kentucky Fried Chicken from going out of business. Wendy was a nickname given to her as she couldn't pronounce her own name when she was young, instead she would say "Wenda", which is how she got the nickname "Wendy".

Arby's: Although some people believe it stands for "roast beef", this isn't true. It actually comes from the initials of its founders, the Raffel Brothers (R.B.'s). They originally planned to name their company "Big Tex", but someone already owned the rights to that name.

eBay: The company was originally supposed to be "Echo Bay Technology Group", but the domain "EchoBay.com" was already taken, so they shortened it and got eBay.com, which was available.

Starbucks: Its name comes from a character in the story of Moby Dick.

Nintendo: This famous company name comes from the Japanese name "Nintendou". Roughly translated "Nin" means "entrusted" and "ten-dou" means "heaven", so basically "leave luck to heaven". It started out making playing cards in 1889.

How Long is a Smoot - The smoot is a unit of length, defined as the height of Oliver R. Smoot, who became the president of the ISO. The unit is used to measure the length of the Harvard Bridge. In 1958 when Smoot was a Lambda Chi Alpha pledge at MIT (class of 1962), the bridge was measured to be 364.4 smoots, plus or minus one ear, using Smoot's body as a ruler. Oliver was 5 feet, 7 inches at that time. Google Earth and Google Calculator include the smoot as a unit of measurement. *You have just been smitten by a smoot fact.*

Grawlix - That is the name we give to a sequence of typographical symbols used to represent a non-specific, profane word or phrase. The term was coined in 1964 by American cartoonist Mort Walker, who is best known as the creator of the Beetle Bailey and Hi and Lois cartoons.

He also created and named an international set of symbols used in comics around the world and called it Symbolia. A few examples.
briffits: clouds of dust indicating that a character left in a rush.
plewds: drops of sweat indicating that a character is hot or stressed.
squeans: asterisks with an empty center indicating drunkenness or dizziness.

This is no #@$%! It is true.*

Couch - Father's Day for some is spent reclining on a couch. How many ways can you say couch? I can think of Couch, Canape, Chesterfield, Divan, Davenport, Loveseat, Sofa, Sectional, and Settee. Variations include sofa bed and futon.

A couch or sofa is a piece of furniture for seating two or more persons in the form of a bench, with or without armrests, that is partly or wholly upholstered, and often fitted with springs and tailored cushions.

The term 'couch' is used in North America, Australia, and New Zealand. The term 'sofa' is generally used in the United Kingdom and Ireland.

The most common types of couches are the loveseat, designed for seating two persons, and the sofa, with two or more cushion seats. A sectional sofa, often just referred to as a sectional, is formed from multiple sections and usually includes at least two pieces that join at an angle of 90 degrees or slightly greater, used to wrap around walls or other furniture.

Other couch variants include the divan, the fainting couch (backless or partial-backed), the canapé is an ornamental 3-seater. To conserve space, some sofas double as beds in the form of sofa-beds, daybeds, or futons.

In the United Kingdom, a Chesterfield is a deep buttoned sofa, with arms and back of the same height. It is usually made from leather and the term Chesterfield in British English is only applied to this type of sofa, but others use the term more generically. The first leather chesterfield sofa, with its distinctive deep buttoned, quilted leather upholstery and lower seat base, was commissioned by Phillip Stanhope, the 4th Earl of Chesterfield.

In Canada, the term chesterfield is equivalent to a couch or sofa. The use of the term was widespread among older Canadians, but is not much used today. Northern California is the only place in the US where chesterfield is a synonym for couch or sofa.

Lacrimal Caruncle - The lacrimal caruncle, or caruncula lachrymalis, is a small triangle-shaped pink bump located in the corner of the eye toward the nose. Within it are sweat and oil glands. Some accessory lacrimal glands, hair follicles, and tiny pieces of fat are also contained inside this small cutaneous mass.

The purpose is to lubricate, cleanse, and moisturize the eye, along with serving as an antibacterial.

The glands in it secrete a thick whitish oily substance that is sometimes seen in the corner of a person's eye after sleeping. On each side of the lacrimal caruncle are two tiny openings called lacrimal puncti that suction tears by vacuum each time the blinking motion of the upper eyelid has ended.

Crayola - Crayola means "oily chalk." The name combines "craie" (French for "chalk") and "ola" (short for "oleaginous," or "oily").

How 7 Companies Chose their Name - Pepsi is derived from the digestive enzyme pepsin.

Starbucks is named after Starbuck from the book Moby Dick.

Amazon is named after the Amazon, because Bezos wanted a name that began with A and the Amazon is the largest river in the world.

eBay was named because the original name Echo Bay was already taken as a dot com name.

Nike is named for the Greek goddess of victory.

Verizon is named after veritas (truth) and horizon.

Reebock is named after an African Antelope, Rhebok.

Emmy - Harry Lubcke suggested the name 'Immy' be used, named after the 'image orthicon tube' that was nicknamed the 'Immy'. The Academy members liked it, but felt is should be more feminine, to match the statuette, so switched it to the name 'Emmy'.

The statuette of a winged woman holding an atom, was designed in 1948 by TV engineer Louis McManus. His wife, Dorothy, served as the model for the statuette. Unlike the Academy Award statuette, where only one design was considered, this design was the 48th looked at by the Academy, with the previous 47 being rejected. The idea behind the design is that the winged woman represents the muse of art and the atom she's holding represents 'the science of television'.

For his design, Louis McManus was awarded a "Special Award" Emmy in the first year the Emmys were given out in 1948. His Emmy was not the statuette he designed, but rather a plaque.

Poker - The card game Poker first was called such around the early 19th century. There are two leading theories where the name originated that more or less coalesce into one likely origin. The first theory is that it came from the name of a French card game that resembled Poker called "Poque". There was also a German card game that is similar to Poker called "Pochspiel", which got its name from the German word "pochen" (also where the French Poque got its name). Pochen at the time meant "to brag or bluff".

Most Poker historians tend to lean towards the French Poque origin, in terms of where the game acquired its name, because Poker seems to have first popped up and spread from New Orleans in the very early 19th century. The French game of Poque was commonly played there.

The term Jackpot originally popped up around the 1870s referencing Jacks or Better Poker. This is much like traditional five card draw, except in this case, if a player does not have a pair of jacks or better in the first round of betting, he has to pass. This does not mean he has to be holding a pair of jacks, queens, or the like. It just means that he has to be holding cards that will beat a pair of tens. Once the first person who has that has placed a bet in the opening betting round, the rest of the participants are free to bet as they will, regardless of the cards they hold.

Ante comes from the Latin "ante", meaning before. *I bet you did not know all that.*

PAM - *PAM* Cooking Spray is an acronym for Product of Arthur Meyerhoff.

NECCO, as in Necco wafers is an acronym for New England Confectionery Company.

Snake Oil - Snake oil is now a generic term meaning a substance with no medicinal value, sold as a remedy for physical ailments. The term most likely comes from the use of oil derived from Chinese water snakes as a topical lotion. Chinese immigrants working on the construction of the Transcontinental Railroad in the 1860s would use it to alleviate joint pain. This ancient Chinese remedy was laughed at by other medicine salesmen, who called it a scam. In time, the term "snake oil" developed a negative connotation.

In the mid-1980s, a California psychiatrist named Richard Kunin decided to explore the question if snake oil was quackery or was it a legitimate treatment for joint pain, like the Chinese laborers claimed it was. He shared his findings in a 1989 letter to the Western Journal of Medicine.

Snake oil, especially the oil from the fatty tissue found in Chinese water snakes was unusually high in omega-3 fats. Kunin concluded, this meant that it could actually do what its advocates claimed, "Snake oil is a credible anti-inflammatory agent and might confer therapeutic benefits. Since essential fatty acids are known to absorb transdermally, it is not far-fetched to think that inflamed skin and joints could benefit by the actual anti-inflammatory action of locally applied oil just as the Chinese physicians and our medical quacks have claimed."

Kunin believed that snake oil actually worked. Subsequent research suggests that he was right. Unfortunately, while Kunin's conclusions are mostly correct, there is one significant omission. The Chinese snake oil came from water snakes, which, perhaps coincidentally fed on fish which themselves contained high amounts of omega-3 fatty acids. American-sold snake oil came from rattlesnakes, which do not have anywhere nearly the omega-3 amounts needed to provide the promised therapeutic benefits.

White Elephant - Sacred white elephants were and are kept by some Southeast Asian monarchs. Possessing a white elephant was regarded, and still is in Thailand and Burma (Myanmar) as a sign that the monarch reigned with justice and power, and that the kingdom was blessed with peace and prosperity.

It derives from stories that the kings of Siam would make a present of one of these animals to courtiers who were obnoxious or unpleasing, in order to ruin the recipient by the cost of its maintenance. A white elephant was a valuable, but burdensome possession, which its owner could not dispose of and whose cost and upkeep was out of proportion to its usefulness or worth.

These days a white elephant can mean an object, business venture, etc., that is without practical use or value. The term is used in business and even more frequently used during the gift-giving holiday season as friends and relatives strive to find unique gifts to give. *Many people consider dried fruit cakes as white elephants.*

Kummerspeck - This German word means excess weight gained from emotional overeating. Literally, 'grief bacon'. *Seems to me, putting grief and bacon together must be an oxymoron.*

Caskets and Coffins - The words coffin and casket are often used interchangeably to describe a box used to bury a dead body in. Although the general purpose of each is the same, there are small differences between the two.

The term coffin has been used since the early 16th century to describe a container that holds a dead body for burial. The shape of a coffin typically resembles the shape of a body and has six or eight sides. It is wider at the top for the shoulders and gradually decreases in width toward the end where the feet are placed. The shape is considered to save wood for construction and can be cheaper than a casket. The word coffin is derived from the Greek word kophinos, meaning basket.

A casket originally described a box used to store jewelry and other small valuable items before coming to have an additional meaning with coffin around the mid-19th century. A casket is typically a four-sided rectangular box and, when used for burying people, often contains a split-lid for viewing purposes.

Interestingly, it is thought that the word casket was adopted as a substitute word for coffin because it was deemed less offensive, especially when morticians and undertakers began operating funeral parlors instead of mortuaries. The shape of a casket also was thought to be less dismal because it did not depict the shape of a dead body.

The main difference between a coffin and a casket is essentially just the shape. A casket may still refer to a jewelry box and not necessarily a box to bury a body in.

When a coffin is used to transport a deceased person, it can also be called a pall, a term that also refers to the cloth used to cover a coffin. The words 'pall bearer' comes from those carrying the pall or coffin.

Taxis - Back in England, the Hansom cab was a two wheel horse-drawn carriage designed and patented in 1834 by Joseph Hansom, an architect from York. The vehicle was developed and tested by Hansom in Hinckley, Leicestershire, England. Originally called the Hansom Safety Cab, Hansom's design was modified by John Chapman (not Johnny Appleseed) and several others to improve its practicality, but retained Hansom's name. Hansom also set up a company in New York in 1869.

Hackney was an area of London, England and before Hansoms, hackney was also a name for carriages for hire to get around the city. It is also where we get the name 'hack' for modern cab drivers.

Harry Nathaniel Allen of The New York Taxicab Co., who imported the first 600 gas-powered New York taxicabs from France, coined the word "taxicab" as a contraction of "taximeter cabriolet", with cabriolet reflecting the design of the carriage.

There are essentially four distinct forms of taxicab, which can be identified by slightly differing terms in different countries:
1 - Hackney carriages, also known as public hire, hailed or street taxis, licensed for hailing on the street. Hansom's were Hackneys.

2 - Private hire vehicles, also known as minicabs or private hire taxis, licensed for pre-booking only.

3 - Taxibuses, also known as Jitneys or Jeepneys, operating on preset routes typified by multiple stops and multiple independent passengers.

4 - Limousines, specialized vehicle licensed for operation by pre-booking.

Taxi service is typically provided by automobiles, but various human-powered vehicles, such as the rickshaw, pedicab, animal-powered vehicles, or boats, such as water taxis or gondolas are also used.

The first taxi service in Toronto was established in 1837 by Thornton Blackburn, an ex-slave from the US. He designed and built a red and yellow box cab named 'The City', drawn by a single horse, and able to carry four passengers, with a driver in a box at the front, which he, himself, would operate. It became the nucleus of a taxicab company, the city's first, a successful venture

The firm Checker, which also made cars in addition to the eponymous cabs, came into existence back then, and stopped manufacturing cabs in 1982. It continued operation at partial capacity making Cadillac parts for General Motors until January 2009 when it declared bankruptcy.

Taximeters and Flag Falls - Taximeter is the device that calculates the charge and has a flag that a cab driver pushes down to start the charge count. The origin is a minimum charge for hiring a taxi, to which the rate per kilometer or mile is then added. It dates back to the old mechanical taximeters, which were equipped with a flag-like lever that could be seen from outside the cab. Think tax (charge) by the meter, as in kilometer.

Flagfall or flag fall is a common Australian expression for a fixed start fee, especially in the haulage and railroad industry. From the Australia mobile phone industry, the expression has spread to other English language countries, as business jargon for an initial fixed fee for establishing each phone call. It is also beginning to find its way into other businesses as a synonym to 'start fee'.

CN Tower - Back in June 1976 this tower solved a few problems for the people of Toronto, Canada. They had been having problems with their TV and radio reception. Interference from the many skyscrapers in the city were causing TV shows to be superimposed on top of each other.

To remedy the situation, the Canadian National Railway Company was commissioned to build an antenna that would tower over every building ever built. The antenna design turned into a tourist attraction. The design was by John Andrews Architects and Webb Zerafa Menkes Housden Architects.

Sixty three million CDN dollars and 1,537 people were needed to complete the tallest free standing structure and building in the world (until 2007). The CN (Canadian National) Tower, including the 335 foot, steel broadcasting antenna, is 1,815 feet, 5 inches tall. At 1,465 feet, you can stand on the public observation Space Deck.

You can take one of six elevators to the Sky Pod level at a speed of 15 miles per hour, or you could climb the 1769 steps up the tower. There

84

is also dining in the world's highest and largest revolving restaurant, aptly named '360'. I have been up there and the views are magnificent.

Sixteen Toronto TV and FM radio stations broadcast their signals from the antenna and all over Southern Ontario, Canada.

Twenty Interesting Names

1. Did you know the Comic Book Guy on The Simpsons has a name? It's Jeff Albertson. Creator Matt Groening says, "I was out of the room when [the writers] named him. In my mind, 'Louis Lane' was his name, and he was obsessed and tormented by Lois Lane."

2. Barbie's full name is Barbara Millicent Roberts. (Ken's last name is Carson.)

3. Cap'n Crunch's full name is Captain Horatio Magellan Crunch.

4. Snuffleupagus has a first name - Aloysius.

5. In the Peanuts comic strip, Peppermint Patty's real name is Patricia Reichardt.

6. The Wizard of Oz' full name is, Oscar Zoroaster Phadrig Isaac Norman Henkel Emmannuel Ambroise Diggs. Frank Baum's Dorothy and the Wizard in Oz relates, "It was a dreadfully long name to weigh down a poor innocent child, and one of the hardest lessons I ever learned was to remember my own name. When I grew up I just called myself O.Z., because the other initials were P-I-N-H-E-A-D; and that spelled 'pinhead,' which was a reflection on my intelligence."

7. Mr. Clean's first name is "Veritably." The name came from a "Give Mr. Clean a First Name" promotion in 1962.

8. In a deleted scene in the 2006 Curious George movie, The Man With the Yellow Hat's name was revealed as Ted Shackleford. The original scene was deleted.

9. The real name of Monopoly mascot Rich Uncle Pennybags is Milburn Pennybags.

10. The policeman in Monopoly is Officer Edgar Mallory.

11. On Night Court, Nostradamus Shannon was better known as Bull.

12. On Entourage, Turtle's real name is Salvatore Assante.

85

13. Sesame Street's resident game show host Guy Smiley was using a pseudonym all these years. He was born Bernie Liederkrantz.

14. The Michelin Man's name is Bibendum.

15. Jonas Grumby was called The Skipper on Gilligan's Island.

16. The Professor on Gilligan's Island was Roy Hinkley.

17. The Shaggy of Scooby-Doo is Norville Rogers.

18. The Pillsbury Doughboy's name is Poppin' Fresh. He has a wife, Poppie Fresh, and two kids, Popper and Bun Bun.

19. The patient in the classic game Operation is Cavity Sam.

20. The true identity of The Lone Ranger was John Reid. He was also the uncle of the Green Hornet. Both radio series originated on Detroit radio.

Insulting Names

Many common words we use to insult people did not begin with our current definition. Here are a few that have changed over the years.

Punk, worthless person - Punk has long been an insult in the English language. Shakespeare used it as an especially dirty word for prostitute in 1602. Eventually it came to mean young male prostitutes. This evolved by the 1920s to mean "young, inexperienced boy." Inexperienced soon translated to good-for-nothing and criminal. During the 1970s, British men in spiky leathers and Mohawk hair styles were called punks.

Brat, - badly behaved child - The worst kind of children in the olden days were very poor. Brat as slang dates from the 1500s in England, and meant beggar's child. Beggars often made sure their children were prominently displayed to garner more sympathy and money, which was annoying to passersby. Bratt is also an old English word meaning 'ragged garment' or 'cloak'. Brats often wore bratts, affirming that they were in fact, brats.

Jerk, obnoxious or dull person - Because older trains ran on steam, they often needed to be refilled with water. Water towers were built periodically along the train tracks and had hanging chains that the boiler man would "jerk" to start the water flowing. Towns sprang up around many of these water-stops and smaller ones were usually called jerk-water towns and their populations' jerks.

Dunce, slow-witted or stupid person - John Duns Scotus was a brilliant 15th century philosopher. He pioneered the idea that we had the exact same kind of goodness inside us that God did, but a lot less. Unfortunately, his followers, known as the Dunses in the century succeeding his death, were reputed to be the most stubborn, closed-minded philosophizers around. Mr. Scotus' name became attached more to his stubborn followers than to his own work.

Bum, one who performs a function poorly - We owe the legendary German work ethic for the introduction of the word bum to mean useless. It meant 'buttocks' since the 13th century (and is still used as such by many). The use of the word became popular during the Civil War, when German immigrants swelled the ranks of the Yankees. The German word bummler was easily shortened to apply to any soldier, because he was a loafer, sitting on his bum all day.

Barbarian, uncivilized or savage - "Bar-bar" was how ancient Greeks imitated the babbling stammer of any language that was not Greek. Thus barbarian came to mean the sort of lowbrow foreigners.

Cretin, stupid or insensitive person - Cretin is an insult that evolved from a real and dreadful medical condition. It comes from a word used in an 18th century Alpine dialect. The word was crestin, used to describe a dwarfed and deformed person. Cretinism was caused by lack of iodine resulting in congenital hypothyroidism.

Real People Facts

Jose Cuervo - Jose Antonio de Cuervo received a land grant in 1758 from the King of Spain to start an agave farm in the Jalisco region of Mexico.

Jose used his agave plants to make mescal, a popular Mexican liquor. In 1795, King Carlos IV gave the land grant to Cuervo's descendant Jose Maria Guadalupe de Cuervo and granted the Cuervo family the first license to commercially make tequila.

The family started packaging it in individual bottles in 1880, and in 1900 the tequila started using the brand name Jose Cuervo. The brand is still under the leadership of the original Jose Cuervo's family. Juan-Domingo Beckmann is the sixth generation to run the company.

Abigail Adams - She was the first Second Lady and the second First Lady. She was the wife of John Adams, who was the first Vice President and second President of the US.

She said something to remember around election time, "Many of our disappointments and much of our unhappiness arise from our forming false notions of things and persons."

Dr. Suess - The "Dr." in "Dr. Seuss" was in homage to Theodore Geisel's father's hope that his son would be a doctor. "Seuss" was his mother's maiden name as well as his own middle name.

Geisel first used the pen name "Seuss" in college after being removed as the editor of the Dartmouth College's humor magazine 'Jack-O-Lantern' and being banned from writing for that magazine after the dean caught him and friends drinking.

He subsequently started publishing under various pen names, including T. Seuss. and Dr. Theophrastus Seuss, which was shortened to Dr. Seuss. He also had an alternate pen name that he also wrote under which was Theo LeSieg. The "Theo" is short for "Theodor", and "LeSieg" is "Geisel" spelled backwards.

After Dartmouth, he attended Oxford, but dropped out of the PhD program. He did eventually receive several honorary doctorates.

The proper pronunciation of Seuss is actually "Zoice" (rhymes with "voice") as it is a Bavarian name. Due to the fact that most Americans pronounced it incorrectly as Soose, Geisel later gave in, stopped correcting people, and decided mispronunciation was a good thing because it is "advantageous for an author of children's books to be associated with Mother Goose."

Theodor Seuss Geisel was born in Springfield, Massachusetts and died in 1991.

Jacuzzi Brothers – The seven Jacuzzi brothers emigrated from Italy to California in the early 1900s. In California, they began developing innovations for the big new craze: the airplane. Their biggest hit was the creation of the first plane with an enclosed cabin, which the US Postal Service bought to deliver mail.

According to legend, their mother was worried about her sons' safety and eventually convinced the brothers to change jobs. They started concentrating on hydraulic pumps for irrigation and hospital use. In the late 1940s, Candido Jacuzzi's young son Kenneth started suffering from arthritis. He received hydrotherapy at a hospital, but his father decided his son needed to have access to it at home as well. He filed a patent for his invention, but it wasn't until another relative, Roy joined the business years later that they started selling their Jacuzzi tubs to the public. *That is just about the hot and cold of it.*

Dr. Samuel A. Mudd - He was the physician who set the leg of Lincoln's assassin John Wilkes Booth and whose shame created the expression, "His name is Mudd."

He was sentenced to life in prison for splinting the fractured leg, but became a hero to guards and inmates of his island prison when he stopped a yellow-fever epidemic there in 1868 after the army doctors had died. President Johnson, Lincoln's successor, pardoned Mudd in early 1869.

Phoebe **Anne Oakley** Mozee - She was five feet tall. She was also a crack shot with rifles, pistols, and shotguns. Annie Oakley was born in a log cabin in Patterson Township, Ohio and starred in Buffalo Bill's Wild West Show for seventeen years.

March 5, 1922, Annie broke all existing records for women's trap shooting by hitting 98 out of 100 clay targets thrown at 16 yards while at a match at the Pinehurst Gun Club in North Carolina. She hit the first fifty, missed the 51st and 67th.

In one day she used a .22 rifle to hit 4,772 glass balls out of 5,000 tossed in the air. She could hit the thin side of a playing card from 90 feet and puncture it at least five times before it hit the ground. It was this display that named free tickets with holes punched in them, Annie Oakleys.

She was immortalized in Annie Get Your Gun, which was later made into a musical for the stage. In 1985, another film, Annie Oakley, was made for TV. It included silent-film footage of the record-breaking sharp-shooter, taken by Thomas Edison. There was also a weekly TV show about her during the fifties.

Johnny Carson - Millions were entertained for decades by the late night TV host of the Tonight Show. Here are a number of YouTube videos of some great moments for your viewing pleasure. LINK *Save it for when you have a bunch of free time.*

Jim Beam - Jim Beam did not actually start the distillery that bears his name. His great-grandfather Jacob Beam opened the distillery in 1788 and started selling his first barrels of whiskey in 1795.

In those days, the whiskey went by the name of "Old Tub." Jacob Beam handed down the distillery to his son David Beam, who in turn passed it to his son David M. Beam, who passed it to his son, Colonel James Beauregard Beam, in 1894.

He was 30 years old when he took over the family business and ran the distillery until Prohibition shut him down. Following repeal in 1933, Jim built a distillery and resurrected the Old Tub brand and also added a bourbon simply called Jim Beam.

Hans Christian Andersen - He was born in 1805 to a poor family. His father, a shoemaker, died when Hans was 11 years old. When he was just 14, Hans left his hometown of Odense, Denmark and traveled to Copenhagen where he became a starving actor, singer, and dancer. It was there that he met the man who became his lifelong friend and benefactor, Jonas Collin. With Collin's help, Andersen received a royal scholarship and completed his education.

By his 25th birthday, Hans was on his way to a writing career that would make him one of the most widely-read authors in the world. His first recognition came for his many plays and novels. Five years later, he penned his first of 168 fairy tales.

Among them are The Tinder-Box, Little Claus and Big Claus; tales that made fun of human faults: The Emperor's New Suit, The Princess and the Pea; tales based on his life: The Ugly Duckling, She was Good for Nothing, The Snow Queen, The Red Shoes, The Little Mermaid, Thumbelina, The Marsh King's Daughter.

As Andersen's popularity rose in the 1840s, he found himself rubbing shoulders with kings and queens, famous composers, poets and novelists. He became wealthy enough to visit throughout Europe, writing about his experiences as he traveled. In Sweden is often considered his best travel book.

He wrote his own story in 1855, The Fairy Tale of My Life. Hans Christian Anderson died a lonely man on August 4, 1875, but his stories and fairy tales live on, entertaining children and adults.

The Hans Christian Andersen Award is presented every other year to an author and an illustrator of children's books. The 'Little Nobel Prize', as it is often called, is the highest international recognition bestowed on an author (since 1956) and to an illustrator (since 1966). It is presented by the International Board on Books for Young People.

Bartholomew Gosnold - He was a prolific explorer and also gave both Martha's Vineyard and Cape Cod their names.

In addition, he pioneered the quickest way to sail from Great Britain to the northeastern seaboard of America. Gosnold recruited John Smith for his Jamestown expedition and a published account of his voyage in 1602 to explore the coast south of Nova Scotia in search of a passage to Asia. He was responsible for popularizing the colonization of New England.

Martha's Vineyard is named after a daughter of Gosnold who died in infancy. Originally the name was applied to a much smaller island; a "place most pleasant" according to a contemporary source. The larger island was actually called Martin's Vineyard, after the captain of the ship Gosnold was sailing on, for much of its history. Eventually the feminine name came to stand for the larger island as well. Martha's Vineyard is the eighth-oldest surviving place name the United States. You can visit the grave of little Martha in the churchyard of Bury St. Edmunds in Suffolk, England.

For centuries, codfish have figured prominently in Cape Cod's history and fortunes. Bartholomew caught a ton of cod near this cape and named it in a note in his logbooks about the plentiful "codfyshes" which "pestered" his ship.

Although many explorers and fishermen had sailed New England's waters in the 1500s, Gosnold is credited with the European discovery of New England decades later.

Walter Lantz - Cartoonist Walter Lantz was born on April 27 1899 in New Rochelle, New York. He was the creator of Woody Woodpecker, Andy Panda, Chilly Willy, and Wally Walrus among others.

Woody Woodpecker made his first appearance in the 1940 film, Knock, Knock with the famous Mel Blanc doing Woody's distinctive laugh. Later on, his wife supplied the laugh.

Walter Lantz was honored by the Academy of Motion Picture Arts and Science in 1979 with the Lifetime Achievement Award at the Oscar ceremonies. Woody received a star on the Hollywood walk of fame in 1990. Walter was active in entertaining Viet Veterans.

Tanqueray - When he was a young boy, Charles Tanqueray, the product of three straight generations of Bedfordshire clergymen, it was assumed he would follow the same path.

He decided to do something different and began distilling gin in 1830 in a little plant in London's Bloomsbury district. By 1847, he was shipping his gin to colonies around the British Empire, where many plantation owners and troops had developed a taste for Tanqueray and tonic.

Madame Curie - Madame Curie was born in 1867 and became an expert in physics, chemistry, and radioactivity.

Marie Salomea Sklodowska was born in Warsaw Poland. Her father was a math and physics teacher and atheist. Her mother was a teacher, operated a boarding school, and was Catholic. Four-year-old Marie taught herself how to read Russian and French and was known to help her four brothers and sisters with their math homework. It was also at age four that she began to demonstrate her incredible memory.

As a teenager, Marie was anxious to attend college, but her family couldn't afford it so she spent five grueling years earning money as a governess. In 1891 she headed for the Sorbonne in Paris. There, she met future husband Pierre Curie. At school she discovered the radioactive elements radium and polonium (She named it after her native Poland). Later, she became the first woman professor at the Sorbonne.

In her thirties, Marie worked closely with her husband, and together they devised the science of radioactivity (she named the term radioactivity), for which they were awarded a Nobel Prize in physics. They had two children Irene and Eve. After Pierre's death in 1906, Marie continued her work, winning her second Nobel, in chemistry at age 44.

It has been determined that Marie contracted aplastic anemia from all the time spent with radiation, of which no one knew the dangers of it. She died from it in 1934.

John Pemberton - Coca Cola was originally used for medicinal purposes and sold at Jacob's Pharmacy in Atlanta, GA. John Pemberton received a medical degree at 19 and worked as a druggist in Columbus, Georgia, before joining the Confederate army during the Civil War. He rose to the rank of lieutenant colonel with the Third Georgia Cavalry and was severely wounded in battle. To control the pain resulting from those wounds, he became addicted to morphine.

After the war, he settled in Atlanta, where he began work on a beverage combining coca leaves and cola nuts. Coca leaves contain traces of cocaine, which was then believed to help control one's dependence on opiates.

His objective was to create a pain reliever, but when his lab assistant accidentally mixed the concoction with carbonated water on May 8, 1886, the two men tasted it, liked it, and decided it might make a profitable alternative to ginger ale and root beer. Vernor's Ginger Ale, created in 1866 by a Detroit pharmacist, preceded Coke.

Three years later, Dr. Pemberton he sold out for $2,300. He had no idea what the still very classified, secret formula would be worth. It now sells about 350 million cans and bottles a day in nearly 200 countries. He died a few years after his accidental invention and only a few months after the Coca Cola Corporation was incorporated.

The original medicine was sold to make people feel better. Some say it still does, minus the cocaine. *Vernor's, especially with Captain Morgan, still makes me feel better than Coke.*

William Henry 'Boss' Hoover - He did not invent the vacuum cleaner, but his name has become a verb and a noun, especially in England, where they hoover the floors with a Hoover.

James Murray Spangler invented the first upright vacuum in 1908, because his asthma was exacerbated by the dust the carpet sweeper used at his work stirred up. He was making one every 2-3 weeks when he loaned a model to his cousin Susan Hoover.

Her husband was looking for a new business venture and seized the opportunity to buy Spangler's patent from him. However, no one was interested in his machine. He decided to put an ad in a popular magazine for possibly the first 'free at home trial'. The gimmick worked and within four years the Hoover Company was an international brand.

Statler Brothers - Two of the group are brothers, but their name is not Statler. The other two are not brothers. Don and Harold Reid, along with Phil Balsley and Lew DeWitt make up the group called the Statler Brothers.

Originally, they called themselves the Kingsmen, until the song "Louie, Louie" by another group called The Kingsmen hit the charts. They decided to call themselves The Statler Brothers, borrowed from a brand of tissue paper.

Lew DeWitt wrote "Flowers On The Wall" one of their biggest hits.

Josiah Wedgwood - He may be remembered today for his eponymous pottery, but his life was far more exciting than just that.

In his day he was a prominent abolitionist, and his pottery company made a medallion with the design of a black slave on his knees with the motto, "Am I not a man and brother?" He produced large quantities of the medallion and distributed them for free through the Society for the Abolition of the Slave Trade.

Fashionable women started wearing them as jewelry and men smoked pipes with the image on the side. It became the most widely recognized image of a black person during the 1700s. Josiah died before slavery was abolished in England. *He also has the distinction of being the grandfather of Charles Darwin.*

Charles E. Hires - Hires Root Beer (now owned by Dr Pepper Snapple) was developed by a pharmacist. According to one of the stories behind the origin of America's oldest root beer, Philadelphia's Charles E. Hires discovered an herbal tea made of roots, berries, and herbs while on his honeymoon.

He introduced a root beer powder mix that consumers could use to make their own root beer. It showcased at the 1876 US Centennial Exposition in Philadelphia, where Alexander Graham Bell showcased his telephone.

Hires developed a soda fountain syrup version of his root beer in 1884 and began bottling the drink in 1893. Only Detroit's Vernor's Ginger Ale is older, and is now also owned by Dr Pepper Snapple.

His decision to market the beverage as a beer rather than a tea, as he had originally considered, appealed to the Pennsylvania miners and added to Hires' popularity during Prohibition. *Incidentally, the R-J on the bottle stood for Root Juices.*

Ellen Henrietta Swallow Richards - She was the first woman to graduate from a scientific institute in the United States. She was the first female student and received a Bachelor of Science degree from the Massachusetts Institute of Technology. She met her husband, Robert Richards at MIT. Ellen Richards was also the first woman to be elected to the American Institute of Mining and Metallurgical Engineers.

In addition, she was a leading figure in the study of nutrition and hygiene. Ellen was an instructor in the laboratory of sanitary chemistry at the Lawrence Experiment Station. She also became the first president of the American Home Economics Association in 1908. In 2011, she was listed as #8 on the MIT150 list of the top 150 innovators and ideas from MIT. Ellen was born in 1842 and died in 1911. She also came up with the word ecology.

Daniel Gabriel Fahrenheit - Fahrenheit is the temperature scale proposed in 1724 by German physicist Daniel Gabriel Fahrenheit, born in 1686. In 1717, Fahrenheit became a glassblower, making barometers, altimeters, and thermometers. After 1718 he was a lecturer in chemistry. At that time, temperature scales were not standardized and everybody made up their own scale. He originally copied another thermometer, but adjusted his scale so that the melting point of ice would be 32 degrees, body temperature 96 degrees, and water boil at about 212 degrees. 180 degrees made for even spacing of his scale.

Other scientists later refined it to make the freezing point of water exactly 32 °F, and the boiling point exactly 212 °F. That is how normal human oral body temperature became 98.6°.

The Fahrenheit scale was replaced by the Celsius scale in most countries during the 1960s and 1970s when converting to metrics. Fahrenheit remains the official scale of the United States, Cayman Islands, Belize (by Guatemala), Puerto Rico, Guam, and the U.S. Virgin Islands. Scientists use Celsius in all countries.

The Fahrenheit and Celsius scales intersect at −40° (−40 °F and −40 °C represent the same temperature).

O. Henry - O. Henry was born as William Sidney Porter in Greensboro, North Carolina. At age three, his mother died of consumption, now called tuberculosis, and he was raised by his physician father and maternal grandmother.

Porter took a number of different jobs over the next several years, first as pharmacist then draftsman, bank teller, and journalist. He also began writing as a sideline.

By 1891, while devoting all his spare time to a self-published magazine 'The Rolling Stone', he took a job as a teller and bookkeeper at the First National Bank of Austin, TX. In 1894, he was abruptly fired for embezzling funds, although no charges were filed. He moved to Houston, TX, where his pieces in The Rolling Stone helped land him a job as a writer for The Houston Post.

After a federal audit of the Austin bank, formal embezzlement charges were brought against him. The day before his trial, he fled to New Orleans and then to Honduras. A year later, after learning that his wife Athol was dying, he returned to Austin and surrendered to authorities. In 1898, he was convicted and sentenced to five years in prison. While serving his sentence at Ohio Penitentiary, Porter worked as a night druggist in the prison hospital, was given a room in the hospital wing, and even provided with access to a typewriter to continue his writing.

He had fourteen stories published in national magazines under various pseudonyms while he was in prison, but became best known as "O. Henry." When asked what the O stood for, he said, "O stands for Olivier, the French for Oliver."

He was released from prison after serving three years and moved to Manhattan, where he lived until his premature death at age 47 in 1910. He died of cirrhosis of the liver, complications of diabetes, and an enlarged heart. During the last decade of his life, he wrote nearly 400 short stories.

Marx Brothers - The five Marx brothers got their nicknames during a poker game. The Marx family comedy act was made up of Julius, Adolph, Leonard, Milton, and Herbert Marx. The five characters became better known as Groucho, Harpo, Chico, Gummo, and Zeppo. Four of the five were given their new names in 1915.

The boys were involved in a poker game with monologist Art Fisher. It was a popular fad around this time to give everyone a nickname that ended in "o". Common nicknames were "Jingo" or "Bongo" or "Ringo, etc.

In this poker game, Fisher was dealing out the cards to the four Marx brothers and he gave them each their nicknames as he dealt. "First, here's a card for 'Harpo'." Adolph Marx played the harp.

"Here's one for 'Chicko'." Leonard Marx was a notorious ladies' man and, in those days, women and girls were often referred to as 'chickens'. Later the slang term became 'chicks'. Supposedly, a typesetter in one town the brothers were performing in, accidentally left the "k" in "Chico" out, and his name became Chico.

Next was Julius, "And here's a card for Groucho." The name derived from Julius' not-so-friendly demeanor.

The fourth was Milton, "And here's a card for Gummo", Fisher said. This one has two popular theories behind it. The one the family (except Harpo) says is because Milton often wore gumshoes (rubber soled shoes), hence "Gummo." The alternate from Harpo is that Gummo was sneaky and would creep up on people like a gumshoe detective. Gumshoe detectives received their name for the same reason, rubber sole shoes.

A few years later, the youngest of the five brothers entered the act, replacing older brother Gummo. Herbert Marx became 'Zeppo'. Harpo said Zeppo was named in honor of a wild monkey named 'Zippo', who played on bars and ran around. Groucho said in 1972 that Zeppo was named after the Zeppelin airships.

Gräfenberg - Gynecologist Dr. Ernst Gräfenberg came to the US from Nazi Germany in 1940. He ran a successful gynecology practice in New York until his death in 1957.

Gräfenberg researched the subject of stimulation and stated in a study, "An erotic zone always could be demonstrated. . ." Although others had studied this before him, he is usually given credit for its 'discovery' and the name 'G-spot' named for him came from a 1981 paper published in the Journal of Sex Research. He also invented the first known ring IUD birth control device, the Gräfenberg ring.

John Josefa Moe - He was born to Samoan father Pulu Moe and Filipino-Hawaiian mother Louisa Moe while they were touring in Hawaii.

He performed with Hawai'i stars Don Ho, Kui Lee, and Ed Kenney during the 1950s 60s, and 70s. He had a vaudeville act in England, carved tiki, created a then-innovative koa Hawaiian Kepi bracelet with names etched in old-English lettering, and designed restaurants and clubs on the East Coast of the US.

He had other skills, such as one of the best fire knife dancers in the world, comedian, musician, singer, middleweight Golden Gloves boxing champion, custom airbrush artist for t-shirts, and surf boarding instructor.

Moe had a thick British accent, because he attended an English boarding school while his parents toured. Another famous Samoan with an accent is Dwayne, The Rock, Johnson, although his is American English. At one time, Josefa was roommates with Sir Roger Moore of James Bond fame and was once considered the most photographed Samoan in the world.

He passed away Nov 3, 2006 at 73 in his Summerlin, Nev. (near Vegas) home. He had 12 children.

John Batman - In 1835, John Batman settled in what was to eventually become Melbourne, Australia. He named it 'Batmania'. Two years later it was renamed Melbourne in honor of the Prime Minister, Lord Melbourne.

Benjamin Franklin - Benjamin Franklin was one of the Founding Fathers of the United States. Franklin was polymath, a leading author, printer, political theorist, politician, postmaster, scientist, musician, and inventor.

He was born January 17, 1706, in Boston, MA and died on April 17, 1790, in Philadelphia, PA. In his will, the left 1,000 pounds each to the cities of Philadelphia and Boston, but the cities were not given access to the money immediately. Franklin required that the money be held in trust for 100 years after his death. After that, the cities could remove a portion of the trust money to establish a trade school, but not all of the money could be withdrawn; some had to remain for another 100 years. Franklin's instructions provided that at the end of the 200 years the balance of the money in the Boston trust be divided, with 26 percent going to the city and 74 percent to Massachusetts. He made a similar arrangement with Philadelphia and Pennsylvania

When the final trusts became due in 1990, Philadelphia's was worth $2 million. It used the money to provide scholarships for area high school children. Boston's trust, which withdrew less money during the trust's second century, was worth $5 million. Boston used it to fund the Benjamin Franklin Institute of Technology, which was established out of the trust's funds which were withdrawn 100 years earlier.

Clarence Leonidas "Leo" Fender - He invented of one of the most popular electric guitar brands in the world, Fender Guitars, but never learned how to play guitar. He was an accountant before losing his job during the Great Depression. When he lost his job, he decided to turn his hobby of tinkering with electronics, radios, amplifiers, etc., into a business, 'Fender Radio and Record Shop'. This eventually led to what is now known as the 'Fender Musical Instruments Corporation' and the creation of his famous guitars and amplifiers.

Despite designing the first commercially successful solid-body electric guitar, the Telecaster, and the most influential of all electric guitars, the Stratocaster, and inventing the solid-body electric bass guitar, the Precision bass, Leo Fender was an engineer, not a musician. He had to bring in musicians to properly test the prototypes of his guitars.

Fender's fascination with electronics started when he was 14 years old. His uncle built a radio from spare parts and the loud music coming from the speaker impressed Leo and repairing radios became his hobby.

He convinced Clayton Kauffman, an inventor and lap steel guitar player, to start 'K & F Manufacturing Corporation', which would design and build electric Hawaiian guitars and amplifiers. Fender began to design steel guitars that rested in the musician's lap while being played with a metal slide. In 1944, Leo and Doc patented a lap steel guitar that had a special electric pickup also patented by Fender. Fender's guitar "Broadcaster" was steadily improved to become a Telecaster, which in turn led to The Esquire Model in 1950, the first six string one pickup Fender guitar.

Fenders designs helped turn electric guitars into the dominate type of guitar used by performing artists. The ultimate goal for Fender was to create an electric guitar which would have no feed-back, even in small settings, and which would be easy to play and to tune. The Fender Stratocaster is still the most popular and copied electric guitar in the world.

Henri Nestlé - He started his company as a pioneer in the baby food industry. He was likely inspired by his family's history as seven of his thirteen siblings died before reaching adulthood.

Nestlé sold the company to his business associates and retired just seven years after he founded the company. Though the name "Nestlé" has since gone on to be associated with many different products, mostly chocolate based products and other sweets, the only Nestlé to be involved with the company left when their only product was baby formula.

Gene Autry - TV viewers were treated to the first performance of The Gene Autry Show in September, 1950. Autry and his sidekick, Pat Buttram maintained law and order in the US Southwest for six years. Gene sang just like he did in the movies and his horse, Champion, would do amazing horse tricks while Pat Buttram would invariably get into silly situations.

Autry went on to become a Country Music Association Hall of Famer, own Golden West Broadcasting, the California Angels baseball team, and he is the only person to have five Hollywood Walk of Fame stars (film, radio, TV, stage, records). He died October 2, 1998.

Fisher and Price - The holidays would not be the same without thinking of toys, and one of the largest toy makers is Fisher-Price. The original founders of the toy company back in 1930 were businessmen Herman Fisher, Irving Price, and Irving's wife, a children's book author and illustrator Margaret Evans Price, and a toy store owner, Helen Schelle.

While the businessmen were instrumental in launching the company, it was actually the two women who collaborated on most of the company's early products, like Dr. Doodle, the duck push-pull toy that was based on a character from Margaret's books. Much of the early success of the company can be attributed to Helen Schelle, who had many connections in the incipient toy industry.

Fisher came from Pennsylvania and went to Penn State. Before founding Fisher-Price, he worked as Vice President and General Manager of All Fair, Inc., a toy and game manufacturer. When Fisher and a group of investors (including Price) unsuccessfully tried to buy All Fair Inc., they decided to start their own company instead. Fisher is credited with coining the term "preschool toys" in 1934.

His partner, Irving Price married into the wealthy Evans family of New York. Irving had a long career as an executive with Woolworth before retiring young and becoming Mayor of East Aurora, New York. His wealth helped start Fisher-Price.

Michelangelo Buonarroti - Michelangelo actively deprived himself many comforts. He told his workshop assistants and friends that he didn't care what food tasted like. He knew of no food that was not palatable, and only ate what was cheapest in providing him a balanced diet. He preferred to drink water, but understood the health benefits of wine and drank only the cheapest he could find.

His house was modest and infested with rats. In the coldest weather, he would simply put on another coat, or go for a jog. He once stated that because he had never been bitten by a flea and the rats did not seem a problem for him. He wore the same old dirty clothes, day after day, washing them and himself about twice a month in the nearest river or lake. He wore a pair of shoes until the soles nearly came off. *Good thing he treated his art better than himself or we would all be deprived of the beauty.*

Clara Peller - Wendy's introduced Clara Peller during 1984, when she was first seen by TV viewers in the famous "where's the beef" commercial campaign for Wendy's fast-food chain.

Dave Thomas spent $8 million on the ads that promoted hamburger sales plus T-shirts, baseball caps, records, greeting cards and many other items bearing her picture and the famous question. *I think the new ads with the real Wendy are boring, but I really do like the tasty new fries.*

W.C. Fields - William Claude Dukenfield was born on February 3, 1880. He became one of the most celebrated comics and actors in the US, starting his career as a vaudeville juggler, then spending several decades on the musical stage before starring in movies.

W.C. Fields, his stage name made his first short, Pool Sharks, in 1915. After silent movies, he performed in many comedy classics like, My Little Chickadee with Mae West, The Bank Dick, and Never Give a Sucker an Even Break.

W.C.'s famous lines became subject matter for nightclub impersonators and comedians. One of the most-repeated quotes was originally directed at the child-actor, Baby LeRoy, his on-screen nemesis: "Go away, kid, you bother me."

His most-quoted, was fired at a party hostess who offered him a glass of water, "Never touch the stuff; fish **** in it." Other W.C. Fields lines: "Doctors say don't worry about your heart, it will last as long as you live.", "Californians talk so much about their climate, it makes their weather vane.", "I am very humble and proud of it.", "It was a woman who drove me to drink and I never even thanked her."

He requested that his headstone read, "All things considered, I'd rather be in Philadelphia." *Ah, Yes!*

Zamboni - The ice making business was booming way before household refrigerators were common. In 1939 Frank Zamboni and his brother had been in their ice block business for years, but refrigerators were becoming popular enough that they saw things quickly changing.

They had an inventory of many large refrigeration units, so they decided to open an ice rink. It was there that Frank came up with a way to resurface the ice. Originally it took three men an hour and a half to get it done, but in 1949 he invented the precursor of the ice machine we know today.

Now one man can resurface an ice rink in ten minutes. Like Xerox and Kleenex, Zamboni is a trademarked word that we now use to refer to all ice resurfacing machines. In April 2012, the 10,000th Zamboni was sold and delivered to the Montreal Canadiens.

Sadism and Masochism These words were named after their first practitioners, Donatien Alphonse Francois de Sade (Marquis de Sade) and Leopold von Sacher-Masoch. Their sexual conduct so shocked the world that their names became synonymous with their activities.

"It is always by way of pain one arrives at pleasure." ~Marquis de Sade Sade was well known for his morally unrestrained sexuality. He was accused of a number of sexual crimes like imprisoning a prostitute and poisoning another one. He also wrote erotic works describing his practices.

Leopold von Sacher-Masoch was also a writer, renowned for his romantic stories. He enjoyed dominating women in furs and once entered into a contract with a woman to become her slave for six months, with the stipulation that she wear furs as often as possible, especially when she was in a cruel mood. "A slap in the face is more effective than ten lectures. It makes you understand very quickly." ~Leopold von Sacher-Masoch.

The terms were first selected as professional scientific terminology, identifying human behavioral phenomena and intended for the classification of distinct psychological illnesses and/or malicious social and sexual orientations.

German psychiatrist Richard von Krafft-Ebing introduced the terms "Sadism" and "Masochism"' into institutional medical terminology in his work "New research in the area of Psychopathology of Sex" in 1890.

The term "Sadomasochism" has been loosely used to refer to the entire umbrella of BDSM. However, BDSM is a shorthand for the three main subdivisions of the culture: B (bondage and discipline), D (dominance and submission) and S&M (sadism and masochism).

Five Interesting People Facts - Shirley Temple always had 56 curls in her hair.

Isaac Asimov is the only author to have a book in every Dewey-decimal category.

Hulk Hogan's real name is Terry Bollea.

Stalin was five feet, four inches tall, his left foot had webbed toes, and his left arm was noticeably shorter than his right.

The only real person to be represented with a Pez head was Betsy Ross.

Mercedes and Benz - Long before there was Daimler Benz and Mercedes, there were two car companies. At the same time that Karl Benz was developing his three-wheeler in Mannheim, Germany, in the 1880s, Gottlieb Daimler was creating the world's first four-wheeled automobile with an internal combustion engine in Stuttgart, 75 miles away.

Incidentally, Benz' wife, Bertha used her dowry to pay off his debts and keep him in business. She also undertook the world's first long-distance car journey, and is acknowledged as the first lady motorist in history.

Daimler received his patent for a "vehicle with gas or petroleum drive machine" in 1885. Benz built three gas engine models between 1885 and 1887, and received the patent for his design in 1886.

In April 1900, Emil Jellinek, an Austrian businessman made an agreement with DMG (Daimler Motoren Gesellschaft, or Daimler Motor Company) to buy and resell its cars. He decided to use his young daughter's name, Mercedes, as a product name. Jellinek ordered 36 vehicles at a total price of 550,000 marks, equivalent to over 2 million dollars today. A few weeks later, he placed an order for another 36 vehicles.

The first 'Mercedes' was developed by Wilhelm Maybach, the chief engineer at DMG, and it is regarded today as the first modern automobile.

After various iterations, in November 1921, DMG applied for patents for a three-dimensional three-pointed star enclosed in a circle and it became a registered trademark in August 1923. Daimler and Benz merged in 1926. Now you know how all the names and pieces fit together.

Real People Extras

In 1871, Clement Vallandigham, a lawyer and Ohio, US, politician was defending a man on a charge of murder. He accidentally shot himself demonstrating how the victim might have shot himself while in the process of drawing a weapon when standing from a kneeling position. The defendant was ultimately cleared, but Vallandigham died from his wound.

In 1974, Basil Brown, a 48-year-old health food advocate from Croydon, England, drank himself to death by consuming 10 gallons (37.85 litres) of carrot juice in ten days, causing him to overdose on vitamin A and suffer severe liver damage.

In 1982, David Grundman was killed near Lake Pleasant, AZ, US, while shooting at cacti with his shotgun. After he fired several shots at a 26 ft (8 m) tall Saguaro Cactus from extremely close range, a 4 ft (1.2 m) limb of the cactus detached and fell on him, crushing him.

555 95472 - One of the characters in the Peanuts universe was "555 95472," or "5" for short. 5 explained that his father was so upset about people being seen as "just a number," he renamed the entire family as a series of digits.

The family's last name is taken from their ZIP Code, though when spoken, 5 insists there's an accent on the 4. The ZIP Code, by the way, is the real one for Sebastopol, California, where Charles Schulz lived at the time.

5's sisters 3 and 4 made a few appearances in the strip before disappearing, but 5 was occasionally a background character until 1981. All three appear in the famous dance sequence in 'A Charlie Brown Christmas'. 3 and 4 are the twin girls in purple dresses, while 5 is the spiky-haired kid in orange.

Charlotte Braun - She was written as a female version of Charlie Brown. In fact, she looked just like him, except she had curly hair. She was also ostracized by her peers, but it was because she was loud and obnoxious, a fact she constantly pointed out during her appearances in the comic strip.

Shortly after her introduction in 1954, Schulz received a letter from Elizabeth Swain, a young fan in Pittsburgh, who told him to get rid of Braun because she found the character annoying and unfunny.

Schulz wrote Swain a letter saying that he would soon "discard" Braun as requested. He added a touch of dark humor by saying that Swain would, "have the death of an innocent child on your conscience. Are you prepared to accept such responsibility?"

Next to his signature, he included a sketch of Charlotte Braun with an ax stuck in her head. Braun showed up in the comic one more time, but then never returned. *He really did have a sense of humor.*

Hansel and Gretel - In the widely known version of Hansel and Gretel, the two little children become lost in the forest and eventually find their way to a gingerbread house, which belongs to a wicked witch. The children end up enslaved for a time as the witch prepares them for eating. They figure their way out and throw the witch in a fire and escape.

In an earlier French version of this tale, The Lost Children, instead of a witch it is a devil. The wicked old devil is tricked by the children in much the same way as Hansel and Gretel, but he works it out and puts together a sawhorse to put one of the children on to bleed. The children pretend not to know how to get on the sawhorse so the devil's wife demonstrates. While she is lying down the kids slash her throat and escape.

The Real Little Mermaid - In the Disney version, the film ends with Ariel the mermaid being changed into a human so she can marry Eric. They marry in a wonderful wedding attended by humans and merpeople.

In the original version by Hans Christian Andersen, the mermaid sees the Prince marry a princess and she despairs. She is offered a knife with which to stab the prince to death, but rather than do that she jumps into the sea and dies by turning to froth.

Andersen later modified the ending to make it more pleasant. In the new ending, instead of dying when turned to froth, she becomes a 'daughter of the air' waiting to go to heaven.

The Simpsons - The inspiration for Homer Simpson came from a character in "The Day of the Locust" book, and Eddie Haskell in "Leave it to Beaver" TV Series.

Life in Hell started in 1977 as a self-published comic book written and produced by Matt Groening and was a story about life in Los Angeles and the things which Groening encountered at school, at work in a succession of seedy jobs, and in his personal love relationships.

The series reached the attention of James L. Brooks who commissioned Groening to create short skits for the Tracey Ullman Show. While waiting in Brooks' office reception for the interview, Groening sketched out a number of basic designs which would go on to become the basis for The Simpsons. He walked in to the office, presented his 10 minute-old drawings and got the job.

He named the characters after members of his own family, his father Homer, mother Marge, and sister Lisa. He substituted Bart for himself. Bart Simpson was named as an anagram of "brat," and Matt's older brother Mark produced much of the early inspiration for Bart's attitude.

The entire Simpson family was designed so that they would be drawn very quickly, allowing the often tight budget to reach further, and be recognizable in silhouette. When designing Homer's hair he initially just sketched his initials, 'M' for the hairline and 'G' for Homer's ear. Matt Groening's initials still remain on the final character to this day. Marge's hair was based on the iconic Elsa Lanchester hairdo as worn in The Bride of Frankenstein (1935), and on a similar style worn by Margaret Groening during the 1960s. Lisa's hair was initially a cluster of hand drawn hairlines, but this was changed to the simpler 'hexagon hair' design before the pilot episode. The show is the longest running animation series of all time.

Four More Simpsons Facts - The show features clips from a movie starring McBain, a movie star in the same vein as Schwarzenegger and Stallone. These clips are dispersed among many episodes, but if you put the clips together, you can actually form a full coherent story.

Many characters are named after streets in Portland, Oregon.

As soon as Matt Groening, creator of The Simpsons, was given a drawing of the characters in yellow by an animator, he knew it was perfect. The idea was that whenever someone was flipping through the channels, they would automatically know The Simpsons was on when they saw the yellow bodies flash by.

All, except one of the characters are a one finger short of a human hand. The only character to have five fingers on a hand is God.

Origin of Porky Pig - The inspiration was Joe Cobb, Joe in the "Our Gang/Little Rascals" TV Series. Joe Cobb starred in 86 episodes of the series and played the ever smiling yet hapless stereotypical fat kid, who often sets up gags for the others.

During the early 1930s, Leon Schlesinger secured a contract to produce the Looney Tunes series for Warner Bros. He asked animator Robert Clampett and studio director Friz Freleng to design a new series of characters and suggested they do a cartoon version of the Our Gang films.

The first short, I Haven't Got a Hat, released in 1935 included: Beans the cat, Oliver Owl, a motherly cow named Mrs. Cud, and Porky Pig in the 'Joe' role. Porky quickly became the star. Porky's name came from Friz Freleng, who remembered two childhood friends and brothers nicknamed "Porky" and "Piggy" and put the two names together.

His trademark stutter comes from Joe Dougherty, the first voice actor to do Porky. Joe had a strong stutter and forced director Freleng to go through many takes of uncontrollable stuttering.

Eventually the studio realized the high production cost of the many hours of wasted material, and replaced Dougherty with Mel Blanc in 1937. By this time the stutter had become so associated with the character that Blanc was asked to use it to create a more precise comedic effect.

Porky's legacy continues with his signature line "Th-th-that's all folks" heard at the end of Looney Tunes episodes. The Warner Bros. other series, Merrie Melodies, which had always used "So Long, Folks" to close its short films, changed to the more catchy Porky line after opinion polls found most people better associated with it.

SpongeBob - Each of the main characters in SpongeBob Squarepants was inspired by one of the seven deadly sins. These seem to fit the characters.

1. Greed (Mr. Krabs) - Eugene Krabs is constantly thinking of ways to turn a profit, even if it involves taking advantage of his friends or putting them in harmful situations.

2. Envy (Plankton) - Sheldon Plankton owns a struggling restaurant called "The Chum Bucket" and is consumed with the desire to achieve the success of his adversary and steal the Krabby Patty formula.

3. Sloth (Patrick) - In one episode Patrick is given an award for 'doing absolutely nothing longer than anyone else'. He then proceeds go back under his rock to protect his title.

4. Pride (Sandy) - The fact that Sandy Cheeks is from Texas alone should almost suffice. She is a squirrel that is very proud of her heritage. Sandy also takes a great deal of satisfaction in being the only land critter living down in Bikini Bottom among all the fish. Sandy is quick to spout off about the greatness of the Lone Star state or to show off her athleticism in a karate match or a weightlifting contest.

5. Wrath (Squidward) - Squidward Tentacles has no qualms about expressing his negative outlook on life by describing how much he hates his job at the Krusty Krab or through outward disdain for his two obnoxious neighbors. He is portrayed as a general failure who refuses to acknowledge his own personal flaws. He has a sarcastic sense of humor and resentment toward the society that does not appreciate his creativity and clarinet skills.

6. Gluttony (Gary) - Gary does not do much other than eating and meowing, and the meowing is often due to the fact that he is hungry. Gary was shown eating parts of their couch. He also ran away from home, because SpongeBob forgot to feed him for a while. Another time Gary ate a year's supply of snail food and became morbidly obese.

7. Lust (SpongeBob) - One definition for lust is simply "a passionate desire for something". In this sense, it cannot be denied that he is an extremely lustful creature. SpongeBob has a lust for life that is incomparable to most other cartoon characters. He yearns for the affections of both friend and foe alike, is eager to please, and will often stop at nothing to complete a task.

Joe Shlabotnik - Charlie Brown's favorite baseball player is a guy whose career was anything but spectacular. After batting .004 in one season in the majors, Joe Shlabotnik was sent back down to the minor leagues, where his most notable highlight was throwing out a runner who fell down between first and second base.

When Shlabotnik became the manager for the Waffletown Syrups, Charlie Brown finally got to meet his hero. While in the stands, Charlie Brown snagged a foul ball, and he wanted Shlabotnik to sign it. Unfortunately, Shlabotnik had been fired in the middle of the game. Like all adults, Joe is never actually seen in Peanuts.

Humpty Dumpty - According to the Oxford English Dictionary, "Humpty Dumpty" was first used in the 17th century and referred to brandy boiled with ale. In the 1700s, it was also a term used to describe a short, clumsy person. It has also been a nickname attributed to someone who has had too much alcohol, as in brandy boiled in ale.

It is most likely that the nursery rhyme was intended as a riddle. The answer to the riddle is an egg. Something that, if it rolled off a wall, could not be mended by any number of people. Today, the answer is so well known that the character of Humpty Dumpty is an egg and the rhyme is not considered to be a riddle, but a story.

Pied Piper - Below is an excerpt from the famous Grimm brothers version of the famous tale of the Pied Piper in which the small German town of Hamelin loses all of its children to the Piper when the mayor refuses to pay him for ridding the town of rats.

"The long procession of children soon left the town and made its way through the wood and across the forest until it reached the foot of a huge mountain. When the piper came to the dark rock, he played his pipe even louder still and a great door creaked open. Beyond lay a cave. In trooped the children behind the pied piper, and when the last child had gone into the darkness, the door creaked shut."

Here is a quote from the wall of the Piper's House in Hamelin today: "In the year of 1284, on the day of Saints John and Paul, the 26th of June, 130 children born in Hamelin were seduced by a piper, dressed in all kinds of colors, and lost at the calvary near the koppen."

The story is largely true, with some exaggerated parts. Many theories abound as to the factual events of that day, but the most logical seems to be that the piper represents death (death was depicted as a skeleton wearing pied clothing in the middle ages) and that the children who died were killed by the plague.

Pied means 'having two or more colors'. The word comes from middle English and is taken from the word "magpie." Thus, the pied piper was a man wearing clothing of many colors.

Five Almost Famous Characters - Arthur Conan Doyle made notes that indicated he considered the name "Sherringford" for Sherlock Holmes.

Holmes' assistant was originally going to be called "Ormond Sacker." Arthur Conan Doyle decided the name was a bit too bizarre and changed it to John H. Watson.

Before "Nancy Drew" it was Stella Strong, Diana Drew, Diana Dare, Nan Nelson, Helen Hale, and Nan Drew.

Small Sam, Little Larry, and Puny Pete were all in the running before Charles Dickens settled on "Tiny Tim" for the sickly lad in A Christmas Carol.

Little Orphan Annie was Little Orphan Otto, until Harold Gray's publisher at the newspaper syndicate suggested his character looked more female than male and told him to make it so.

Food Facts

Boiling Tips - Here is an easy way to remember what to put in boiling water vs. room temperature water. Whatever grows below ground, like potatoes, should be placed in room-temperature water and brought to a boil. Whatever is grown above ground, like spinach, should be placed in boiling water and then cooked until done.

Rhubarb - The first shipment of rhubarb was sent to the United States in 1770 from London. Most of the world recognizes it as a vegetable, but the US classifies it as a fruit. There are rhubarb festivals around the country, but mainly in the northeast, where it grows abundantly.

Rhubarb is a perennial and grows rather wild if you do not keep up with it. Easy to grow and exciting to watch it come back each year in the spring. We always had some in the yard along with strawberries, which will also grow wild.

I was in the store last spring, picked up some rhubarb and the person at the register did not know what it was. I had to explain what it was and how it was used. My mother used to make rhubarb pie and stewed rhubarb (cook it down and eat it like applesauce). It also makes great jam. Ah, it has a wonderful tart taste and also good for you.

When taken internally in small doses, rhubarb acts as an astringent tonic to the digestive system, when taken larger doses rhubarb acts as a very mild laxative. It is a useful alternative to prunes to keep things flowing. People claim that rhubarb enhances the appetite when it is taken before meals in small amounts, that it also promotes blood circulation and relieves pain in cases of injury or inflammation, inhibits intestinal infections, and can also reduce autoimmune reactions.

If you're in the vicinity of Knott's Berry Farm you will get stewed rhubarb with your meal, whether you want it or not. Children in the UK and Sweden dip a stalk in sugar and eat it raw. You do not want to eat the leaves or flowers because they can be toxic. *Another delicious reason to look forward to Spring.*

World's Biggest Happy Meal - Where else but in Texas could you find the world's biggest anything. Dallas is home to this one.

The McDonald's PlayPlace is in the box, and the building is adorned with gigantic hamburgers, French fries, Cokes, and a Ronald McDonald. The exterior is the only Happy Meal-shaped McDonald's in the world. The interior has Austrian crystal chandeliers, Ralph Lauren wallpaper, granite floors, and mahogany booths. It is at 13105 Montfort Drive, Dallas.

Calorie Cutter - You can eat two Egg McMuffins from McDonald's for fewer calories and fat than a bagel with two tablespoons of cream cheese.

Ice-Cream is Good for You - Ice-cream is a low GI (glycemic-index) food. This means that it is a slow sugar release food that keeps you satisfied for a longer period of time than a high GI food. For that reason, you are less likely to binge after eating ice-cream.

Nutrients in ice-cream are biotin, iodine, potassium, selenium, vitamins a, B12, D, and K. 75 grams of Ben and Jerry's Cookies and Cream ice-cream contains only 114 calories compared to a slice of cheesecake with 511 calories.

Milk and Calcium - The long held myth that milk is the best thing for healthy bones is not true. Many confuse "dairy" with "calcium," and assume they are the same thing. Dairy products contain calcium, but so do dark-leafy greens. Milk is fortified with vitamin D, but bone health goes beyond calcium and vitamin D.

Vitamin K is important for bone health (dark leafy greens have it, dairy doesn't). Magnesium, also missing in dairy products, plays an important role in bone health.

Milk isn't the only, or even the best, source of calcium. If you are looking for good sources of calcium and Vitamin D, consider dark greens, mustard greens, kale, and bok choy instead of milk. Toss in some almonds, cashews, and potatoes for magnesium.

Bratwurst Bust - The beloved Nürnberger Bratwurst is the latest victim of escalating tensions over Iran's nuclear program. German butchers complained that the diplomatic crisis was driving up the price of sausage casing. In shock news for Germans everywhere, the sausage industry is feeling the rising cost of importing sheep intestines from Iran, leading Nürnberger Bratwurst producer Claus Steiner reported.

The Nürnberger Bratwurst is made of finely ground pork, cased in intestinal lining and seasoned with marjoram. By European Union regulations, it can only be called a Nürnberger Bratwurst if it's made in the Nuremberg area.

Sheep intestinal lining, a key ingredient in making the sausage, is largely imported from Iran, which has a 500-year history of trading animal by-products. This may change, as the price of sheep gut has recently almost tripled.

Not long ago 90 meters of intestinal lining cost just €6.30, but now the same length costs €17.20. *War is hell.*

Origin of Tea Bags - In 1904, tea bags were invented accidentally. The inventor was a tea merchant named Thomas Sullivan. He decided that it was cheaper to send small samples to prospective customers in silk bags, rather than boxes. The recipients mistakenly believed they were meant to be dunked and Sullivan was overrun with orders for his tea bags.

Nutmeg and Potatoes - Add a small dash of nutmeg to your next potato dish for a great taste.

Rosemary Makes You Smart - Rosemary is one of many traditional medicinal plants that yields essential oils.

The Brain, Performance and Nutrition Research Centre at Northumbria University, UK designed an experiment to investigate the pharmacology of one of rosemary's main chemical components.

The investigators tested cognitive performance and mood in 20 subjects, who were exposed to varying levels of the rosemary aroma. Using blood samples to detect the amount of 1,8-cineole participants had absorbed, the researchers applied speed and accuracy tests, and mood assessments, to judge the rosemary oil's affects.

Results indicated that concentration of 1,8-cineole in the blood is related to an individual's cognitive performance, with higher concentrations resulting in improved performance. Both speed and accuracy were improved. The oil did not appear to improve attention or alertness. The same 1,8-cineole is also found in aromatic plants, such as eucalyptus, bay, wormwood, and sage.

Enhancing Tomato Flavors - When cooking tomatoes, add a piece of the branch to heighten the flavor. Also, when eating tomatoes, salt adds to the already natural acidity, try a pinch of sugar instead to really bring out the taste of the tomato.

Cashew Facts - The thing we normally think of a cashew nut is really a seed. Cashews grow on short evergreen trees and are originally from South America, but now more commonly found in India, the Philippines, and Africa.

The accessory fruit is the oval or pear or bell-shaped structure that develops from the receptacle of the cashew flower which ripens into a yellow and/or red and delicately soft body, called cashew apple.

The nut is attached to the fruit and inside the nut is the seed, which we call a cashew nut. The seed has within itself a whole kernel and is covered by a membrane and a thick outer shell.

The bark of the tree is scraped and soaked overnight or boiled as an antidiarrheal and also yields a gum used in varnish. Seeds are ground into powders used as antivenom for snake bites. The nut oil is used topically as an antifungal and for healing cracked heels.

The cashew apple is five to ten times richer in Vitamin C than an orange and may be consumed fresh, but its high tannin content yields a slightly bitter taste and dry mouth after-feel. The soft flesh packs a rather large quantity of nutritious sweet juice but with extreme astringency that puckers up the mouth.

Cashew fruit juice is popular in Brazil and the Philippines. The juice is also fermented into liquor in many countries.

Hamburger Culture - A researcher recently announced that his lab will soon have an artificial hamburger fit for human consumption. Growing meat without raising livestock has long been a goal and now it seems it may finally be practical.

He made the announcement at the annual meeting for the American Association for the Advancement of Science in Vancouver. He said soon they will have enough tissue to make a hamburger.

Cultured meat begins with muscle cells taken from the rear of a cow for sirloin steak or from the area surrounding a pig's spine for growing pork chops, etc. The cells are then placed in a nutrient mixture that helps them to proliferate. A biodegradable scaffold guides the cells as they grow together to eventually form tissue. I withheld the pics, because it does not look pretty at this stage. *Hey, maybe they should grow the pork and beef together in the dish and make bacon burgers.*

PB&J Vodka - The fragrance is predominately of peanuts, but it is complimented by the fresh fruit aroma of the raspberry. On the tongue, the roles are reversed and the raspberry flavor is more focal, giving it a velvety texture with a hint of vanilla on the side.

After I read about this I made and ate a peanut butter and jelly sandwich. Mmmm!

Flutie Flakes - Have you ever heard of these? Buffalo Bills quarterback Doug Flutie released his brand of corn flakes cereal in 1998 to raise money for autism awareness in honor of his son, who is autistic. The cereal ended up being a hit, selling more than 3 million boxes. He also branched out into other foods, including a fruit snack called Flutie's Fruities.

Cheddar Cheese - Cheddar cheese gets its name from the town of Cheddar in southwest England. Unlike other cheeses named for their town of origin, like Gorgonzola and Parmesan, Cheddar is not covered by a Protected Designation of Origin, which means no matter where it is produced it can still legally be called Cheddar cheese.

Sticky Tip - Use nonstick cooking spray in votive candle holders and the remaining wax after burning will easily slip out.

Soft Drink Facts - Soft Drink refers to nearly all beverages that do not contain significant amounts of alcohol as hard drinks do.

The term soft drink is typically used mostly for flavored carbonated beverages and that is because of advertising. Flavored carbonated beverage makers were having a difficult time creating national advertisements due what people call their product varies from place to place.

In parts of the United States and Canada, flavored carbonated beverages are referred to as "pop"; in other parts "soda"; in yet other parts "coke"; and there are a variety of other names commonly used as

116

well. In England these drinks are called fizzy drinks and in Ireland called minerals.

Since beverage makers can't refer to their product in the generic sense in national or international advertisements due to the varied terms, they have chosen the term soft drink to be more or less a universal term for flavored carbonated beverages.

Picnics and Germans - Just about all the ingredients to make a perfect 'All-American' picnic come from German origins.

There is the hot dog, wiener, or a Frankfurter; a pork sausage that originated in 13th century Germany. We also cannot forget the Brats or Bratwurst and Knackwurst, both great grilled. All of these washed down with a chilled beer, while not originating in Germany, was certainly made popular there many years ago.

Ketchup was developed by Heinz, and Mayonnaise, developed by Hellman, both German immigrants. Some of those items are based off earlier recipes (Ancient Rome: ketchup; France: mayonnaise) but the favorites eaten today are definitely German.

Then, of course, there is the Potato Salad. There are many different versions to this dish, one of the most popular variations is the traditional German potato salad.

Yogurt Breath - Research shows that the live bacteria in yogurt can suppress levels of bad breath causing bacteria. "Good" bugs in yogurt may crowd out the "bad" stink-causing bacteria or create an unhealthy environment for it.

Sliced Bread Fact - Claude R. Wickard, the head of the War Foods Administration as well as the Secretary of Agriculture, got the idea to ban pre-sliced bread in America, which he did on January 18, 1943.

He said it was about conservation of resources, such as to conserve wax paper and secondary goals of conserving wheat and steel.

However, there was no shortage of wax paper at the time the ban was put in place. He also thought that by banning pre-sliced bread, the amount of bread consumed would go down and reduce the demand for flour and wheat, and thus, decrease prices of those products while increasing stockpiles of wheat. However, at the time of the ban, the US had already stockpiled over 1 billion bushels of wheat, which would be enough to meet the United States' needs for about two years, even if no new wheat was harvested.

After a severe consumer backlash, the ban was rescinded three months later on March 8, 1943. Upon rescinding the ban, Wickard stated, "Our experience with the order, however, leads us to believe that the savings are not as much as we expected..."

Automatic Bread Slicer - As long as we are talking of bread slicing, The world's first automatic bread slicer was invented by Otto Frederick Rohwedder in Davenport, Iowa. He first built a prototype of his bread slicer in 1912. Unfortunately, his blueprints and machine were destroyed in a fire in 1917. It took him until 1927 to re-build the machine and produce a model ready to use in an actual bakery.

The first pre-sliced loaf of bread using his machine, was sold on July 7, 1928. The Chillicothe Baking Company in Missouri installed the bread slicing machine. Sliced bread sales skyrocketed.

Pre-sliced bread became a national hit thanks to Wonder Bread, then owned by Continental Baking, who began commercially producing the pre-sliced bread in 1930 using a modified version of Rohwedder's machine. Crumb is a term bakers use to define the part of bread inside the crust. *Unrelated, Jackie Gleason, on his TV show called his drinking buddies crumb bums.*

Vanilla Truth - Vanilla comes from a special species of orchid. Consuming natural vanilla causes the body to release catecholamines, including adrenalin and for this reason it is considered to be mildly addictive.

When vanilla plants were first exported from Mexico to other tropical climes, they flowered, but wouldn't produce vanilla pods. It was discovered that a bee native to Mexico was the only creature that could pollinate vanilla flowers.

Attempts to move the bee to other countries failed and it was not until a slave boy discovered a method of artificial pollination that Mexico lost its monopoly on vanilla. As well as being mildly addictive, vanilla has also been found to block bacterial infections. *Ice cream with real flecks of vanilla beans (and maybe some bacon bits) is probably doubly addictive.*

Seven Handy Kitchen Tips - Keep your onions in the refrigerator. A chilled onion is easier to chop, and causes fewer tears.

If you use seltzer instead of tap water or milk, you get fluffier pancakes, waffles, and scrambled eggs.

To freeze berries, spread them on a pan or plate and freeze, then take out and put into freezer bags. That way they stay separate and not in one big lump.

Keep milk fresher for longer by adding a dash of salt into the carton right after opening it for the first time.

Take your eggs out of the refrigerator and let sit out so that when you begin breakfast the eggs are at room temperature. They cook better and make especially fluffy omelets. For other dishes, eggs separate better when cold but whip better when warmed.

Glue a few magnets under your upper kitchen cabinets to attach your frequently used metal items, like kitchen scissors, mixing spoon, etc. It keeps them handy, but out of site and reduces drawer clutter.

Use a cheese grater for easier spreading of cold, hard butter. When you are buttering bread, pastries, etc., it is difficult when the butter is hard. Rather than waiting for the butter to soften, you can quickly solve the problem with a cheese grater. Grate the butter over whatever you are making. This process generates a little bit of heat and the smaller pieces of butter will melt faster and spread better when they hit a warm piece of toast or while mixing dough for pastries.

Origin of Chocolate Milk - Chocolate milk was not just a clever ploy built up by a marketing team as a way to sell more milk to children. In fact, Sir Hans Sloane first created chocolate milk over 350 years ago. He had tasted chocolate while in the West Indies, but said it made him nauseous, so he added milk and sugar to make it more appealing. By 1700, people would often go to 'chocolate houses' instead of coffee houses, where they could choose from a range of different chocolate milk mixes.

Soft Drinks and Sugar - A typical carbonated soft drink will have 200 calories in a 16-ounce serving. All of those calories come from sugar, and sugar contains 16 calories per teaspoon. Divide those two and you find a 16-ounce serving contains about 12.5 teaspoons of sugar.

A 12 ounce soda, which has about 140 calories or about 8.75 teaspoons of sugar. Standard coffee cups (not mugs) contain about 6 ounces of fluid. Take half the calories and sugar of a 12 ounce soda and it would take about 4.38 teaspoons of sugar to make coffee as sweet as soda.

Milk Duds - They really are duds. The Milk Duds name came about because the original idea was to have a perfectly round piece. Since this was to be impossible to do at the time, the word 'dud' was used. Each piece was a dud, because it was not round.

In 1928, Milton J. Holloway took over F. Hoffman & Company of Chicago, the original manufacturer of Milk Duds chocolate covered caramels. The brand passed through many other hands in subsequent years and is now owned by Hershey.

Fortune Cookies - The commonly held notion that they were invented in China typically comes from the fact that they are primarily served in American Chinese restaurants. However, you will not find fortune cookies in actual Chinese restaurants or in China.

The largest manufacturer of fortune cookies, Wonton Food, based in New York, even once tried to introduce fortune cookies to the Chinese in the late 1980s. After three years, it gave up, as they simply were not a popular food item in China.

The people often credited with inventing fortune cookies were Japanese immigrants to America. Fortune cookies were actually invented in Japan.

A researcher, Yasuko Nakamachi, encountered a fortune cookie-shaped cracker, called a Tsujiura Senbei, made by hand in a family bakery near a Shinto shrine outside of Kyoto, Japan. This cracker only looked like a fortune cookie and contained an "omikuji" (fortune slip), and was traditionally sold in shrines and temples.

About three billion fortune cookies are consumed annually world-wide, with most consumed in the United States. Wonton Food produces about 4.5 million fortune cookies per day.

As an aside, Chop Suey, which translates to "break into many pieces," is commonly believed to be a Chinese food invented in America. Not so. It was invented in Taishan, a district of Guangdong Province, China.

Hawaiian Punch - Hawaiian Punch was originally supposed to be used as an ice cream topping and was originally called 'Leo's Hawaiian Punch'.

The recipe for the confectionery was created by Tom Yates, A.W. Leo, and Ralph Harrison in a garage in Fullerton, California in 1934. They started out by selling the tropical fruit flavored ice cream topping to local restaurants, stores, and ice cream makers.

Over the next decade as the syrup's popularity spread, people started using it not just as an ice cream topping, but also mixing the syrup with water to make a tropical drink. By 1946, this was a common practice. In 1946 Reuben P. Hughes and other investors purchased the company and began offering it in the drink forms most commonly associated with it today. In 1955 it became a national selling brand.

The name Hawaiian Punch came from several of the original recipe ingredients, which included apple, apricot, guava, orange, papaya, passion fruit, and pineapple, being imported from Hawaii. Hawaiian Punch is currently owned by Dr. Pepper Snapple Group, Inc.

MSG Facts - It is a common misconception that monosodium glutamate (MSG) is bad and must be avoided. That is not exactly true, MSG is a naturally occurring substance found in foods like tomatoes, mushrooms, and more. It was first isolated and presented in pure powder form in 1909 and is a flavor enhancer that excites the fifth taste sense umami, like sugar enhances sweet.

Most good chefs use natural MSG by using tomatoes or mushrooms, etc., but many will also use the powder directly. MSG does not make you ill. It is found in seasonings, chips, many fast-food and pre-packaged foods, and sauces.

Apple Facts - Greek and Roman mythology refer to apples as symbols of love and beauty. This time of year we often think of warm apple cider on a cold night.

Apples contain Vitamin C, Beta-Carotene, iron, potassium, and more. Apples have very high mineral contents, pectins, malic acid which are good in normalizing the intestines. Apples are good for treatment of anemia, dysentery, heart disease, headache, eye disorders, and kidney stones. Apple juice is an excellent means of providing essential fluids to the body.

A number of components in apples have been found to lower blood cholesterol with a reduced risk of ischemic heart disease, stroke, prostate cancer, type II diabetes, asthma, and a new study findings published in the Journal of Alzheimer's Disease show there may be some help for those patients. Apples are also good for treatment of the Acid reflux condition also called gerd (gastro esophageal reflux disease).

Green Apples - Good for strong bones and teeth, aids in vision, anti cancer properties.

Yellow Apples - Good for heart and eyes, immune system, reduce risk of some cancers.

Red Apples - Good for heart, memory function, lower risk of some cancers and to maintain urinary tract health. *Maybe there is some truth to the old saying that an apple a day keeps the doctor away.*

Rosemary for Memory - Scientists have found that aromas can profoundly affect people's cognitive abilities. In a 2003 study, psychologists asked 144 volunteers to perform a series of long-term memory, working memory, and attention and reaction tests. Some subjects worked in a scent-free cubicle, some in a cubicle infused with essential oil from rosemary, and the rest worked in cubicles scented with lavender oil.

Those in the rosemary-infused cubicles demonstrated significantly better long-term and working memory than those in the unscented cubicles. Also, those exposed to the smell of rosemary reported feeling more alert than the control (scent-free) group.

Participants working in the lavender cubicles reported feeling less alert and those in the lavender-scented cubicles performed worse than the others in tests of working memory.

If you need your brain to perform at its best, you can try placing a rosemary plant on your windowsill. *Research also shows that eating chocolate may improve memory and cognition, because it is rich in antioxidants called flavanols.*

Why Milk is White - Milk is 87% water and 13% solids. It consists of about 5 percent lactose, 3.7 percent fats, and 3.5 percent proteins. Casein is the most common protein and makes up about 80% of the proteins in milk. Also, casein's molecular structure is very similar to that of gluten. This is why many gluten free diets also are casein-free. It is the combination of casein and fats that give milk its color.

The color white results from all the wavelengths of visible light being reflected into the eye. Casein and certain fats reflect wide ranges of wavelengths, causing milk to appear white. Fat free milk appears a bit bluish due to reduction of fats reflecting light.

The pasteurization process that kills microorganisms in milk, also destroys the Vitamin C content, as well as significantly diminishes various other health benefits of milk.

Frozen and Canned Fruit - Have you ever wondered if the benefits of frozen or canned fruit are equal to fresh fruit?

Frozen fruit can be equal, or even nutritionally superior to fresh fruits. As a general rule, fruits are at their nutritious best when they are left on the vine for the longest possible time, so ideally we pick and eat them right away when they are at their ripest. When you buy whole fruits that are not in season, chances are they were harvested before they were fully ripe and left to ripen off the stem on their way to the market. Frozen fruits have the advantage of staying on the stem longer and freezing them at their peak locks in their nutrients.

Canned fruits, like frozen are usually harvested when they are fully ripe and very nutritious. It is important to check how the fruit was prepared and packed. Some canned fruits are packed in sugary heavy syrup and adding sugary calories. Fortunately canned fruit comes in several varieties, including light syrup and the best is packed in its own juice.

Benefits of Peanut Butter - According to the US National Peanut Board, the average American eats about three pounds of peanut butter each year. Peanut butter is a great source of unsaturated fats and vegetarian protein. Over 80 percent of the fats found in peanut butter are unsaturated, with 50 percent being monounsaturated fats that can help cut bad cholesterol (LDL).

Peanuts contain B vitamins, potassium, and resveratrol a powerful antioxidant known to have cancer fighting properties. Check the amount of carbohydrates on the nutrition label, because less fat sometimes comes with not-so-healthy trade-offs, such as added salt and sugar. *Instead of that PB&J, spread some peanut butter on apple slices for a great taste and fiber boost.*

Mustard - The oriental mustard plant originally started growing in the foothills of the Himalayas, but migrated to the USA, UK, Denmark, and Canada.

Mild white mustard grows wild in North Africa, the Middle East, and Europe and has also spread. Black mustard is grown in Argentina, China, the US, and Canada.

Canada and Nepal are the world's major producers of mustard seed, between them accounting for about 57% of world production in 2010. The United Sates receives 43% of Canada's total output of mustard seeds.

Chicken Noodle Soup - "Chicken with Noodles" soup was a variety introduced to the public by Campbell's in 1934. It is now considered a comfort food, but sales back did not pick up until the product's name was misread during an episode of the popular Amos 'n' Andy radio show.

Once listeners heard the words "chicken noodle soup," and consumer interest was captured. Folks began to ask Campbell's about the "new" soup. It quickly renamed the soup to match the blooper.

I make no bones about adding the following to the discussion about soup. *To make no bones about a matter means to speak frankly and directly. A form of this expression was used since the 1400s, meaning to have no difficulty. The allusion is to the occurrence of bones in stews or soup. Soup without bones would offer no difficulty, so one would have no hesitation to swallow soup with no bones.*

Sugarloaf - Sugar used to be refined into what was called a sugarloaf, a tall cone shape with a rounded top. People have been making sugarloaves since at least the 12th Century. Raw sugar was refined by a series of boiling and filtering processes. When, at the final boiling it was considered ready for granulation it was poured into a large number of inverted conical molds. The popularity of sugarloaves declined as new processes were invented making it easier to refine and be sold as the small cubes and granulated sugar we are familiar with.

Pieces were cut from it by hand using sugar nips, pliers-like cutters. Typically, the bigger the sugarloaf, the lower the grade of sugar.

Portuguese explorers who discovered Rio de Janeiro in 1502 named Sugarloaf Mountain, due to its resemblance to a sugarloaf cone.

Ten Oreo Cookie Facts - More sweet stuff. Oreos are the world's best-selling cookie. The first Oreo cookie was made in 1912 in two flavors, original and lemon meringue at the original Nabisco bakery in New York City

The origin of the name Oreo is unknown, but a leading theory is that the name was derived from the French word "Or", meaning gold (the early packaging was gold tin).

The cookie-to-creme ratio of an original Oreo cookie is 71% to 29%.

Double Stuf Oreos were introduced in 1974.

Big Stuff Oreos were introduced in 1987, and were about 10 times larger than a regular Oreo. They were discontinued in 1991.

Oreos became kosher in 1998.

50% of all Oreo eaters pull apart their cookies before eating them. Also, women twist them open more often than men.

In 1998, they introduced Oreo'Os cereal. The cereal was discontinued because Post and Kraft are no longer co-branding. Post owns the recipe to the cereal and Kraft owns the rights to Oreo

----

Ten Weird Fast Foods - Here are a few weird fast food menu items from around the world.

1. Pork and seaweed doughnut (Dunkin' Donuts China)
2. Darth Vader burger (Quick, France) all black bun
3. Kimchi croquettes (Dunkin' Donuts Korea) made with real kimchi
4. Bacon Potato Pie (McDonald's Japan) mashed potatoes and bacon deep-fried in the familiar apple pie shell *Mmmm!*
5. Shrimp burger (McDonald's Japan) fried shrimp patty
6. Chicken Nugget burger (Burger King, Poland) ground chicken with curry sauce
7. Coffee Jelly Frappuccino (Starbucks, Japan) a regular Starbucks Frappuccino (frozen coffee drink) with coffee jelly, made from actual brewed coffee.

8. Cheese and marmite panini (Starbucks UK) Marmite is a brown, sticky spread made from yeast byproduct.

9. Tuna Pie (Jollibee, Phillipines) the tuna pie comes stuffed with cooked tuna and vegetables

10. Winter double king pizza (Pizza Hut, Japan) a pizza topped with mayonnaise, king crab, shrimp, beef, broccoli, onion, corn, egg, and potato and a removable crust made of fried, mayonnaise-stuffed shrimp that look like little pigs in blankets.

Jollibees is a chicken and burger franchise like McDonalds. It is also in a number of states including California, New York, and Nevada. Mascot is Jolly bee.

Oysters Alive - Did you know that most oysters are served while still living? Oysters are generally served live because they deteriorate much faster than most other animals when dead. When their shells are cracked open, they can survive for a significant amount of time.

It is only when the flesh is actually separated from the shells that they begin to die; this is why oysters are almost always sucked directly out of their shells.

Biggest and Smallest Eggs - The Ostrich lays the smallest egg for its size. Although the Ostrich egg is the largest single cell in nature, it is less than one and a half per cent of the weight of the mother. A wren's egg, by comparison, is 13 per cent of its weight.

The largest egg in comparison with the size of the bird is that of the Little Spotted kiwi. Its egg accounts for 26 per cent of its own weight. That would be the equivalent of a woman giving birth to a six-year-old child.

An ostrich egg weighs as much as twenty-four hen's eggs. *Can you imagine how much bacon it would take to go with an Ostrich egg omelet?*

Worcestershire Sauce - This is difficult to spell and more difficult to pronounce liquid is made of vinegar and soy sauce, spices, and liquefied anchovies. The anchovies are soaked in vinegar until they are totally dissolved, including the bones. It is named for the town in England where it was originally brewed. (woos teh shur) Here is one Heinz pronunciation LINK

126

Another Use for Basil -You already know that fresh basil is delicious in many of your favorite recipes, but did you also know it is great for repelling bugs naturally? Snip a few fresh leaves and hang them in doorways or put on top of an outdoor table to repel mosquitoes and flies.

Fairy Floss - William James Morrison was a dentist, lawyer, and author from Nashville, Tennessee in the late 19th and early 20th centuries. Because he became President of the Tennessee State Dental Association in 1894 and wrote several children's books, it might seem a little odd that he would go on to invent cotton candy.

Dr. Morrison patented several inventions. He developed a process for extracting the oil from cottonseeds and converting it to lard substitute, and developed a chemical process to purify the public drinking water in Nashville.

In 1897, he and a Nashville candy maker named John C. Wharton conceived and co-patented an "electric candy machine" which produced what was then called Fairy Floss and today is called Cotton Candy. The product was brought to the public in 1904 and became a huge instant success.

Eight Real People Inspired Food Names - We usually do not think about how foods are named, but here are a few inspired by their inventor, or other inspiration.

German Chocolate cake is named for an American, Sam German.

Boysenberry is named for Rudolph Boysen.

Eggs Benedict is named for Lemuel Benedict.

Tetrazzini is named for Louisa Tetrazzini.

Alfredo Sauce is named for Alfredo Di Lelio.

Nachos are name for Ignacio "Nacho" Anaya.

Clementine oranges named for Father Clément Rodier.

Chicken a la King named for E. Clark King.

Brussels Sprouts - If you hate the taste of Brussels sprouts it might be due to your DNA.

Brussels sprouts are among the group of cabbages grown for edible buds. The leafy green vegetables are typically small, and look like miniature cabbages. The Brussels sprout has long been popular in Brussels, Belgium, and may have originated there.

In Europe, the largest producers are the Netherlands and Germany. Mexico tends to cultivate them in the Baja region from December through June.

Brussels sprouts have potent anticancer properties. Although boiling reduces the level of the anticancer compounds, steaming and stir frying do not result in significant loss.

Many people seem to not like Brussels sprouts. Scientists explain that there is a mutated gene possessed by about half of the population that prevents a person from tasting the bitter-tasting chemical used to grow Brussels sprouts. If a person does not possess this gene they can taste the chemical, thus making them much more likely to dislike Brussels sprouts. *Apparently, I do not have that gene.*

Taco Bell Meat - Taco Bell says its meat is 88% beef. Other ingredients include water to keep it juicy and moist (3%), Mexican spices and flavors, including salt, chili pepper, onion powder, tomato powder, sugar, garlic powder, and cocoa powder (4%), and the rest is oats, caramelized sugar, yeast, citric acid, and other ingredients (5%).

Fruits and Veggies - Beans, corn, bell peppers, peas, eggplant, pumpkins, cucumbers, squash, and tomatoes are all fruits. That is because, botanically speaking, fruits are the part of flowering plants that contain the seeds and are the means by which such plants disseminate those seeds. Nuts are also fruits. Grains, which are really over-sized seeds, are also fruits. Botanically speaking, some spices, such as allspice and chilies, are fruits.

Also, botanically speaking, vegetables are all the other parts of the plant, including the leaves (e.g. lettuce and spinach), roots (e.g. potatoes and carrots), bulbs (e.g. onions and garlic), flowers (e.g. artichokes, broccoli, and cauliflower), and stems (e.g. rhubarb and celery).

If it is from a plant and has seeds (or would have seeds if it wasn't genetically engineered or cultivated to not have them, as with seedless grapes) it is a fruit; if it does not naturally have seeds, it is a vegetable.

The reason we learn peppers, corn, and cucumbers are vegetables and are found in the veggie section is due to tradition. Culinary traditions (with no scientific value) tell us the part of the plant we are eating does not matter, taste does. Fruits are generally sweet tasting and vegetables are more savory and less sweet. Fruits are also typically served as part of dessert or as snacks, and vegetables are often part of the main dish.

Scientific classification system makes a clear dividing line between fruits and vegetables, while the culinary system of classification is much more ambiguous. Not to be outdone, The United States Supreme Court entered the debate and gave a legal verdict about whether a tomato should be classified as a vegetable or a fruit. They decided unanimously, in Nix vs. Hedden, 1883, that a tomato is a vegetable, even though it is a botanical fruit. *I use a much more simple method - If I like it, it's a fruit, if I do not like it, it's a vegetable.*

Calories - Nutrient labels on food products in the United States list their percentages based on a 2,000 calorie per day diet. However, energy requirements can vary significantly based on age, sex, weight, height, physical activity, and base metabolic rate, ranging between 1,000 to 4,000 calories.

Another number on labels is the portion, or suggested serving size, which is also arbitrary and should be looked at closely. A package stating 90 calories on the front might show 90 calories per serving with three servings, so 270 total calories.

The Merck Manual states 1,600 calories per day are needed for young children and sedentary women; 2,000 for active adult women and sedentary men; and 2,400 for active adolescent boys and young men. These values are also a bit arbitrary, because the average person uses different amounts of energy almost daily. One day you might go for a hike and the next sit on the couch watching football. One month you could lose five pounds and increase your base metabolic rate in the process. The next month with the same caloric intake gain ten pounds and decrease your base metabolic rate. *Bottom line, the numbers are arbitrary and should be used with caution.*

Granny Smith Apples - Fall is the perfect time of year to enjoy fresh apples and apple cider. While working on her farm near Sydney, Australia, Maria Smith found a small sapling growing where she had discarded some rotten apples. She replanted the tree and it eventually bore fruit, green apples with a tart flavor. She shared these apples with her friends and neighbors and they grew in fame. Maria died in 1870 but her "Granny Smith" apples are still popular around the world.

Egg Fact - I know at least one person has been wondering about which end of the egg comes out first. Not exactly breaking news, but the egg initially moves through the chicken's oviduct small end first. When it reaches the uterus, the shell calcifies, rotates 180 degrees, and moves on big end first. When the muscles of the chicken's uterine and vaginal walls finally contract to squeeze the small end, it helps to expel the egg forward.

Yogurt Debate - Almost 28% of Americans eat yogurt on a daily basis. Yogurt comes from milk that has healthy bacteria added for fermentation. During this process, yogurt thickens and takes on a slightly tangy taste. Yogurt is then strained through a cheesecloth, which allows the liquid whey part of milk to drain off. Regular yogurt is strained twice and Greek yogurt is strained three times to remove more whey, making it thicker.

Greek yogurt has almost double the protein and double the cholesterol of regular yogurt. Eight ounces of Greek yogurt has about 20 grams of protein and regular yogurt 11-13 grams. Greek yogurt has fewer carbohydrates than regular yogurt. Regular yogurt has about twice the calcium of Greek yogurt. Greek yogurt has half the sodium of regular yogurt. Greek has a bit more calories than regular yogurt. Greek yogurt does not curdle when heated like regular yogurt. Greek yogurt, on average costs twice as much as regular yogurt. *Bottom line, for one serving a day, not much difference, except a little texture, maybe taste, and a much higher cost for Greek.*

Barbecue vs. Grilling - These usually fit in any conversation about sausage. Barbecue or Barbeque or BBQ is slow cooking for several hours. Grilling is cooking fast, at a high temperature.

Barbecue is a method and apparatus for cooking food with the indirect heat and hot gases of a fire, smoking wood, or hot coals of charcoal and may include application of a marinade, spice rub, or basting sauce to the meat.

Grilling or broiling is a form of cooking that involves direct heat. Devices that grill are called grills. The definition varies widely by region and culture. In the United States and Canada, use of the word refers to cooking food directly over a source of dry heat, typically with the food sitting on a metal grate that leaves 'grill marks'. In the UK and other Commonwealth countries this would be referred to as barbecuing.

Grilling in the United Kingdom and Commonwealth countries (except Canada) generally refers to cooking food directly under a source of direct, dry heat. The grill is usually a separate part of an oven where the food is inserted just under the element. This is referred to as broiling in North America. *To sum it up, whether grilled or barbecued, broiled or boiled, marinated or rubbed, slathered or dry, sausage is almost as good as bacon.*

Corned Beef - The term 'corned beef' refers to the 'corns' of salt used to preserve the meat. Meat is treated with large grains of salt (corns) in a process known as salt-curing. Corn is used to describe any small hard particles or grains, in this case, salt. That is why corned beef tastes salty. The salt draws water out of the meat via osmosis, making it more difficult for microorganisms to breed in the meat.

Food for Thought - Oranges and bananas are berries, but strawberries are not technically berries, they are aggregate fruits.

Kiwifruit was once called Chinese Gooseberry, but changed for marketing reasons. Kiwifruit has more vitamin C than oranges and about as much potassium as a banana. *Kiwi also tastes great.*

Six Cooking Tips From HGTV - When you deep-fry, hold each piece of food with long tongs as you add it to the oil. Hold it just below the oil's surface for five seconds before releasing it. This will seal the exterior and stop it from sticking to the pot or the other food.

If you need more oil in the pan when sautéing, add it in a stream along the edges of the pan so that by the time the oil reaches the ingredient being cooked, it will be heated.

Do not use oil in the water when boiling pasta, because it will keep the sauce from sticking to the cooked pasta. Also, After you drain pasta, while it is still hot, grate some fresh Parmesan on top before tossing it with your sauce to give the sauce something to stick to.

When making burgers, add in a bit *(or a lot)* of bacon bits or pork bits while mixing for added flavor.

When making mashed potatoes, after you drain the potatoes, return them to the hot pan, cover tightly and let steam for five minutes. This allows the potatoes to mash with a beautiful texture and soak up the butter and cream more easily.

Use By/Sell By Dates - Holiday feasts are usually followed by leftovers and the trick is to consume the leftovers before they go bad. Below are some tips to help. The only food federal law that says must have a use-by date is infant formula.

Some states also have their own rules about dates for bottled water or foods, such as milk. Other dates are voluntary by manufacturers to tell consumers when the food tastes best, not when it's going to make a person sick. The 'use by,' 'sell by', 'code dates', and 'best by' dates are all used for quality reasons not for safety reasons.

One group, the Natural Resources Defense Council, a New York City-based, non-profit environmental advocacy group, report calls for putting sell-by dates meant for businesses, into code so they are invisible to consumers, *although I do not understand how that will help.*

A few guidelines follow. Bagged produce, such as spinach and lettuce should be tossed by the dates on the package. Bacteria does not grow in condiments such as mustard and catsup. It is OK to cut the mold off hard cheese, cured meats, and hard vegetables such as bell peppers and carrots.

Additional foods and their shelf lives, according to the USDA. Every food product listed should be stored at a refrigerator temperature of 40 F and below for the following shelf life to pertain.

Eggs 21 to 35 days
Lunch meat 14 days [unopened]; 3 to 5 days [opened]
Bacon 14 days [unopened]; 7 days [opened]
Cured Ham 5 to 7 days
Beef, Veal, Pork and Lamb 3 to 5 days
Apples 90 to 240 days
Grapefruit 28 to 42 days
Strawberries 5 to 7 days

Raspberries 1 to 2 days
Grapes 56 to 180 days
Carrots 28 to 128 days
Cherries 10 to 21 days
Asparagus 10 to 20 days
Bunched Broccoli 10 to 14 days
Celery 3 to 5 days
Lettuce 14 to 21 days

Interesting Use for Black Pepper - Next time you nick yourself in the kitchen, reach for the black pepper. Run cold water over the wound to clean it, using soap if you were handling meat. Then sprinkle on pepper and apply pressure. In no time, the bleeding will stop. Black pepper has analgesic, antibacterial, and antiseptic properties. *In addition, pepper doesn't sting.*

Mealtime Definitions

Dinner is usually the name of the main meal of the day. Depending upon culture, dinner may be the second, third, or fourth meal of the day. It is still occasionally used for a noontime meal, if it is a large or main meal.

Dinner was the first meal of a two-meal day with the dinner heavy meal at noontime. The word is from the Old French disner, meaning "breakfast."

More meals were added and the morning meal became breakfast, because we 'break the fast' of not eating since the day before. Eventually, dinner shifted to referring to the heavy main meal of the day, even if it had been preceded by a breakfast meal. The (lighter) meal following dinner has traditionally been referred to as supper.

Luncheon, commonly abbreviated to lunch, is a midday meal, and is generally smaller than dinner, which is the main meal of the day whenever dinner is eaten. The origin of the words lunch and luncheon relate to a small meal originally eaten at any time of the day or night, but during the 20th century gradually focused toward a small meal eaten at midday.

So, there it is - Breakfast, Lunch, Dinner for some. Others say it is Breakfast, Dinner, Supper. Still others say Breakfast, Lunch, Supper. None of these are to be confused with Brunch, which is a combo of the words breakfast and lunch. *Snacks are not meals, so they contain no calories.*

Blue Raspberry

Do you know why some candy makers color their concoctions? Cherry, strawberry, raspberry and watermelon all lend themselves to the color red, and if any two of those flavors were in the same pack, they had to be distinguishable by color.

At first, the problem was solved by making cherry and strawberry slightly different shades of red. Watermelon pops were often made a lighter pink-red, and raspberry ones a dark wine-red. Scientists soon found out, though, that the most inexpensive and widely available dye for this deep red, Amaranth, or Red No. 2, provoked severe reactions, and was deemed a possible carcinogen and banned by the FDA.

The ice pop folks had access to blue dye, but no flavors that needed it. It was just an extra color sitting around, so they started to marry the flavor of blue raspberry, with the bright blue synthetic food coloring Brilliant Blue, or Blue No. 1).

Blue raspberry flavor is a now common flavoring for candy, snack foods, sweet syrups and soft drinks. It is more often used in the United States and originates from Rubus leucodermis, or Blue Raspberry for the blue-black color of its fruit. This species is also related to the black raspberry. *Of course, all of this has nothing to do with giving someone the raspberries, which term is used over much of the globe or a Bronx cheer as many in the US call it.*

Facts About Coffee

Four Coffee Seed Facts - Coffee bean is not actually a bean, it is a seed. Beans are always seeds, but seeds are not always beans. A bean is just one kind of a seed. Specifically, the bean is a name for seeds of the family Fabaceae, of which the coffee plant is not a member.

- A coffee bean is actually the seed of the coffee plant, the pit inside of the coffee fruit.

- Only one US state produces coffee, Hawaii.

- English chemist, George Constant Washington invented instant coffee.

- Put used coffee grounds in houseplant soil to help the plants.

How to Not Spill Coffee - Rouslan Krechetnikov is a mechanical engineer at the University of California at Santa Barbara, and he spends most of his time working on fluid dynamics, the flow of air on a plane's wings, the stability of a rocket, and other weighty problems. None of that brought him as much attention as his paper in the journal Physical Review E: "Walking with coffee: Why does it spill?"

Krechetnikov and a graduate student, Hans Mayer, decided to divert from weightier subjects after a scientific conference, where they had watched fellow researchers stumble to their tables, trying not to get coffee all over themselves and the floor.

"The project was certainly fun. We just wanted to satisfy our curiosity and, given the results, to share what we learned with the scientific community through peer-reviewed literature," Krechetnikov wrote.

They set up a simple experiment, watching a person walk in a straight line, mug in hand. They had their test subject look at the coffee cup. They had their test subject look at the floor ahead. They shot video of it all, recording how the coffee oscillated and how long it took to spill.

The results. Don't rush. You may think the coffee will spill less if you get it to the table quickly, but the opposite is true. Slow down and the sloshing will too. Watch the cup, not the floor. You will spill less.

The abstract concludes: "The studied problem represents an example of the interplay between the complex motion of a cup, due to the biomechanics of a walking individual, and the low-viscosity-liquid dynamics in it." *Isn't science wonderful?*

Origin of the Coffee Break - Pan American Coffee Bureau's 1952 advertising campaign made this widely acceptable. According to Mark Pendergrast's book, Uncommon Grounds: the History of Coffee and How It Transformed Our World, PACB's $2 million dollar annual advertising budget created this daily routine.

The bureau launched a radio, newspaper, and magazine campaign with the theme, 'Give Yourself a Coffee-Break--And Get What Coffee Gives to You.' The bureau gave a name and official sanction to a practice that had begun during the war in defense plants, when time off for coffee gave workers a needed moment of relaxation along with a caffeine jolt.

'Within a very short space,' Charles Lindsay, the manager of the bureau, wrote in late 1952, 'the coffee-break had been so thoroughly publicized that the phrase had become a part of our language." After the campaign, 80% of polled firms introduced coffee breaks.

Eight Coffee Facts - A coffee bean tree takes five years to mature.

- It takes the yield of a complete coffee tree to make one pound of coffee.

- There are fifty species of coffee, but only two, Arabica and Robusta are used for commercial coffee.

- The first coffee house opened in Venice in 1683.

- Starbucks uses about 2.3 billion paper cups each year.

- Coffee is the second most traded commodity after oil.

- Americans drink an average of 450 million cups of coffee per day.

- The name java comes from the place, Java, Indonesia, which was the primary source of coffee in the nineteenth century.

Five Household Uses for Tea

Tea is a great, natural way to clean and polish wood furniture. Brew a full pot of tea and allow it to cool to room temperature. Then dip a light colored, clean towel in the tea and gently rub the wet end of the towel along the surface of wooden furniture. The tea removes light stains and scratches and leaves the furniture shining.

If you wipe mirrors down with room temperature tea, they will be clean and streak-free. A microfiber towel or newspaper both work well.

Empty wet tea leaves into a bowl and sprinkle them across the fireplace before cleaning. The wet tea leaves absorb the ash, making it easier to clean the fireplace and with less dust.

Add a few used tea bags to the bottom of a planter before adding soil. The tea bags absorb excess water.

Used tag bags actually absorb odors in small spaces, much like baking soda does. Let tea bags dry completely and add to sock drawers or toss a bag into shoes or sneakers. The bags soak up odors for a few weeks.

Bacon Tidbits

Overdone Bacon - Now I know I must have crossed the line with so many bacon comments. LINK This site page title from Grupthink is 'Mmmm. . . Bacon' and my Bloginalia 2010 book is posted with two other food books.

More Salt Less Bacon- I think not. Some people are beginning to say that salt is the new bacon. However, bacon is not so hoidy toity. Bacon lovers love bacon and do not need fancy names and additional flavors to make it better. The price of bacon has gone up over twenty percent in the past three years, but that is nothing compared to the price of specialty salts.

New salt types include Himalayan or alder-smoked and many more. Salt is in chocolate, on caramels, and even chocolate covered bacon.

SaltWorks sells Black Hawaiian sea salt, Bolivian Rose salt, Merlot-infused crystals, and Yakima apple wood smoked sea salt. It even has salt and pepper tastings. Some specialty salts can cost $8 per ounce, or $128 per pound. *Bacon salt is much cheaper.*

Bacon Shake - It seems fitting after discussing the Bacon Queen to add this new menu item for Jack in the Box. It is the Bacon Milkshake. The food chain felt the need to create some bacon buzz. It is all part of a new ad campaign that asks: If you like bacon so much, why don't you marry it?

Alas, Jack sold us out, it is just a bacon flavored syrup added to a shake. Word from reporters is that the real taste is Ugh! *Oh, well, give them credit for trying to get on the bacon bandwagon. Too bad it doesn't pass the sniff test.*

Bacon Peanut Butter Cups - They combine delicious milk chocolate, creamy all natural peanut butter, and yummy bacon.

Giant peanut butter cups are filled with all natural peanut butter and Applewood smoked bacon with no nitrates or nitrites and no preservatives. Each cup is 4" across and weighs 6 oz. They can be ordered on the web at LINK.

Bacon Fat - Almost half of bacon fat is monounsaturated, just like what is found in olive oil. It can actually lower your bad cholesterol.

Bacon Coffee - Starbucks subsidiary brand Seattle's Best have combed state fairs across the country and are officially gearing up to release a bacon coffee drink.

The new flavor combines Level 5 Seattle's Best Coffee, caramelized bacon, and subtle hints of pumpkin pie spice. It is a result of a country-wide search for the most "imaginative new coffee drink."

The winner was Des Moines native Eileen Fannon, who calls her concoction the "How to Win a Guy with One Sip." The key to America's collective male heart is apparently coffee with a hint of bacon.

According to a Starbucks press release, Eileen "will have the chance to see her coffee drink featured in participating Seattle's Best Coffee locations across North America."

PS - The Texas State Fair has breaded, deep fried, bacon crusted cinnamon rolls, Yumm.

Bacon or Ham - The difference between bacon and salted pork or ham is primarily the composition of the brine that is used to cure it. Brine for bacon often includes sodium nitrite, sodium nitrate, and saltpeter (for curing the meat); sodium ascorbate (for setting the color, as well as speeding up the curing process); and brown or maple sugar (for flavor), among other ingredients. Brine for ham tends to have a significantly higher concentration of sugar. Incidentally, the USDA defines "bacon" as "the cured belly of a swine carcass"

Bacon - Traditional pork bacon has many good points. It is high in protein, vitamins, and minerals, including B6, B12, niacin, thiamin, riboflavin, iron, magnesium, potassium and zinc, as well as choline, a nutrient which helps improve cognitive performance, memory, mood and mental alertness. Bacon has about 30 calories per regular slice.

Bacon flavored salt is low in sodium, zero calories and fat, kosher and vegetarian. It allows bacon lovers to enjoy all the flavor of their beloved treat without a side of guilt. Sprinkle it over eggs, potatoes, meats, baked beans, soups, salads and sandwiches.

If you want to find more about bacon, in fact almost everything about bacon, try my book 'Bacon Orgazmia'. It is veritable plethora of all things porcine and available on Amazon.

FDA Food Label Folly

The US FDA uses common words to mean something different. FDA evaluates certain terms with reference to a typical portion size known as an RACC (Reference Amounts Customarily Consumed). An RACC of eggnog, for example, is ½ cup. For croutons, it is 7 grams, and for scrambled eggs, 100 grams. Many labels use artificially low or high portion size to reduce or increase the amount of calories, fat, etc. perceived by the consumer.

Imitation - A food only has to be labeled as "imitation" if it has a lower amount of protein or some other essential nutrient than the food it is trying to look like.

Free - To be labeled "free" of calories, the food must have less than 5 per RACC. For fat and sugar, less than .5 grams. For sodium, less than 5 milligrams. Also, the food must somehow be processed to be "free" of those things in order to get the simple "free" label. You cannot have "fat free lettuce," only "lettuce, a fat free food."

Low - Low is also defined with respect to set portion sizes and varies with whether it refers to calories, fat, or sodium. For fat it is less than 3 grams. For calories, it is less than 40, unless it is a prepared meal, in which case it's 120 per 100 grams.

Reduced/less - Sometimes manufacturers want to make a relational claim about a food, not just that it is "low" in some substance, but lower than it usually is (which may mean it doesn't meet the standard for "low"). Relational claims are evaluated with respect to a reference food. A reference food should be the same type of food, as yogurt vs. yogurt. The "reduced" substance must be less than 25 percent of what it is in the reference food.

Light/lite - This is also evaluated with respect to a reference food, and a rather complicated set of conditions is taken into account for different substances. For example, if a "light" product has more than half of its calories from fat, the fat must be reduced by half per reference serving amount. If less than half its calories come from fat, it can be "light" if the calories per serving are reduced by 1/3. Sometimes foods that meet "low" requirements can also be labeled as "light."

High - High means that the food has 20 percent or more of the recommended daily value for that nutrient per reference serving.

Good Source - "Good source of" is a little lower than "high." A food with this label should have 10 to 19 percent of the recommended daily value.

Lean - "Lean" applies to seafoods or meats that have less than combined specified levels of fat, saturated fat, and cholesterol (10g, 4.5g, and 95mg, respectively).

Natural - The FDA has not established an official definition, but endorses the general understanding that it implies nothing artificial or synthetic has been added that would not normally be expected to be added.

Glucose, Fructose, Sucrose

Glucose, fructose and sucrose are three types of sugar. Sugar production has been around for a few thousand years. In 2011, worldwide production of table sugar was about 168 million tons.

Glucose, also known as dextrose, is the most common sugar. It is rarely found in food in its single molecular form, but is found as a building block for more complex carbohydrates. Foods containing glucose include: bread, pasta, cereals, rice, most fruits and vegetables, dairy products, maple syrup, pancake mixes, commercial salad dressings, and spices, and all foods containing sugar. Brain cells show a marked preference for glucose.

Fructose is the sugar that sweetens fruits, and it is also naturally present in some vegetables. One of the major differences between fructose and glucose is that cells require insulin to take up glucose from the bloodstream, but fructose is absorbed directly without insulin. Fructose a healthier choice for individuals with diabetes than glucose or sucrose. Foods rich in fructose include, agave, apricots, blueberries, figs, dates, grapes, honey, and raisins.

Sucrose is made up of two smaller sugar units, glucose and fructose. Sucrose is the type of sugar you use in your kitchen and in cooking. It is usually derived from either sugar cane or sugar beets. An apple contains both fructose and glucose. Sucrose is digested into glucose and fructose before it enters the bloodstream.

Glucose, fructose, and sucrose contain identical amounts of energy. Each provides four calories per gram. Glucose and fructose units are absorbed across the intestinal wall by active transit into the portal vein. They are then transported to the liver where they are converted to energy units. When reading food labels, sucrose can be listed as sugar, glucose can appear as dextrose, and fructose as corn syrup or high-fructose corn syrup.

Bottom line - Cells require a constant supply of energy to keep running. Glucose and fructose have identical chemical formulas. Glucose and fructose can be burned for immediate energy or stored as body fat. It is not important where sugar comes from. Too little and your body is deprived of much needed nutrients, too much and your body stores sugars as fat. *There is a correlation between increased soda consumption and obesity, but no proven causation. Headlines about soda and obesity are mostly non-scientific mumbo jumbo designed to titillate, but not educate.*

Novel Use for Sugar - Healers in Africa have been putting crushed sugar cane on wounds for generations. Moses Murandu is a nurse who grew up watching his father use the remedy in Africa and was surprised to find that doctors in England didn't use it. He started a study to research the idea and tested it on patients with bed sores, leg ulcers, and amputations before dressing the wounds. They found that sugar can reduce pain and kill bacteria that slow healing. Sugar is hygroscopic, meaning it naturally absorbs water, which bacteria needs to survive. Sugar is also much cheaper than modern antibiotics. *The next time you cut yourself, give it a sprinkle of sugar (or pepper) before putting on a band-aid.*

Saccharin - The artificial sweetener in "Sweet'N Low," is about 400 times sweeter than sugar. It was discovered in 1879 by Constantine Fahlberg who was actually working on substitution products of coal tar.

After a long day in the lab, he forgot to wash his hands before eating dinner. When the bread and everything he touched tasted sweet, he remembered he spilled a chemical on his hands earlier.

Fahlberg patented saccharin in 1884 and began mass production. The artificial sweetener became widespread when sugar was rationed during World War I. In 1907 diabetics started using the sweetener as a replacement for sugar and it was soon labeled as a non-caloric sweetener for dieters. Because the body can not break it down, we do not get any calories.

All About Gluten

We read about way too many headlines and diets about gluten these days. It appears to be the latest fad ingredient to pick on. It is serious for some, but less than one percent of the population may have Celiac disease, an autoimmune disorder. Some people have been found to be allergic to wheat only, but not gluten.

Gluten is a naturally occurring protein composite found primarily in wheat, but may also be found in rye, barley, and some types of oats. The US FDA considers foods containing less than or equal to 20 ppm to be gluten-free, but there is no regulation or law in the US for labeling foods as 'gluten-free'. There still is no general agreement on the analytical method used to measure gluten in ingredients and food products.

Gluten may be added as a stabilizing agent or thickener in products such as ice-cream and ketchup. It is also found in ingredients of many over-the-counter and prescription medications and vitamins. Items such as lipstick, lip balms, lip gloss, soy sauce, barbecue sauce, salad dressings, gravy, canned soups, ground spices to prevent clumping, instant powdered drinks, and imitation and pasteurized cheeses. Glue used on envelopes may also contain gluten.

Many types of alcoholic beverages are considered gluten-free, provided no gluten colorings or other additives have been added. Distillation removes proteins, including gluten in bourbon and corn whiskey. Spirits made without any grain such as gin, vodka, scotch, rye, brandy, wine, mead, cider, sherry, port, rum, tequila, vermouth, and some beers generally do not contain gluten.

Gluten consists of gliadin and glutenin. Gliadin is one of the proteins that forms gluten. Doctors test for anti-gliadin antibodies if celiac disease or gluten hypersensitivity is suspected. Gliadin triggers immune response in celiac disease. Glutenin is the other protein of gluten. It is responsible for the strength and elasticity of dough.

Several grains and starch sources are considered acceptable for a gluten-free diet, such as corn, potatoes, rice, some oats, tapioca, quinoa, sorghum, taro, chia seed, and yam. Flours, such as bean, soybean, almond, gram derived from chickpeas, and buckwheat are used as alternatives to wheat flour.

Most humans naturally digest gluten. The human mouth contains symbiotic bacteria colonies that help break down gluten. Gluten allergies and sensitivities are different. Celiac disease sufferers are allergic. Others may have similar symptoms, such as bloating, flatulence, irritable bowel syndrome, and abdominal pain, but these same symptoms may also be caused by any number of other dietary items.

Top Ten Benefits of Cinnamon

Did you know cinnamon:

- *Can Lower Cholesterol* - Studies have shown that 1/2 teaspoon per day can lower LDL cholesterol.

- *Helps Regulate Blood Sugar* - Several studies suggest that it may have a regulatory effect on blood sugar, beneficial for people with Type 2 diabetes.

- *Helps with Yeast Infection* - In some studies, it has shown an ability to stop medication-resistant yeast infections.

- *Helps with Cancer Prevention* - The US Department of Agriculture in Maryland showed cinnamon reduced the proliferation of leukemia and lymphoma cancer cells.

- *Aids Anti-Clotting* - It has an anti-clotting effect on the blood.

- *Provides Arthritis Relief* - In a study at Copenhagen University, showed half a teaspoon of cinnamon powder combined with one tablespoon of honey every morning before breakfast had significant relief in arthritis pain after one week.

- *Is Anti-Bacterial* - When added to food, it inhibits bacterial growth and food spoilage.

- *Aids Brain Health* - One study found that smelling cinnamon boosts cognitive function and memory.

- *Fights E. Coli* - Researchers found that cinnamon fights the E. coli bacteria in unpasteurized juices.

- *Is High in Nutrients* - It is a great source of manganese, fiber, iron, and calcium.

- The cinnamon in Cinnabon rolls is actually not 'true' cinnamon. True cinnamon has a citrusy fragrance and complex yet mild taste without the "bite" we associate with the spice. Cinnabon trademarked its supply of Korintje cassia as "Makara Cinnamon."

- Cinnamon is produced from the inner bark of a small evergreen tree belonging to the Laurel family with the genus Cinnamomum. Although there are four commercial species of Cinnamomum, the global cinnamon market recognizes the product from one species as true cinnamon. The last two are more closely related to cassia than cinnamon

True cinnamon – Cinnamomum verum
Cassia – Cinnamomum aromaticum
Indonesian - Cinnamomum burmannii
Vietnamese - Cinnamomum loureiroi

- About a hundred years ago, American traders started importing cassia, because of a rise in the price of Ceylon cinnamon. Cassia continues to be the main variety sold in supermarkets in the US and Canada. American labeling laws do not require that a distinction be made between cassia and cinnamon in the retail market.

- The "cinnamon" found in Cinnabon and your kitchen is cassia, derived from Cinnamomum burmannii, a tree native to Indonesia. Of all the Cinnamomum species, this form of cassia (known as Indonesian cassia or Korintje cassia) has the lowest oil content and is therefore the cheapest. *Cinnamon and cassia have numerous health benefits.*

Interesting Facts About Nuts

Nuts can reduce the risk of diabetes and bring down cholesterol and you only need just a handful of nuts a day, raw if possible.

Tree nuts are increasingly regarded as wonder foods that lower the risk of heart disease, some forms of cancer and type 2 diabetes while providing essential vitamins and minerals including niacin, zinc, folic acid, selenium, and magnesium.

They contain more unsaturated fats than animal proteins and can cut levels of LDL or "bad" cholesterol, according to numerous studies. Their mix of omega-3 fatty acids, protein and fiber will help you feel full and suppress your appetite. The fat content helps release satiety hormones in the digestive system, which also helps to curb hunger, and lessen your desire to overeat later in the day.

Almonds are rich in vitamin E.

Brazil nuts are rich in selenium, a vital mineral and antioxidant. Just two Brazil nuts a day may prevent heart disease and can also enhance mood.

Cashews are high in magnesium and are good sources of phytochemicals and antioxidants.

Hazelnuts, the most fiber-rich of all the nuts, contain significant levels of B-group vitamins including folate and vitamin B6.

Macadamia nuts are high in healthy mono-unsaturated fats, contain all the essential amino acids and have been shown to lower blood cholesterol.

Pecans reduce cholesterol and may delay age-related muscle nerve degeneration.

Pine nuts, the edible seeds of pine trees removed from pine cones contain zinc, niacin, and manganese, and are rich in mono-unsaturated acids.

Pistachios are packed with protein, vitamin E and are an excellent source of copper and manganese.

Walnuts are loaded with natural plant omega-3s called alphalinoleic acid or ALA.

Peanuts, technically legumes, but commonly referred to as nuts, are high in vitamin E, folate (for brain development) and may reduce cognitive decline.

Benefits of Nuts - The holidays always include snacks for family and friends and now you can be good to them without cooking. A study in The New England Journal of Medicine, comes from the Nurses' Health Study and the Health Professionals Follow-Up Study, which together have followed nearly 119,000 women and men from 1980 - 2010. Both studies recorded what the participants ate and analyzed their diets in relation to the causes of death among the 27,429 people who died since the studies began.

The more often nuts (pistachios, almonds, Brazil nuts, cashews, hazelnuts, macadamias, pecans, pine nuts, peanuts, and walnuts) were consumed, the less likely participants were to die of cancer, heart disease, and respiratory disease, and not because nut eaters succumbed to other diseases. Their death rate from any cause was lower. Those who ate nuts seven or more times a week were 20 percent less likely to die. Among those who consumed nuts less often than once a week, the death rate was still 11 percent lower than for those who did not eat them.

Of course, moderation is key, because an ounce of nuts has 160 to 200 calories. However, findings revealed the more often people ate nuts; the leaner they tended to be. In a Mediterranean study that tracked the effect of nut consumption on weight gain over the course of 28 months, frequent nut consumers gained less weight than those who never ate nuts, and were 43 percent less likely to become overweight or obese. One reason it found may be the fat, fiber, and protein in nuts suppresses hunger between meals. Every study has indicated that nuts make a contribution to health and longevity, even after taking other factors into account.

Nuts provide rich sources of unsaturated fat and also contain protein, fiber, plant sterols that can lower cholesterol, and micronutrients copper and magnesium. Nuts have less cholesterol-raising saturated fat than olive oil. On average, 62 percent of the fat in nuts is monounsaturated, the kind that supports healthy levels of protective HDL cholesterol and does not raise blood levels of harmful LDL cholesterol.

Nuts contain omega-3 fatty acids that can lower triglycerides and blood pressure, slow the buildup of arterial plaque, and prevent abnormal heart rhythms. Walnuts contain rich sources of alpha-linolenic acid, some of which is converted to heart-protective omega-3 fatty acids. Almonds are good sources of vitamin E. Peanuts and pistachios are rich in resveratrol. The nurses' study also linked tree nuts to a reduced risk of pancreatic cancer.

A Taiwanese study of about 24,000 people found a 58 percent lower risk of colorectal cancer among women who ate peanuts, although a similar effect was not found among men. The nurses' study and a study of 64,000 women in Shanghai found strong evidence that frequent consumption of tree nuts, peanuts, and peanut butter reduced the risk of developing Type 2 diabetes.

As with all studies, especially many with exaggerated claims, no food is a panacea and eating nuts will not heal the sick or raise the dead. However, there seems to be enough evidence that adding a moderate amount of nuts to your diet is better for you than not.

Peanuts and Almonds are not Nuts - Notwithstanding the above, peanuts are not nuts. They are legumes. The plant has seeds that grow inside pods such as peas or beans. Nuts grow on trees, peanuts grow underground. Peanut seeds flower above ground and then migrate underground to reach maturity. Peanuts are also called goobers, goober peas, groundnuts, earthnuts, monkey nuts, and grass nuts.

Also, almonds are not nuts. An almond is the seed of the fruit of the almond tree. The tree bears fruits with a seed within. Fruits with these characteristics are called drupes. A drupe is a fruit that has an outer fleshy part surrounding a shell that contains a seed. Other drupes include fruits from walnut trees and coconut trees. The seed inside the almond fruit is called an almond nut, even though it is not a nut. A nut is a hard shelled fruit that doesn't open to release its seed.

Graham Cracker Facts

During the 1820s, Sylvester Graham created the eponymous cracker as part of his diet plan thought to increase physical wellness, sexual purity, and spiritual health. The Presbyterian minister's mission was to rid the world of sexual immorality. He believed a vegetarian diet, devoid of spices and sugars, combined with avoiding foods made with overly processed flours would do away with the greatest evils of his day, lustful thought and masturbation. Of course, neither Graham crackers nor his diet have ever been shown to cure sexual urges.

Graham flour is essentially a type of non-bleached, finely ground whole wheat flour. Among other things made with this flour, Graham made bland crackers. They were not the sweet treat we enjoy today.

Nabisco began making Graham crackers with bleached white flour and oils. The germ is rarely used today so the crackers have a longer shelf life.

Dr. John Harvey Kellogg and his brother Will found the minister's ideas useful at their Sanitarium in Battle Creek Michigan. Dr. Kellogg imposed the vegetarian diet on his patients with the belief that it could cure some of their troubles.

The brothers made their own Graham crackers on the premises. Once, Will left out some prepared wheat used to make Graham crackers. When he came back to finish the cooking, the dough had become hard and stale. Because he could not afford to waste a whole batch's ingredients, he used it in the baking process anyway. Rather than get thin wafers after extruding the dough through rollers, he ended up with hard crispy flakes, similar to the corn flakes we eat today. *Now you know how Graham crackers and Kellogg's corn flakes are related.*

Facts about Olives

Did you know the main difference between green and black olives is when they were picked? Green olives are picked before they are ripe, while black olives are allowed to ripen on the tree.

After that, green olives are soaked in a solution containing lye, then fermented in brine for anywhere between 6 to 12 months after being picked. The longer the olive is fermented, the less bitter and more flavorful it becomes. Green olives are usually pitted, and often stuffed with items such as pimientos, anchovies, jalapenos, garlic, or onions.

Black olives are also soaked in lye to lessen their bitterness, then cured in brine, but rarely stuffed. Green olives contain about twice as much sodium as black olives, while black olives contain more oil than green.

Olive oil has been considered sacred since ancient times and is still used in religious ceremonies today. It was used to anoint kings in ancient Greece, for grooming bodies and hair in Ancient Rome, burnt in sacred lamps of temples, rubbed on the first Olympic athletes to cure muscle aches. Victors in Olympic games were crowned with wreathes made of olive branches and leaves.

Olive trees can live for over a thousand years.

Speaking of olives and long living, Popeye's friend Olive Oyl was the main star of the comic strip for ten years before Popeye took top billing. She was also the supposed fiancée of Harold Hamgravy before Popeye stepped into her life.

Olive's family included her brother, Castor Oyl, Castor's estranged wife, Cylinda Oyl, their mother, Nana Oyl (after banana oil), their father, Cole Oyl. Olive's nieces Diesel Oyl and Violet Oyl, her two uncles, Otto Oyl and Lubry Kent Oyl and cousin, sultry blonde Sutra Oyl.

Olive Oil - Calories per tablespoon: 119, Total fat: 13.5g, Saturated fat: 1.82g, Cholesterol: 0mg, Vitamin E: 4% Daily Value

Olive oil comes from California, France, Greece, Italy, and Spain. All olive oils are graded in accordance with the degree of acidity they contain. The best are cold-pressed, a chemical-free process that involves only pressure, which produces a natural level of low acidity.

Extra virgin olive oil, the cold-pressed result of the first pressing of the olives, is only 1 percent acid. It's considered the finest and fruitiest of the olive oils and is therefore also the most expensive. Extra virgin olive oil can range from a crystalline champagne color to greenish-golden to bright green. In general, the deeper the color, the more intense the olive flavor. After extra virgin, olive oils are classified in order of ascending acidity.

Virgin olive oil is also a first-press oil, with a slightly higher level of acidity of between 1 and 3 percent.

Fino olive oil is a blend of extra virgin and virgin oils (fino is Italian for "fine").

Olive oil (once called pure olive oil) products contain a combination of refined olive oil and virgin or extra virgin oil.

Light olive oil contains the same amount of beneficial monounsaturated fat as regular olive oil and has exactly the same number of calories. Light" refers to an extremely fine filtration process and this olive oil is lighter in both color and fragrance. The rather nondescript flavor makes 'light' olive oil good for baking and cooking. The filtration process for the light-style oil also gives it a higher smoke point than regular olive oil. Light olive oils can be used for high-heat frying, whereas regular olive oil is better suited for low to medium-heat cooking, as well as for salad dressings and marinades.

Olive oil can be stored in a cool, dark place for up to six months. It can be refrigerated and last up to a year. Chilled olive oil becomes cloudy and too thick to pour. However, it will clear and become liquid again when brought to room temperature.

Olive oil is obtained from the pulp of olives by separating the liquids from solids. To make the finest or extra-virgin olive oil, the fruit is gathered when fully ripened, ground to a paste under granite or steel millstones, layered over straw mats, and pressed in a hydraulic press. Today, most olive oil is produced by just one pressing. The resulting oil is separated from the juice by settling or by centrifuge and then filtered. Olive oil of good quality is ready to use, without further refinement.

Although olive oil is chiefly used as a food or in food preservation, it is also used in soaps, certain pharmaceuticals, and cosmetics.

Other Uses for Food

Garlic for Feet - Garlic is a great food enhancer, but is also a potent natural antifungal, making it ideal for treating fungal infections like athlete's foot. Add a few cloves of crushed garlic to warm water in a foot bath and soak the affected feet for 30 minutes. *I swear it is not trading one smell for another.*

Hot Pepper for Pain Removal - Capsaicin, the thing that makes peppers hot, is fat soluble and thus water does not counter the burning sensation. If it is cold water it will temporarily overpower the capsaicin's effect on the nerve receptors and tell your brain you are feeling a cold sensation, but once the cold water is swallowed the heat will come back.

Dairy products work best to counteract capsaicin because they contain a protein called casein which binds to the capsaicin, hindering its ability to bind to your nerve receptors.

Drinking milk before or while eating the peppers will help reduce irritation in your intestines for the same reason it helps in your mouth. It could save you from that awful day after burn.

Hiccup Cure - Rub an ice cube on your Adam's apple for a minute. The coldness interrupts the reflex arc from your brain to your diaphragm that causes hiccups.

Walnuts for Scratches - My brother, a carpenter, among other skills, says to rub a walnut over a wood scratch to hide the scratch.

Seven More Uses for Rice

You can use rice to get at those hard-to-reach bottoms of narrow-necked bottles and flower vases. Add rice, soap, water, and then shake and swirl.

Get your coffee grinder squeaky clean by wiping grinder clear of debris then add enough rice to cover the blades, grind. The rice will absorb all the lingering oils that carry the coffee aroma.

Use rice water as a facial by saving the water from rinsing your cooking rice. Let it cool and use a wash cloth to rub the liquid into your face and rinse clean. Rice is high in vitamin E.

Make an easy heating pad by filling a sock with a couple cups of rice, and then tie the open end. Pop it in the microwave for a few minutes, and you have an instant heating pad.

When finished with that heating pad, let the kids or pets play with it like a bean bag.

Bury wet electronic devices in a bowl of rice. It extracts moisture like silica gel.

Make DIY glue by boiling down rice until it degrades and releases the starch.

Nine Things You Never Thought of Freezing

Here are a few things we usually do not think about freezing, but might be worth a try.

Fruits: Cut up and freeze season fruits such as peaches, cantaloupe, honeydew melon, pineapple, grapes, or apples. Add a spritz of lemon juice to your frozen fruits to prevent browning.

Nuts: Bag up and freeze almonds, pine nuts, honey toasted pecans and others.

Berries: Freeze blueberries, blackberries, raspberries, and strawberries.

Fresh Bread: Store specialty breads in the freezer. The cold temperature will preserve the crumb and texture while prolonging staleness. A quick oven re-bake will bring back the aroma, crispness, and moisture.

Semi-Soft Cheese: Freezing cheese slows down mold in super-melts like mozzarella, Colby, pepper jack, or Gouda.

Whole Grains: Whole grains like flax, millet or oats can stay fresh by freezing them in insulated bags.

Herbs: Fresh herbs, such as basil, parsley, mint, dill, cilantro and chives can benefit from a deep-freeze treatment. To retain their vibrant color, let herbs air-dry before freezing.

Juices: Freshly squeezed citrus like lemon, lime, orange, and grapefruit. Store in ice-cube trays for future use.

Fresh Vegetables: Freeze asparagus, beets, broccoli, green beans, peas, carrots, and greens.

Cheesy Facts

The root of the English word cheese comes from the Latin caseus, which also gives us the word casein, the milk protein that is the basis of cheese. In Old English, caseus became chese in Middle English and cheese in Modern English. Caseus is also the root word for cheese in other languages, including queso in Spanish, kaas in Dutch, käse in German, and queijo in Portuguese. Caseus Formatus, or molded (formed) cheese, brought us formaticum, the term the Romans employed for the hard cheese used as supplies for the legionaries. From this root comes the French fromage and the Italian formaggio.

Cheese consumption predates recorded history, with scholars believing it began as early as 8000 BC, when sheep were first domesticated. It is believed to have been discovered in the Middle East or by nomadic Turkic tribes in Central Asia, where foodstuffs were commonly stored in animal hides or organs for transport. Milk stored in animal stomachs would have separated into curds and whey by movement along with the rennet and bacteria.

Monks were responsible for inventing some of the classic varieties of cheese we know today. According to the British Cheese Board, Britain has approximately 700 distinct local cheeses. France and Italy have about 400 each. The varying flavors, colors, and textures of cheese come from many factors, including the type of milk used, the type of bacteria or acids used to separate the milk, the length of aging, and the addition of other flavorings or mold.

The United States is the top producer of cheese in the world, with Wisconsin and California leading the states in production. Although the US produces the most cheese, Greece and France lead in cheese consumption per capita. Cheese consumption in the US has tripled since 1970 and is continuing to increase.

I recently discovered nutritional yeast as a great cheese substitute that is gluten free, salt free and loaded with protein, Vitamin B, 18 amino acids, 15 minerals, etc. The only thing it is low in is calories.

Chocolate Facts

People who eat chocolate regularly tend to be thinner according to new research. The findings come from a study of nearly 1,000 US people that looked at diet, calorie intake and body mass index (BMI). It found those who ate chocolate a few times a week were, on average, slimmer than those who ate it only occasionally.

Even though chocolate is loaded with calories, it contains ingredients that may favor weight loss rather than fat synthesis, scientists believe. Despite boosting calorie intake, regular chocolate consumption was related to lower BMI in the study published in Archives of Internal Medicine.

The link remained even when other factors, like how much exercise individuals did, were taken into account and it appears how often you eat chocolate that is important, rather than how much of it you eat. The study found no link with quantity consumed.

Other studies have claimed chocolate may be good for the heart and linked to some favorable changes in blood pressure, insulin sensitivity, and cholesterol level. Chocolate, particularly dark chocolate, contains antioxidants which can help to clean harmful free radicals, unstable chemicals that can damage our cells.

Dr Golomb and her team believe that antioxidant compounds, called catechins, can improve lean muscle mass and reduce weight.

Chocolate Reduces Coronary Heart Disease - Eating high levels of chocolate could reduce the risk of coronary heart disease and stroke. Data from 114,009 patients suggested risk was cut by about a third, according to a study published on the BMJ website.

The analysis, conducted by scientists at the University of Cambridge, compared the risk to the brain and heart in groups of people who reported eating low levels of chocolate, fewer than two bars per week, with those eating more than two bars per week. It showed that the "highest levels of chocolate consumption were associated with a 37% reduction in cardiovascular disease and a 29% reduction in stroke compared with the lowest levels". It also found chocolate is known to decrease blood pressure. They recommended people should avoid binge-eating and eat small amounts of chocolate on a regular basis.

Eleven Benefits of Chocolate - A recently completed European study of chocolate eating among teens showed those who regularly consumed chocolate have less total and abdominal body fat than those who do not. The findings are based on data from 1,458 youths ages 12 to 17, who were part of the Healthy Lifestyle in Europe by Nutrition in Adolescence study, which examines lifestyle habits among youths in nine countries in Europe. The study did not differentiate between dark or light chocolate.

Although most studies claim dark chocolate is better for you, there is no need to rule out light chocolate. Benefits of eating chocolate show:

- A 20% reduced risk of stroke,
- Lower blood pressure,
- Lower risk of heart attack,
- Helps keep you feeling fuller longer,
- Increases insulin sensitivity (reducing risk of diabetes),
- Dark chocolate flavonoids are good for your skin,

- Theobromine in chocolate reduces activity of the vagus nerve to ease coughing,
- Increases a positive mood and reduces stress,
- Cocoa has blood thinning properties,
- Improves vision.

White chocolate is really not chocolate, because it does not contain cocoa solids. It is a chocolate derivative and usually consists of cocoa butter, sugar, milk solids, and salt.

Four Cookie Facts

The **Fig Newton** is named for Newton, Massachusetts where it was originally made.

Lorna Doones were introduced in 1912. The shortbread biscuits were considered a product of Scottish heritage, and back then, Lorna Doone character was symbolic of Scotland.

Nabisco created 'Barnum's Animals' in 1902 and sold them in a little box designed like an animal cage with a string attached to carry and hang on Christmas trees. In 1948, the company changed the name to its current **'Barnum's Animal Crackers'**. Fifty Four different animals have been represented by animal crackers since 1902. Currently, each package contains 22 crackers consisting of a variety of animals. The newest, a koala was added in September 2002, but later retired. Current animals include bear, camel, crocodile, elephant, giraffe, gorilla, horse, lion, seal, tiger, and zebra.

The name **Oreo** was inspired by the gold color used on early package designs. The French word for gold is Or. A number of other versions for the name persist, but this is most widely accepted. The original name was Oreo Biscuit. It was renamed in 1921, to "Oreo Sandwich. In 1948, the Oreo Sandwich was renamed the "Oreo Creme Sandwich." It was changed in 1974 to the Oreo Chocolate Sandwich Cookie. Oreos are a knockoff of the Sunshine Hydrox cookie invented two years earlier. Today, China has become the second largest Oreo market, after the United States.

Seven Cracker Facts

The first cracker was made in 1792 by John Pearson. He was looking to make a type of biscuit that would last longer than traditional sailor's biscuits without spoiling. He eventually mixed just flour and water, baked it, and called his invention 'Pearson's Pilot Bread'. This later became known as hardtack or sea biscuit and was popular among sailors due to its long shelf life without spoiling.

The name cracker came to be when Josiah Bent accidentally burned a batch of what we now call crackers. As they burned, they made a crackling noise, which inspired the name. He invented soda crackers, which were precursors to saltine crackers we enjoy. Some folks still call saltines soda crackers. In 1810 Bent's cracker business was acquired by the National Biscuit Company (Nabisco).

Crackers have holes for a reason, because the holes allow steam to escape during cooking. This keeps the crackers flat and the holes also help crisp the crackers. If the holes are too close together, the cracker will become extra dry and hard, due to too much steam escaping. If the holes are too far apart, parts of the cracker will rise a bit forming little bubbles on the surface of the cracker, which is undesirable in most types of crackers, except Cheez Its. There are hundreds of varieties of crackers now and sales are over $10 Billion a year.

Top Ten Vitamin C Foods

Top ten foods that have more vitamin C than oranges: Guava with 376 mg of vitamin C for 1 cup. Next are red bell peppers followed by lychee, a small Asian fruit, followed by parsley, kiwi, broccoli, Brussels sprouts, papaya, strawberries, and pineapple. Bringing up the rear are oranges.

Top Twelve Ice Cream Facts

July is National Ice Cream Month (created by Ronald Reagan in 1984) and (third Sunday in July (July 21) is National Ice Cream Day). Here are a few frozen goodie facts.

Ice cream has the following composition by weight: greater than 10% milkfat by legal definition, 9 to 12% milk solids-not-fat, 12 to 16% sweeteners, 0.2 to 0.5% stabilizers and emulsifiers, 55% to 64% water which comes from the milk or other ingredients.

The history of ice cream dates back to the second century B.C.

The ice cream cone was invented in 1896 with a patent being issued in 1903 to Italo Marchiony.

The United States is the top ice cream consuming country in the world.

It takes 12 lbs. of milk to make a gallon of ice cream.

Vanilla is the number one selling flavor at 27.8%, followed by chocolate 14.3%, strawberry 3.3% *(hot dog flavored ice-cream is made by Udder Delights in Arizona)*.

Chocolate syrup is the favorite topping to put on ice cream.

The major ingredient in ice cream is air.

Depending on conditions of storage, ice cream might last one year, or it might be two weeks or less.

PETA urged Ben & Jerry's to replace cow's milk in its ice cream with human breast milk.

In the late 19th century, America's soda shops bowed to pressure from local churches to not serve ice cream sodas on Sundays. They removed the soda from the recipe and invented the ice cream sundae.

Ice cream is made from milk fat and milk solids. Sorbet is non-dairy and usually high in sugar. Yogurt is usually tart with low or no fat milk substitute. Custard is rich and smooth with lots of egg in it.

An average dairy cow can produce enough milk in her lifetime to make a bit over 9,000 gallons of ice cream.

Eight Fun Food Facts

Several states used to require margarine to be dyed pink to appease the dairy lobby and keep butter sales strong.

The Quaker Oats guy's name is Larry.

Twinkies originally had banana-flavored filling. Hostess switched to vanilla after bananas were rationed during World War II.

Oklahoma's official state vegetable is the watermelon.

The eight juices in V8 are tomato, spinach, celery, carrot, beet, lettuce, watercress and parsley.

NECCO Wafers - New England Confectionery COmpany.

Barbie's full name is Barbara Millicent Roberts.

Kool-Aid was originally marketed as "Fruit Smack."

Six Uses for Lemons

Summertime always means refreshing lemonade to quench your thirst. Here are some other uses for those yellow goodies.

Realtors say a nice bowl of lemons makes a colorful and inexpensive arrangement for the table or counter top.

Finger nails looking dull and yellowed after a long period covered in dark polish? Just squeeze a lemon into a small dish, clean your nails and soak them in the lemon juice for a minute or two. Some women claim that this treatment will also make nails stronger, particularly when adding a tablespoon or so of olive oil to the dish.

Keep cut fruit and vegetables like apples, pears, avocados, and potatoes from turning brown by squeezing on a little bit of lemon juice.

You can perk up droopy lettuce by soaking it for an hour in a bowl of cold water and the juice of one lemon.

Simmer lemon peel in water on the stove-top as a natural air freshener

A few drops of lemon juice added to simmering rice will keep it from sticking to the pot, making clean-up a lot easier.

Eleven Twinkie Facts

Another fun treat anytime is Twinkies. Here are some facts that might surprise you.

- Twinkies were first thought up by James A. Dewar, Vice President of Continental Bakeries, which sold the Hostess brand. Dewar was trying to come up with a way to utilize the machines used to make cream filled strawberry shortcake when strawberries were out of season and the machines normally sat idle.
- The name Twinkies was also thought up by James Dewar. On the way to a marketing meeting, he saw a billboard advertising "Twinkle-Toes Shoes" and came up with the name Twinkies.
- Exploding the common belief that Twinkies can last forever, Twinkies stay good for about 25 days.
- According to Hostess, it takes about 45 seconds to explode a Twinkie in a standard microwave.
- In 2006, Hostess briefly brought back a banana filled Twinkie as part of a promotion for the release of King Kong on DVD.
- During the 1980s, Hostess introduced a strawberry cream filled Twinkie, but it was not successful.
- Among the artificial ingredients in Twinkies is cellulose gum, which gives Twinkie cream its smooth feel.

- Another ingredient in Twinkies is corn dextrin. This gives Twinkies their sticky crust.
- Of the 39 ingredients that make up a Twinkie, only one of them is strictly a preservative. Some of the other chemicals in Twinkies have preserving side effects, but their use is primarily as substitutes for dairy ingredients.
- Despite their the 150 calories each, Hostess makes more than 500 million per year.
- Twinkies are made by baking the Twinkie for 12 minutes; injecting it with cream; and flipping it over so the round bottom becomes the top.

Four Uses for Butter

Butter isn't just good for topping toast and popcorn. There are plenty of other things it is useful for, such as:

- **Swallowing pills**: Coat the pills with a thin layer of butter to make them go down easier, especially bigger pills and ones that have no coating.
- **De-stress cats**: If you're moving or throwing a party, your cat can get a bit stressed by the sudden change in the environment. Put a little dab of butter on the top of her paws. She'll be distracted by cleaning herself.
- **Prevent cheese mold**: Put a thin coat of butter on cheese after you cut it so it won't get too hard or start molding, especially harder cheeses.
- **Preserve onions**: If you cut an onion in half and decide to leave the other half in the fridge, coat the exposed side with a bit of butter to keep it fresh longer.

Eight Ways to Keep Food Fresher Longer

- Put onions in pantyhose, and tie knots between each onion - will last up to 8 months.
- Freeze green onions in a plastic bottle. Make sure the green onions are completely dry before storing or they will get freezer burn.
- Use a vinegar solution to make your berries last longer.
- Spray leftover guacamole with cooking spray before putting it back in the fridge.
- Store potatoes with apples to keep them from sprouting.

- Wrap celery, broccoli, and lettuce in tin foil before storing in the fridge.
- Keep ginger in the freezer.
- Keep mushrooms in a paper bag, not a plastic bag.

Salt Facts

Saltiness is one of the five primary basic tastes the human tongue can detect. Those five tastes are: salt, bitter, sweet, sour, and umami (it is from glutamic acid, which is found in many foods, particularly some meats, and is the basis of the flavor enhancer monosodium glutamate, also known as MSG).

Extra salt has other effects, beside simply making things more salty it helps certain molecules in foods more easily release into the air, thus helping the aroma of the food, which is important in perception of taste.

Adding a bit of salt will also decrease the bitter taste perception in food, which is why it is often sprinkled on grapefruit.

Salt does not suppress sweet or sour flavors as with bitter flavors, but balances out the taste by making the perceived flavor of sugary candies or lemons, less one dimensional.

Salt Reduction Myth Debunked - There continues a myth that originated in the 1940s when a professor used salt-reduction to treat people with high blood pressure. Science has since found out that there is no reason for a person with normal blood pressure to restrict salt intake.

Decades of scientific research have failed to prove any benefits of a low-salt diet, and in fact tend to show the opposite. Studies have also failed to prove salt's connection to heart disease.

Salt is essential for life. Natural salt is important to many biological processes, including: Being a major component of your blood plasma, lymphatic fluid, extracellular fluid, and even amniotic fluid; Carrying nutrients into and out of your cells; Increasing the glial cells in your brain, which are responsible for creative thinking and long-term planning; and helping your brain communicate with your muscles, so that you can move on demand via sodium-potassium ion exchange.

A Scottish Heart Health Study was launched in 1984 by epidemiologist Hugh Tunstall-Pedoe and colleagues at the Ninewells Hospital and Medical School in Dundee, Scotland. The researchers used questionnaires, physical exams, and 24-hour urine samples to establish the risk factors for cardiovascular disease in 7,300 Scottish men. This was an order of magnitude larger than any intrapopulation study ever done with 24-hour urine samples. The BMJ published the results in 1988: Potassium, which is in fruits and vegetables, seemed to have a beneficial effect on blood pressure. Sodium had no effect.

A review published in the Journal of the American Medical Association. University of Copenhagen researchers analyzed 114 randomized trials of sodium reduction, concluding that the benefit for hypertensives was significantly smaller than could be achieved by antihypertensive drugs, and that a "measurable" benefit in individuals with normal blood pressure of even a single millimeter of mercury could only be achieved with an "extreme" reduction in salt intake.

Recent studies, including those cited by Harvard University at St. George's Medical School in London, have shown that potassium rich foods are an essential defense in helping to relieve high blood pressure. Potassium is an essential mineral that enables the body to maintain a healthy fluid and electrolyte balance, while also promoting optimal nerve and muscle functions.

If a person has high blood pressure he or she may become salt-sensitive. Hypertension is actually promoted more by excess fructose than excess salt. This can be relieved by reducing salt intake or increasing potassium intake, because it is the balance of the two that is important. Eating more potassium is likely more important than reducing salt.

Potassium is found in orange colored fruits and vegetables, including pumpkins, carrots, and apricots. Tomatoes and bananas are another source of high potassium. It is also found in artichokes, avocados, broccoli, dark chocolate, spinach, potatoes, yogurt, fish, and a variety of beans.

Table Salt vs. Kosher Salt - Salt is another game day treat that goes on almost everything. The primary ingredient in each type is sodium chloride. US requires food-grade salt be a minimum of 97.5% pure.

Table salt usually contains an anti-clumping agent, like calcium silicate, and also iodine. Kosher salt usually does not contain either. In the old days, people used to put a few grains of rice in their salt shaker to keep the salt from clumping.

The main difference between Kosher salt and regular salt is the grain size, with table salt being much smaller, because Kosher salt is less processed.

Kosher salt is not called "Kosher" because the salt is certified as kosher, but because this type of salt was used in the process of koshering meat to remove surface blood from meat without making the meat too salty.

Incidentally, iodine was first added to salt commercially in the United States in 1924 by the Morton Salt Company at the request of the government, because people weren't getting enough iodine in their diets. This caused many people to develop goiters or swelling of the thyroid gland. The practice was taken from the Swiss, who began adding iodine to salt many years earlier. Today most people get enough iodine in their diets, but many government health agencies around the world still recommend adding it to salt.

Morton Salt Facts - Difficult to imagine Morton Salt without thinking of the umbrella girl (*when it rains it pours*).

During the 1880s, Joy Morton invested in a Chicago-based salt company. Salt was big business in those days, largely fueled by the demand of the explorers and pioneers who were settling the American West. Salt is a critical component of any diet and throughout history has been critical to various types of food preservation.

Salt is hygroscopic, which causes it to absorb water from the air around it. When water is absorbed, the salt tends to clump. Morton's solved this problem in 1911 by adding an anti-caking agent, magnesium carbonate, to its product. It also put the salt in a cylindrical package to aid in keeping water out.

Morton hired an advertising agency to put together a marketing campaign to promote the anti-caking properties of his salt. The ad team came up with a long list of marketing plans. Morton's son chose the umbrella-wielding girl, accidentally pouring salt in the rain. The illustration epitomized wholesomeness, innocence and the value of Morton salt to pour easily, even if you are standing in the rain.

The additional ingredients did help, but salt still tended to clump and people put a few grains of rice in salt shakers to absorb moisture. Today there are more than a half dozen common additives to reduce clumping, reduce health defects, and add flavors. About 17% of all salt production is used for food. The bulk of the rest is used in manufacturing, dyeing, and in soaps and detergents.

Judas Iscariot is depicted knocking over a jar of salt in Leonardo da Vinci's famous painting The Last Supper. Spilled salt was considered a bad omen and still is for some people.

Iodized Salt is Good - The "iodized" emblazoned on the vast majority of salt sold in the US might go by largely unnoticed, but it turns out that it may have had such a profound effect on public health that it raised the national IQ.

Iodine deficiency is the number one cause of preventable mental retardation, and a recent paper published by the National Bureau of Economic Research (NBER) shows that after iodized salt was introduced in 1924, the most deficient quarter of the US population saw its IQs rise by a full 15 points, or one standard deviation. Averaged over the entire country, that equates to a 3.5 point bump per person — the equivalent of a whole decade's worth of IQ growth according to the Flynn effect, which holds that IQ tends to increase over time. While salt has virtually extinguished iodine deficiency in the US, it remains a problem in much of the developing world, where some 30 percent of citizens do not have access to it.

Salt Water Myth Debunked - The myth is that adding salt to water changes the boiling point and cooks food faster. This is one of those food myths that does not want to die. You hear it repeated by home cooks and professional chefs, but any first year Chemistry student can show you how minor the effect is to alter the boiling point. In order to change water's boiling point appreciably, you would have to add so much table salt that the resulting salt water would be nearly intolerable. *In spite of the boiling point myth, adding a bit salt to pasta water makes the pasta more tasty.*

Another Use for Salt - One way to keep your clothes from fading is to turn them all inside-out before putting them through the wash. If yours have already faded, adding a couple of pinches of salt to your detergent will brighten your clothes in just one wash.

Spuds, Potatoes, and Fries

Among other definitions, a "spud" is a "sharp, narrow spade" used to dig up large rooted plants. Around the mid-19th century (first documented reference in 1845 in New Zealand), this implement began lending its name to the things it was often used to dig up, potatoes. This caught on throughout the English speaking world and this slang term for a potato is still common today.

The word "potato" comes from the Haitian word "batata", which was their name for a sweet potato. Potatoes were grown about 2000 years ago in South America. This later came to Spanish as "patata" and eventually into English as "potato". Potatoes were first introduced to Europe through the Spanish.

Exactly who introduced French fries to the world isn't entirely known. Among the various theories, historical accounts indicate that the Belgians were possibly frying up thin strips of potatoes during the late 17th century.

It was very common for the people to fry up small fish as a staple for their meals. However, when the rivers froze up thick enough, it was difficult to get fish. Instead of frying up fish in these times, they would cut up potatoes in long thin slices, and fry them up as they did the fish. Today, the Belgians still eat more French fries or Frites than any country in Europe.

The French originally thought potatoes caused various diseases. In fact, in 1748, the French Parliament even banned cultivation of potatoes as they were convinced potatoes caused leprosy. However, while in prison in Prussia, Antoine-Augustine Parmentier was forced to cultivate and eat potatoes and found the French notions about the potato weren't true.

The French appeared to be the ones that spread fries to America and Britain and it, in turn, was the Americans, through fast food chains, that eventually popularly introduced them to the rest of the non-European world as 'French fries'. Because of this spread by American fast food chains, in many parts of the non-European world, 'French fries' are more often than not known as 'American fries'.

One of the ingredients of almost all Thanksgiving and other holiday meals is the potato. The starchy, edible tuber was introduced to the world around 400 years ago from regions around the Andes. Originally they were grown almost 10,000 years ago in Peru and Bolivia and are now found growing in most countries around the world, although the Andes continues have major production.

Currently, potatoes are the fourth largest food crop in the world and there are more than a thousand different types. They are versatile and can be enjoyed baked, boiled, fried, and more. They can be mashed, sliced, chopped, diced or eaten whole. They can be eaten cold or hot, raw or cooked. *I will need some chips to hold me over until dinner with mashed potatoes, cheese, and bacon. Mmm!*

Potato Facts - China grows the most potatoes of any nation on earth, followed by Russia, India, and US in fourth place. China consumes almost half of all potatoes produced and the Europeans, per capita, consume the most potatoes annually.

A fresh potato contains about 80 percent water and 20 percent dry matter. About 60 to 80 percent of the dry matter is starch. On a dry weight basis, the protein content of potato is similar to that of cereals and is very high in comparison with other roots and tubers. In addition, the potato is low in fat. Potatoes are rich in several micronutrients, especially vitamin C, if eaten with its skin. A single medium sized potato provides nearly half the daily adult requirement. The potato is a moderate source of iron, and its high vitamin C content promotes iron absorption. It is a good source of vitamins B1, B3, and B6 and minerals such as potassium, phosphorus, and magnesium, and contains folate, pantothenic acid and riboflavin. Potatoes also contain dietary antioxidants and dietary fiber.

Boiling potatoes in their skins prevents loss of nutrients. Baking causes slightly higher losses of vitamin C than boiling due to the higher oven temperatures, but losses of other vitamins and minerals during baking are lower.

More than 5,000 native varieties are still grown in the Andes. While the Incas called it papa (as do modern-day Latin Americans), Spaniards called the potato patata, apparently confusing it with another New World crop, the sweet potato, known as batata. In 1797, the English herbalist Gerard referred to the sweet potato as "common potato", and for many years S. tuberosum was known as the "Virginia potato" or "Irish potato" before finally displacing batata as the potato.

Four Healing Spices

Cinnamon significantly decreased the blood sugar in people who had type II diabetes and ate a 1/2 teaspoon of cinnamon a day. This powerful bark decreases cholesterol, keeps your teeth and gums healthy, improves digestion and alleviates the congestion that comes from colds and allergies. It is also anti-inflammatory and improves blood circulation. All that and it tastes good.

Turmeric is perhaps a less well-known spice, unless you love Indian food and curry. This spice is bright orange and comes from the root of a plant in the ginger family. It is a powerful antioxidant (just as strong as vitamins C and E) and works as an anti-inflammatory agent. In fact, it can be drunk in the form of golden milk to reduce inflammation and joint pain, or put on a swollen area as a poultice. People with liver problems or hepatitis also drink turmeric or take turmeric capsules, because this spice increases the production of bile in the liver and protects it from toxins.

Basil is not only delicious on pizza or ground up in pesto, but also boosts the cardiovascular system. People who have colds or asthma drink basil tea to make breathing easier and to invigorate the lungs.

Basil also has a calming effect on the nerves, relieves headaches, brings down fevers, and promotes healing from insect bites and skin infections.

Oregano has always been known to help relieve bad breath. It is also great against swollen throats, coughing, insomnia, and headaches. This herb is also a powerful antioxidant. Oregano has "42 times more antioxidants than apples, 30 times more than potatoes, 12 times more than oranges, and four times more than blueberries."

Not often the we find so many good tasting things that are actually good for us.

Origin of Breath Mints

Bad breath in ancient Egypt often was a symptom of poor dental health. Seems the stones they used to grind flour for bread contributed a lot of sand and grit to their diet, which wore down tooth enamel to expose the pulp of the tooth and making it vulnerable to infection.

The Egyptians did not have dentists to fix their deteriorating teeth and gums. Instead, they simply suffered, and scientists who examined mummies have found severely worn teeth and evidence of abscesses, even in youthful Egyptians. To cope with the unpleasant odors from their rotting mouths, Egyptians invented the first mints, which were a combination of frankincense, myrrh, and cinnamon boiled with honey and shaped into pellets.

Archaeologists also found toothpicks buried alongside mummies, apparently placed there so that they could clean food debris from between their teeth in the afterlife. Along with the Babylonians, they are also credited with inventing the first toothbrushes, which were frayed ends of wooden twigs.

The Egyptians also contributed toothpaste. Early ingredients included the powder of ox hooves, ashes, burnt eggshells, and pumice. They also found what appears to be a more advanced toothpaste recipe and how-to-brush guide, written on papyrus that dates back to the Roman occupation in the fourth century A.D. It explains how to mix precise amounts of rock salt, mint, dried iris flower, and grains of pepper, to form a "powder for white and perfect teeth."

Eight More Egg Facts

We all know dinosaurs laid eggs. Ostriches and turkeys also lay eggs, but the ones we eat most often are chicken eggs.

- Eggs take about 24 to 26 hours to form inside a hen.
- An average hen can lay 250 to 270 eggs per year.
- In China, approximately 390 billion eggs are produced a year, while the US produces about 75 billion eggs a year.
- An egg shell is made of calcium carbonate and makes up 9-12 percent of an egg's total weight. It contains pores that allow oxygen in and carbon dioxide and moisture out.
- The blood sometimes seen in an egg comes from the rupture of small blood vessels in the yolk. It does not indicate the egg is unsafe to eat.
- An average person on Earth consumes 173 eggs a year (less than one chicken lays).
- The world record for eating hard-boiled eggs is 65 in 6min 40sec, by Sonya Thomas in 2003. She would have eaten more but they ran out of eggs.

Here is the big answer to the big question of which came first, the chicken or the egg. The egg came first, because dinosaurs laid eggs before chickens evolved.

Origin of Doughnuts

No one really knows when donuts were invented or who invented them. One theory suggests they were introduced into North America by Dutch settlers, who were responsible for popularizing other American desserts, including cookies, cream pie, and cobbler. Another theory is the English brought the recipes over when they settled in the US.

Doughnut is the more traditional spelling, and still dominates outside the US. Doughnut and the shortened form donut are both pervasive in American English.

Donuts were originally made as a long twist of dough. It was also common in England for doughnuts to be made in a ball shape and injected with jam after they were cooked. Both methods of cooking involved no human intervention as the balls and twists turn over when the underside is cooked.

Hansen Gregory, an American, claimed to have invented the ring donut in 1847 when he was traveling on a steam boat. He was not satisfied with the texture of the center of the donut so he pressed a hole in the center with the ship's tin pepper box. *Excuse me; I feel the need to graze on a glazed.*

Marshmallows

Origin of Marshmallows - I would be remiss if I mentioned Graham crackers and did not speak about marshmallows in the same book. Marshmallows date back to as early as 2000 BC and Egyptians made individual marshmallows by hand by extracting sap from a mallow plant and mixing it with nuts and honey.

The official name of the mallow plant is Althea officials and it is a pink-flowered plant. Marshes are the native growing ground for the mallow plant; hence the name marshmallow. Mallow plants are native in Asia and Europe and are also grown in eastern United States.

During the 1800s, candy makers in France took the sap from marshmallow plants and combined it with egg whites and sugar. The mixture was whipped by hand and took the form of the marshmallow we know today.

Candy makers replaced the sap taken from the marshmallow plant with gelatin, which enabled the marshmallow mixture to maintain its form and reduced the labor intensive process of extracting sap from the mallow plant. The gelatin was combined with corn syrup, starch, sugar, and water to create the fluffy texture of the marshmallow. The gelatin ingredient is essential for extending the shelf life of marshmallows, because of the moisture it infuses into the candy. Thus, by replacing the previous egg whites with gelatin, marshmallows maintain their elastic and spongy qualities much longer than they had previously.

The marshmallow made its way to the United States in the 1900s and grew in popularity in the 1950s when it was used in a variety of recipes. Even though Americans were a little behind when it came to the marshmallow, they are now the number one consumers of the fluffy candy, buying more than 90 million pounds per year.

In 1948, Alex Doumak created an extrusion process to make marshmallows. Through this process, the marshmallow substance was pressed through tubes, cut into equal pieces, cooled, and then packaged - just the perfect size for s'mores.

Uses for Marshmallows - Stash a few marshmallows in a box of brown sugar or the sugar bowl to prevent the sugar from hardening or clumping.

Make ice cream cones less messy by sticking a few marshmallows in the bottom of the cone to prevent the ice cream from leaking out.

Eat three or four marshmallows to sooth a sore throat. Apparently, the gelatin is very helpful when it comes to relieving irritation and soothing pain in your throat.

Eleven More Uses for Butter

Butter has many more uses than just for sandwiches and sautéing.

- If you have anything sticky on your hands, like glue, tar, or paint, rub with butter, then wash with soap and water.

- Gum in hair comes off easier if rubbed with butter.

- Tree sap on a car comes off easier if rubbed with butter before washing.

- Cutting things like marshmallows, pies, toffee, dates is easier if you slice the knife through butter first so it does not stick.

- Butter works like oil to shine shoes, baseball gloves, etc. Just put some on a cotton swab and rub in.

- Large pills can go down a bit easier if rubbed with a bit of butter before swallowing.

- Butter works like expensive skin oils to soften cuticles and nails and to soften dry skin. it can also be used in a pinch to replace shaving lotion.

- Rubbing butter on hard cheese helps keep down mold if you rub it on the cut edge before wrapping.

- Dingy dusty holiday candles can be brought back to life by rubbing with butter. It cleans and brings back the shine.

- Difficult to remove rings slide off easy if you apply butter first.

After handling and cleaning fish, rub some butter on your hands before washing with soap and water to remove the smell. *(Butter is not good to rub on burns, use an ice cube instead.)*

Watermelon Facts

The watermelon grows on vines on the ground. It is a member of the Cucurbitaceae family and is related to cantaloupe, squash, and pumpkin. Some varieties of watermelon come with a variety of rind and flesh colors. The inside flesh of the popular varieties are red or yellow. The watermelon grows in many different shapes. Watermelon has 92% water. Watermelon contains vitamins A, B6, and C. You can eat every part of a watermelon, including the seeds and rinds.

Thought to be the ancestor of the original watermelon, the white-skinned citron first grew in the Kalahari Desert of Africa. Egyptians recorded the earliest harvest of them 5,000 years ago. Watermelons were depicted in hieroglyphics that adorned the ancient walls of their structures. They buried the fruit in the tombs of their kings, because they believed it nourished them in the afterlife.

Watermelons spread by merchant ships to other countries as they traveled to conduct their business. The plants flourished along the Mediterranean Sea, and by the 10th century they made their way to China. Later in the 13th century the Moors helped spread the watermelon throughout Europe.

The watermelon may have made its way to the United States during the African slavery trade via slaves carrying the seeds on the ships. The word watermelon made its first debut in the English Dictionary in 1615. There are five states that currently lead watermelon production in the US - Florida, Texas, California, Georgia, and Arizona. The United States ranks as number four in worldwide production of watermelon. China is number one. Ninety six countries grow watermelons. Chinese and Japanese often give watermelons to the host when they visit. Israelis and Egyptians enjoy salads made with sweet watermelon and salty feta cheese.

Watermelons come in 1,200 different varieties. Recent cultivations led to development of several desirable characteristics of the fruit, including seedless varieties and ones with thin rinds.

Candy Tidbits

The *3 Musketeers* bar was originally split into three pieces with three different flavors – vanilla, chocolate, and strawberry. When vanilla and strawberry flavoring became hard to come by during WWII, Mars decided to go all chocolate.

When *M&Ms* were first introduced in 1941 they were red, brown, yellow, green, and violet. The first M&Ms came in a cardboard tube and were given to soldiers in their rations, because the chocolate was a good energy source, and the candy-coated shell kept the chocolate from melting in their hands.

Milky Way was the first commercially distributed, filled candy bar in 1923. It came in chocolate and vanilla flavors. The vanilla version came covered in dark chocolate. They were sold separately for several years, then sold as a two-piece candy bar just like 3 Musketeers was sold as a three-piece candy bar. Mars continued to sell the vanilla and dark chocolate version under a new name – the *Forever Yours* bar. It was rebranded again as the Milky Way Dark, and these days you'll find it on shelves under the name "Milky Way Midnight." The name of the bar was inspired by the flavor of a milkshake.

Starbursts were originally named Opal fruits and came in four flavors: orange, lemon, lime, and strawberry. When the name switched to Starburst in 1967, lemon and lime were combined into one flavor so blackcurrant chews could be added to the mix.

When *Jelly Bellys* were first launched, there were eight flavors; Very Cherry, Tangerine, Lemon, Green Apple, Grape Jelly, Licorice, A&W Root Beer, and A&W Cream Soda. Now Jelly Bellys have 50 official flavors, nine rookie flavors, five Cold Stone Creamery-inspired flavors, and lines that include soda flavors, sour beans, sport beans, Harry Potter's Bertie Bott's Every Flavor Beans, and smoothie blends.

Life Savers first came in Pep-O-Mint when they were introduced in 1913 Later they added Wint-O-Green, Cl-O-ve, Lic-O-Riche, Cinn-O-Mon, Vi-O-let and Choc-O-Late. The familiar fruit flavors of today were developed in 1925: grape, orange, lemon, and lime.

PEZ gets its name from the first flavor it ever came in – Pfefferminz, German for peppermint. They came in little cigarette lighter-like cases to conveniently dispense mints to smokers. In the 1950s PEZ decided to expand their market to children and used the fun dispensers to do so. Santa, a robot, and a Space Gun were the first dispensers for children.

Tootsie Pops started with Chocolate, Cherry, Orange, Grape and Raspberry. There is a sixth flavor that alternates between Lemon Lime, Blue Raspberry, and Banana.

The first *Mentos* flavor was a peppermint flavored caramel candy when it was introduced in 1932. Cinnamon Mentos in the US and fruit-flavored Mentos in Europe came 40 years later. Mentos around the world now come in raisin, lemon yogurt, cola, grape 'n' cream, black licorice, red orange, and others.

Kit Kat - It dates back to the 18th century, when mutton pies called Kit-Kats were served at the political Kit-Cat Club. The origins of today's product go back to 1935, when a York based candy maker, Rowntree's trademarked 'Kit Kat'. The Kit Cat, as it was called, was produced for a while, before being discontinued. Eventually, it relaunched and was relabeled as "Rowntree's Chocolate Crisp" before being renamed to its modern title.

Medicine and Healthcare

FACTS ABOUT OUR BODIES

Homo Sapiens - Homo sapiens is Latin for 'wise man'. It is the scientific name for the human species. Homo is the human genus, which also includes Neanderthals and many other extinct species of hominid. H. sapiens is the only surviving species of the genus Homo. Modern humans are the subspecies Homo sapiens sapiens (sic).

German anthropologist Friedrich Blumenbach divided Homo sapiens into five distinct races based on their physical characteristics. There was the Mongolian, or yellow race, the red American race, the brown Malayan race, the black Ethiopian race, and the white Caucasian race.

He looked at many physical traits to carve out his categories and thought characteristics of the skull, the size and angle of the forehead, jawbone, teeth, eye sockets, etc. were especially important.

He thought that the skulls of Georgians were exemplary of the characteristics of his white race and named the group (Caucasian) after the Caucasus Mountain Range that runs along Georgia's northern border.

Butt Detector - Here is an interesting development. Apparently butt prints left on car seats are like finger prints. The University of Tokyo has already developed a prototype smart car seat capable of detecting when its occupant is on the verge of falling asleep. The seat features respiration-monitoring sensors and pressure sensors that monitor the pulse. The system can identify the physiological changes that occur 10 minutes before a driver actually falls asleep.

A new company is hoping to use pressure sensors built into car seats to help detect when a car is being driven by an unauthorized person. The seats will use 360 sensors to measure a person's bum in order to confirm their identity. The system tested was able to identify drivers with 98% accuracy during experiment. The company will work with car companies to commercialize it as an anti-theft system. *It will be interesting to see how it measures the same person who adds or loses weight.*

Obesity is Shrinking - A new Gallup report shows that obesity in America has declined between 2010 and 2011, from 26.6 percent to 26.1 percent. The shift is likely caused by more Americans reporting that they were of normal weight, from 35.4 percent in 2010 to 36.1 percent in 2011, according to the report, based on data taken from the Gallup-Healthways Well-Being Index.

Lets check the math - 26.1 percent obese, 36.1 normal - that leaves 37.8 percent as either skinny or otherwise abnormal. This is another of those great headline making studies. People are less obese, because they say they are. Hmmm, Gallup was actually paid to ask people if they were obese, then reported that those people said they were not? Maybe it was a blind study.

Losing Weight - Did you know that it is actually easier to lose weight than it is to gain weight? It is mathematically easier to lose than to gain. For example, if you eat 3,500 calories more than you burn, you will gain 0.3 pounds, but if you burn 3,500 calories more than you eat, you will lose 1 pound.

Also, if you want to lose weight, you can expose yourself to significant changes in temperature which speeds up your metabolism. This information is based on a pure fat diet.

Excess Weight and Acne - Here is another one of those headlines from a national newspaper that is overshadowed by the details within the article. It begins with the statement that researchers have found that weight gain and moderate to severe acne go hand in hand, particularly among young women.

The most recent study highlighting a link was recently published in The Archives of Dermatology and included 3,600 teenagers. The researchers looked closely at their weight and its relation to their skin and several variables that could also play a role, including age, puberty, and diet.

After adjusting for these and other factors that could affect acne risk, the researchers found that overweight or obese teenagers, particularly young women were significantly more likely to develop acne than normal-weight adolescents.

Researchers have proposed several explanations for the link. One is that an excess of androgen caused by obesity provokes acne. As for why girls would be more greatly affected than boys, it is possible that having bad skin and being overweight cause them greater psychological strain, which in turn prompts the release of stress hormones that worsen the problem. *So the cause is bad skin and hormones, not excess weight. I wonder if bad skin causes acne or acne causes bad skin? Yes someone actually paid them to come up with this stuff.*

Relieve Eye Strain - Near-point stress can be caused by staring at your computer screen for too long. Here is a simple solution that is cost free. Every few hours close your eyes, tense your body, take a deep breath and, after a few seconds release your breath and muscles at the same time. Tightening and releasing muscles such as the biceps and glutes can trick involuntary muscles, like the eyes into relaxing as well.

Tooth Patch - The Japanese have developed a tooth-patch made of an ultra thin biocompatible film made from hydroxyapatite, the main mineral in tooth enamel. The microscopically thin film can coat individual teeth to prevent decay or to make them appear whiter. It could also mean an end to sensitive teeth. They are aiming to create artificial enamel.

Researchers can create film 0.00016 inches thick by firing lasers at compressed blocks of hydroxyapatite in a vacuum to make individual particles pop out. These particles fall onto a block of salt which is heated to crystallize them, before the salt stand is dissolved in water. The film is scooped up onto filter paper and dried, after which it is robust enough to be picked up by a pair of tweezers. The sheet has a number of minute holes that allow liquid and air to escape from underneath to prevent forming bubbles when it is applied onto a tooth.

The film is currently transparent, but it is possible to make it white for use in cosmetic dentistry.

It might be five years before the film could be used in practical dental treatment such as covering exposed dentin, the sensitive layer underneath enamel, but it could be used cosmetically within three years. The technology is currently patented in Japan and South Korea and applications have been made in the United States, Europe, and China.

Feet Facts - As we enjoy the holidays sitting in front of a warm fire with our feet up and pondering our toes, here are a few interesting feet facts.

Human feet can sweat up to a pint of fluid a day. Feet have more sweat glands than any other part of the body, approximately 125,000 in each foot. The toughest skin on your body is on your feet. Toenails grow fastest during your teenage years, in hot weather, and when you are pregnant.

American actor Matthew McGrory, 7'6" had the record-breaking foot size until he passed away in 2005. He was in the Guinness Book of World Records for being the tallest actor and having the largest toe. His shoe size was 29 1/2.

What Causes Gray Hair - A few of these gray things have begun to sprout and it made me wonder why. A person's hair color is the result of pigments known as melanin produced by a specialized group of cells known as melanocytes. Melanocytes are found throughout our body and the melanin they produce is what gives our skin, hair, and eyes their color. Scientists can determine what color your eyes and hair are from DNA.

The melanocytes responsible for hair color are found in the bulbs of your hair follicles.

There are two main types of melanin. Eumelanin produces dark browns and blacks, and pheomelanin produces reddish/yellow. How these cells blend together determines what color hair will be. It is not fully known what makes the melanocytes blend together in the ways they do, but it appears to be genetic.

Once melanin is produced, their granules are transferred to adjacent keratinocytes, also found in the bulbs of your hair follicles. Keratinocytes are what produce keratine, the dead protein cells that make up our visible hair. Gray hair is the result of less melanin within the keratin. The less melanin, the more gray your hair will be and white hair has no melanin.

As we age our melanocytes decrease in number. The result is less and less melanin, until none are present, so hair slowly turns gray, and then white.

In 2009, scientists in Europe found that hair follicles produce small amounts of hydrogen peroxide. Normally this small amount of hydrogen peroxide is broken down by an enzyme called catalase. As we age, catalase production is reduced and there is a build up of hydrogen peroxide, which blocks melanin production by melanocytes.

There are several other things that can cause our hair to turn gray, including: genetic defects; abnormal hormone production, such as stress; abnormal body distribution of melanin; and climate factors, such as pollutants, toxins, and chemical exposure. The time and speed at which you will gray varies greatly.

As an aside, in Britain, Canada, Australia, Ireland, New Zealand, and South Africa, the spelling is commonly grey. In the United States, the preferred spelling is gray, but grey is accepted.

Fingernail and Toenail Facts - Fingernails grow about one nanometer every second or 3.5 mm per month and toenails grow about 1.6 mm per month on average. The exact rate at which your nails grow depends on several factors, such as age, sex, diet, exercise, etc. Nails also grow faster in summer when it is warmer. Fingernails can be seen on babies after the tenth week of pregnancy.

Nails consist of many different parts. The visible part is known as the nail plate and below that is the nail bed. The white, half-moon shaped part at the base is called the lunula or distal matrix. The tissue over the top of the matrix is called the cuticle, and the soft tissue directly over the cuticle, is called the eponychium.

Ninety percent of nail growth comes from the matrix. Pressure within the matrix forces dead karatinized cells out. Speed of growth is caused by blood supply and it seems the increased activity of our fingers vs. our toes causes more blood supply to our fingers which leads to faster growth.

The longest fingernails ever recorded on a women belonged to Lee Redmond of Las Vegas. After growing for 30 years, they measured a combined length of 28 feet 4.5 inches. Unfortunately, she lost her fingernails in a car accident in February 2009.

Clean trimmed nails are more noticeable to the beholder than the owner.

Redhead Facts - Redheads, when compared to blondes or brunettes are more than twice as likely to avoid going to the dentist. The same genetic variant that explains their hair also makes them more resistant to local anesthesia, such as Novocain and they might need as much as twenty percent more as reported in Journal of the American Dental Association.

Researchers report that, on average redheads are also more sensitive to heat and cold and three times more susceptible to skin cancer than the rest of us.

Other disorders, all backed by studies, that disproportionately affect redheads include: Parkinson's disease, Endometriosis, and Tourette's syndrome.

At a seminar on hair color and health, Scottish researcher Jonathan Rees reported that throughout history the "ginger gene" may have "played a big role" in protecting many redheads from rickets (soft, weak bones triggered by vitamin D deficiency).

Unlike blondes and brunettes, their natural red hair retains its original color longer than any other hair color, although eventually it tends to turn blond, and ultimately white. On average, redheads have thicker hair, but fewer strands (about 90,000), compared to blondes (110,000) or brunettes (140,000).

The world's highest rate of redheads is found in Scotland, where an estimated 13 percent of Scots, about 650,000 people have red hair compared to 4 percent of Europeans and less than 2 percent of the global population, according to STV News. In the US, there are an estimated 6 million redheads.

Nose Facts - Did you know we all have four nostrils? We have two you can see and two you can't. This discovery came from watching how fish breathe. Fish get their oxygen from water; most of them have two pair of nostrils, a forward facing set for letting water in and two for letting water out.

Our other two nostrils, migrated toward the back of the head, to become internal nostrils called 'choannae' – Greek for 'funnels'. They connect to the throat and allow us to breathe through our noses.

Cryptomnesia - The emergence in the mind of previously learned information that is treated as a new, original idea is cryptomnesia. A fragment of a song or a line of poetry comes to you, for instance, that you think you have invented, until someone else informs you it was Seeger or Lennon. The act of remembering, without knowing that is what you are doing.

It was first used by the nineteenth-century psychologist Théodore Flournoy, who studied mediums, psychics, and others. The ability to generate vivid recollections of past lives under hypnotic regression is, perhaps facilitated by cryptomnesia. From Greek kryptos, "hidden," + mnesia, "memory."

How Fingerprints Are Formed - By the 17th week of pregnancy, the fingerprints of a fetus are set. The uniqueness of fingerprints has been recognized and studied scientifically for two centuries, but researchers have not been able to explain exactly how they form. A new theoretical computer model describes how the patterns are likely created, beginning in the 10th week of gestation, when a fetus is about 3 inches (80 mm) long.

Researchers at the University of Arizona found that creation of the patterns involves stresses in a sandwiched sheet of skin called the basal layer. In a fetus, the basal layer grows faster than surrounding layers, the outer epidermis and the inner dermis. The basal layer buckles and folds in several directions, forcing complex shapes. Stresses are created at skin boundaries, including fingernails and knuckle creases, as well as around shrinking fingertip pads.

The fingerprint pattern is coded underneath the skin surface, does not change as we age, and the pattern cannot be destroyed by superficial skin injuries.

General characteristics of fingerprints can be inherited, so family members do tend have similar, but still unique fingerprint patterns. Even Siamese twins and identical twins have varying fingerprints.

Fingerprints are impressions made by the ridges on the ends of the fingers and thumbs. These ridges provide friction, or traction, when we grasp objects so that those objects do not slip through our fingers. Fingerprints are on the fingers and palms, but not on any other places of the skin. Scientists also believe that they may enhance our sense of touch.

Koalas have ridges on their fingers which create fingerprints very much like those of human beings.

Fingers Have No Muscles - Each finger consists of three bones called phalanges. Tendons generally connect muscle to bone, and ligaments generally connect bone to bone. The tendons that control the bones in fingers are attached to seventeen muscles in the palm of the hand and eighteen in the forearm. Some are very small and help control each individual finger.

Of the 206 bones in a body, 106 are located in the hands and feet.

When rock climbers and others exercise, they are actually strengthening the muscles in hands and forearms, not fingers. The average grip strength for men ages 20 to 75 is 104.3 pounds for the right hand and 93.1 pounds for the left. Women averaged 62.8 pounds and 53.9 pounds respectively.

Several studies have shown that it is easier to handle wet objects when you have wrinkled fingers vs. smooth ones. Wrinkling skin in water is caused by constriction of blood vessels. If you sever the nerve to a specific part of your finger, that part will never again wrinkle when wet. *Now you have a handle on how fingers work.*

Memory Tricks - Have you ever wondered if you closed the garage door, or turned off the stove? How about putting out food for your pet, or watering the plants. Aging reduces these mundane acts far to the back of our consciousnesses. If these niggling things bother you from time to time, try clapping. When you close the door or other mundane activity, clap your hands. Alternatively, you can say it out loud, "I closed the garage door."

Sounds silly, but your mind will file those actions away much more prominently than the act itself. When you doubt whether you turned off the stove, your mind will rapidly remember you said it out loud or clapping.

Here is another mind trick for those times you go into another room to find or do something, only to discover you forgot why you are there. Going through the doorway is like passing through a barrier and it changes your thought process. When you decide to go to another room to retrieve an item, say it out loud, "I am going to the kitchen to get some potato chips". *Of course, that is one activity that I would never forget, but you get the idea.*

Hypnagogic Jerk - Most of us have had them, but few know the proper name. It is an involuntary muscle spasm that occurs as a person is drifting off to sleep. The phenomenon is so named in reference to the hypnagogic state, or the transitional period between wakefulness and sleep. Hypnagogic jerks are also commonly known as hypnic jerks or sleep starts.

The muscle spasms may occur spontaneously or may be induced by sound, light, or other external stimuli. Some people report hypnagogic jerks accompanied by hallucinations, dreams, the sensation of falling, or bright lights, or loud noises coming from inside the head.

Sleep starts are quite common, with some research suggesting 60 to 70 percent of people experience them. Many individuals may be visited by nightly hypnic jerks without even knowing it, as the twitches often go unremembered, particularly if they do not cause a person to wake up.

Some scientists believe certain factors, such as stress, anxiety, fatigue, caffeine, and sleep deprivation may increase the frequency or severity of hypnagogic jerk. Researchers are also unsure exactly why hypnic jerks occur. One hypothesis is that hypnagogic jerks are a natural part of the body's transition from alertness to sleep, and occur when nerves "misfire" during the process.

Blood Type Defined

Blood consists of red and white blood cells, platelets, and plasma (the goop in which everything sits). Antigens and various proteins float in the plasma and on red blood cells. An antigen is any substance that causes the immune system to produce antibodies to fight intruders.

The ABO grouping system refers to genetically-determined individual differences in the presence of two antigens (A and B), which stimulate the production of different antibodies. Type-O blood has both the antibodies produced in type-A and type-B, whereas type-AB has neither.

The human heart creates enough pressure while pumping to squirt blood 30 feet.

There are 8 main types of blood separated into 4 groups. The groups are A, B, AB, and O. They are grouped together by the presence or absence of an antigen. Antigens are substances within the blood that cause our immune systems to create antibodies. These antibodies kill anything the immune system thinks is a threat.

The specific antigens that create the different blood types are found on the surface of red blood cells and are known as type A and type B. They are separated by the presence of another type of antigen known as rH factor. If this rH antigen is present, blood is considered positive, if absent, negative.

Someone that has type A antigens and rH factor is considered type A+. If someone has both types of antigens and no rH factor would be type AB- blood. If no A or B antigens then it is type O.

All of this matters because of those antibodies your immune system creates. Someone with type A blood will have antibodies for type B, and someone with type B will have antibodies for type A. Type O has antibodies for both A and B. If you were to give type B blood to someone who was type A, their antibodies would attack the type A red blood cells causing very unwanted side effects, including possible death.

Red blood cells make up nearly 45% of blood volume. White blood cells make up less than 1%. What is left over is blood plasma at approximately 55% of blood volume.

Red blood cells and most white blood cells are predominantly created within the bone marrow of large bones. White blood cell production is controlled within the immune system.

In 2004 researchers from University College London proposed that the presence of certain bacteria and intracellular viruses may have put evolutionary pressure on certain antigen-producing genetic mutations. In populations where viruses prevailed, gene O dominated. Those with bacteria-heavy environments found themselves more likely to have A or B type.

The major blood groups were not known until the early 1900s. Before then blood transfusions sometimes were fatal, because the different blood groups are incompatible. In 1940, experiments on Rhesus monkeys revealed additional antigen factors now known as positive or negative "Rh factors." This led to the types "O positive" or "AB negative." Since then, hundreds of other less-significant antigen differences have been identified, most of which do not lead to transfusion problems.

Blood Vessels - Every pound of fat gained causes your body to make 7 new miles of blood vessels. Knowing this, it is easy to see why obesity and heart disease often go together. Most of the new blood vessels are tiny capillaries, but also include small veins and arteries. This means if you are "only" 10 pounds overweight your heart has to pump blood through an extra 70 miles of blood vessels.

Blood vessels in a human body can be as long as 60,000 miles.

The good news is that this also works in reverse. If you lose a pound of fat, your body will break down and reabsorb the no longer needed blood vessels. This is encouraging to dieters, as one pound does not seem like a lot to lose, but even that little bit of difference will result in a large benefit for your heart.

The Human Body

- People with higher number of moles tend to live longer than people with fewer moles.
- When filming summer scenes in winter, actors suck on ice cubes just before the camera rolls. It cools their mouths so their breath does not condense in the cold air.
- Thinking about your muscles can actually make you stronger.
- Grapefruit scent will make middle aged women appear six years younger to men. The perception is not reciprocal and has no effect on women's perception.
- The world's youngest parents were 8 and 9 and lived in China in 1910.
- The colder the room you sleep in, the better the chances are that you will have a bad dream.
- There are more people alive today than have ever died.
- Women's hair is about half the diameter of men's hair.
- Humans are born with over 300 bones, but this number reduces to 206 in adults because some naturally fuse together as we grow.

- The liver is the largest solid organ and it contains 10% of the blood in a human body.

The little piece of cartilage that sticks out at the front external opening of your ear is called a tragus.

- The stirrup bone in the middle ear is the smallest bone in the human body and is about .11 inches long.
- The average person has 100,000 hairs on his or her head. Hair grows about five inches per year.
- The strongest muscle in the human body is the tongue in proportion to its size. The hardest bone is the jawbone.
- The tooth is the only part of the human body that cannot repair itself.

- It takes twice as long to lose new muscle if you stop working out than it did to gain it.
- We use 200 muscles to take one step and we average 10,000 steps a day.
- Women blink twice as many times as men do.
- The average person who stops smoking requires one hour less sleep a night.
- After eating too much, your hearing is less sharp.
- Your nose can remember 50,000 different scents.
- Laughing lowers levels of stress hormones and strengthens the immune system. Six-year-olds laugh an average of 300 times a day. Adults only laugh 15 to 100 times a day. *Am glad I have not grown up.*
- Intelligent people have more zinc and copper in their hair.
- The brain operates on the same amount of power as 10-watt light bulb. Your brain generates as much energy as a small light bulb even when you are sleeping.
- The brain is much more active at night than during the day.
- The brain itself cannot feel pain. The brain might be the pain center when you cut your finger or burn yourself, but the brain itself does not have pain receptors.
- The fastest growing nail is on the middle finger and the nail on the middle finger of your dominant hand will grow the fastest of all. Nail growth is related to the length of the finger, with the longest fingers growing nails the fastest and shortest the slowest.
- The lifespan of a human hair is 3 to 7 years on average.

- Human hair is virtually indestructible. Aside from its flammability, human hair decays at such a slow rate that it is practically non-disintegrative. Hair cannot be destroyed by cold, change of climate, water, or other natural forces and it is resistant to many kinds of acids and corrosive chemicals.
- The acid in your stomach is strong enough to dissolve razorblades. Hydrochloric acid, the type found in your stomach, is not only good at dissolving pizza, but can also eat through many types of metal.

> *Borborygmus is the rumbling noises your stomach makes.*

- The surface area of a human lung is equal to a tennis court.
- Sneeze outputs usually exceed 100 mph.
- Approximately 75% of human waste is made of water.
- Earwax production is necessary for good ear health. It protects the delicate inner ear from bacteria, fungus, dirt and even insects. It also cleans and lubricates the ear canal.
- Babies are always born with blue eyes. The melanin in a newborn's eyes often needs time after birth to be fully deposited or to be darkened by exposure to ultraviolet light, later revealing the baby's true eye color.
- Every human spent about half an hour as a single cell.
- Women can smell better than men. (which is different than women do smell better than men.)
- The average person expels flatulence 14 times each day.

MEDICAL FACTS

Six Operations now Unpopular

New on the list of operations that have fallen into disfavor is appendectomies. Four trials involving 900 patients with appendicitis found almost two-thirds of them (63 per cent) were successfully treated with antibiotics, and avoided the complications of surgery.

- Tonsillectomy, the removal of tonsils to prevent repeated sore throats. More than 200,000 were carried out every year in the 1950s, but only 49,000 in 2009. There is no evidence that it works.
- Grommets, or valves are inserted in the ear drum to treat inflammation of the inner ear. Most children grow out of it naturally.
- A mastectomy for breast cancer. Today, many surgeons remove only the lump, and survival is just as good.
- Hysterectomy for fibroids or benign growths in the womb can now be treated by an injection.
- Surgery for stomach ulcers can now be treated by an over-the-counter drug.

Leprosy

Contrary to popular belief, leprosy does not cause rotting flesh or the loss of limbs. It is actually a disease (now called Hansen's disease, named after Gerhard Hansen a Norwegian physician who discovered the leprosy bacteria that damages nerve endings and effects the skin. Because of the numbness caused by leprosy, a sufferer can be unaware of harming himself accidentally. It is this accidental harm that can lead to infections and, consequently, the loss of limbs.

Leprosy has been treatable since the 1930s, but to this day there remain leper colonies in some nations such as India, Japan, and China.

Armadillos also carry leprosy and can transmit it to humans. Ninety five percent of humans are naturally immune to the disease, and the remaining five percent can be easily and successfully cured of it.

Scratch Remedies

Most folks under 30 have never heard of using the relatively painless Mercurochrome in lieu of that nasty stinging Iodine. It stained your flesh pinkish-red. The FDA put limitations on the sale of Mercurochrome in 1998 and stated that it was no longer considered 'Generally Recognized As Safe' over-the-counter product. The main active ingredient in Mercurochrome is mercury.

Speaking of Iodine, it burned like fire when applied to an open wound, because it had an alcohol base. Many doctors today use a water-based iodine as an antiseptic, as it has one of the broadest germ-killing spectrums. This old school remedy is rarely found in home first aid kits anymore. *Alas, change comes too late for some of us.*

Smarter Pills

The Food and Drug Administration recently approved a device that is integrated into pills and let's doctors know when patients take their medicine and when they don't.

The device, made by Proteus Digital Health, is a silicon chip about the size of a sand particle. With no battery and no sensor, it is powered by the body itself. The chip contains small amounts of copper and magnesium. After being ingested the chip will interact with digestive juices to produce a voltage that can be read from the surface of the skin through a detector patch, which then sends a signal via mobile phone to inform the doctor that the pill has been taken.

Sensors on the chip also detect heart rate and can estimate the patient's amount of physical activity. It will allow doctors to better assess if a person is responding to a given dose, or if that dose needs to be adjusted.

It has been in clinical trials since 2009, but currently the FDA has only approved the chip for placebo pills, which were used in trials showing the chip to be safe and highly accurate. Proteus hopes to gain approval to use the digestible chip with other medicines. Andrew Thompson, chief executive of Proteus, says the chip has already been tested with treatments for tuberculosis, mental health, heart failure, hypertension, and diabetes.

The company is currently working with makers of Metformin, a drug used to treat type 2 diabetes and the most commonly prescribed drug in the world. The company also plans on adding a wireless glucose meter to their device so that dosage amount and frequency can be correlated with changes in blood glucose levels.

Sugar Cure

Healers in Africa have been putting crushed sugar cane on wounds for generations. A study was conducted testing sugar on patients with bed sores, leg ulcers and amputations before dressing the wounds.

Results showed sugar can reduce pain and kill bacteria that slow healing. Sugar is hygroscopic, meaning it naturally absorbs water which the bacteria need to survive. Sugar is also much cheaper than many antibiotics. Try giving that cut a sprinkle of sugar before putting on a band-aid.

Common Cold and Flu

Most flu viruses last a week or less, while others last for weeks. There is no cure, due to the many varieties of viruses.

The name "common cold" came into use in the 1500s, because its symptoms seemed to appear in cold weather. Of course, we now know that a common cold is not limited to cold weather. It seems more prevalent, because people spend more time indoors in close proximity to each other and sharing the virus.

Antibiotics do not cure a cold as they work on bacteria and most colds are caused by virus.

Good news, kissing reduces levels of the stress hormone cortisol, thereby lowering blood pressure and optimizing immune response. Also, kissing a person with a cold will not cause you to catch it. The quantity of virus on the lips and mouth are miniscule.

Zinc, echinacea, vitamin C, garlic, eucalyptus, honey, lemon, menthol, steam, hot toddies, alcohol, Zicam, chicken soup, and many other "cures" have been repeatedly tested and have been scientifically proven to not prevent or shorten the duration of a cold. At best they provide some physical relief.

Flu shots are designed to prevent the most common types of virus. Most are effective for only those types.

Antibiotics do not cure a cold as they work on bacteria and most colds are caused by virus. However, if it is bacterial, such as half of pneumonia strains, it does help. Bacterial pneumonia usually comes on suddenly and viral types take some time to develop.

Pigs DNA

Scientists announced that they have mapped the entire genome of the domestic pig, revealing that besides providing tasty bacon and sausages, the animal may also be useful in fighting human diseases.

The study published in the journal Nature found that pigs and humans share more than 100 DNA mutations that have previously been linked to diseases like obesity, diabetes, dyslexia, Parkinson's, and Alzheimer's, according to US and European researchers.

"In total, we found 112 positions where the porcine protein has the same amino acid that is implicated in a disease in humans," researchers wrote.

Researchers said that because pigs share many of the same complex genetic diseases as humans, the animals would serve as excellent models for studying the underlying biology of human disease.

A domestic pig breed is already being used extensively in medical research because of its anatomical similarity to humans. Pig heart valves have long been used by doctors to replace faulty human ones.

Scientists can use the new genome map to improve meat production by breeding a new generation of super-pigs that will grow faster, survive longer, produce more offspring, and yield more meat for less feed.

"This new analysis helps us understand the genetic mechanisms that enable high-quality pork production, feed efficiency, and resistance to disease," Sonny Ramaswany, director of the US Department of Agriculture's National Institute of Food and Agriculture said.

Scientists in the sequencing project compared the domestic pig's genome to that of the wild boar, human, mouse, dog, horse, and cow.

A recent study also revealed that pigs had the most olfactory receptor genes, which highlights the importance of smell in the scavenger animal's lifestyle. It also found that pigs also had fewer bitter taste receptors, meaning that pigs can eat food that is unpalatable to humans, which is one of the reasons why pigs have become such a highly valued farm animal. *I am still trying to figure out how they will know if a pig has Alzheimer's.*

Clean Houses Cause Allergies

Here is another one of those studies that makes me wonder. It contends that children who grow up in hygienic households develop more allergies, eczema, and other disorders that result from a depressed antibody response. Scientists have theorized that children from middle class and affluent families have weaker immune systems, because they live in cleaner homes.

In spite of increases in medicated and vaccinated children in the past 20 years, the number of children with allergies has also doubled, with the sharpest increase among the middle classes.

Their study examined 8,306 patients, 776 of which also had some form of reaction to peanuts, and the findings were presented at the annual meeting of the American College of Allergy, Asthma, and Immunology.

Lead study author, allergist Dr Sandy Yip, said, "Overall household income is only associated with peanut sensitization in children aged one to nine years. This may indicate that development of peanut sensitization at a young age is related to affluence, but those developed later in life are not." *Am not sure of the relationship between dust bunnies and peanuts, but why take chances. Was going to clean my house today, but think it might be healthier if I wait a few weeks.*

Heart Attack vs. Cardiac Arrest

The terms "heart attack" and "cardiac arrest" are often used interchangeably. However, they are not equivalent. Cardiac arrest implies the heart has stopped pumping blood. A heart attack is a lack of blood flow to a specific area of the heart caused by some blockage, spasm, or rupture.

People who have a heart attack are significantly more likely to survive than those who suffer cardiac arrest. While both are bad, cardiac arrest is worse.

Life Span vs. Life Expectancy

There are two kinds of life span. One is maximum life span, the greatest age reached by any member of a species. In humans this is currently about 120 years. (The oldest confirmed recorded age for any human is 122 years). The other is average life span, the average age reached by members of a population.

Life expectancy is the number of remaining years an individual can expect to live, based on his or her current age and average life spans. Life expectancy generally quoted is the "at birth" number which is an average that includes all the babies that die before their first year of life as well as people that die from disease, war, etc. For example, the Life Expectancy table at the University of Texas shows "at birth" the life expectancy was 25, but at the age of 5 it jumped to 48. So life expectancy changes with your age.

Mozambique has the lowest life expectancy for its population at 39.2. Japan is the highest at 82.7 and the US is 38th at 78.2 years.

Pacemaker Origin

Wilson Greatbatch was working on a device that would record human heart beats when he accidentally inserted an incorrect resistor. It ended up perfectly mimicking the heart's rhythm and led to the first implantable pacemaker.

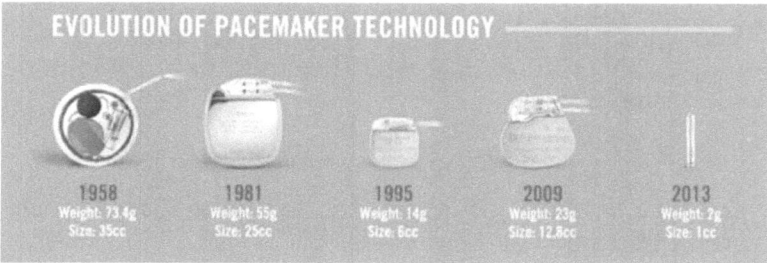

In 1958, he designed the first practical implantable pacemaker, a device that has preserved millions of lives. Mr. Greatbatch patented more than 325 inventions, including a long-life lithium battery used in a wide range of medical implants. He also created tools used in AIDS research and a solar-powered canoe.

Three Types of Burn Relief

Milk is an excellent compress for minor burns. Soak the burned area in milk for about 15 minutes or apply a milk-soaked cloth to the area. Whole milk's fat content soothes burns and promotes healing. Of course, rinse your skin and the cloth in cool water after or the milk will begin to stink.

A less known option is to use *Preparation H*, the hemorrhoid treatment cream for treating minor burns. Pat it on the area and you can reduce a few days off the healing time. This is because it contains a yeast derivative that speeds healing.

The most common option is to use *cold water* to soothe a new burn. However, using ice water can risk making the burn worse, because extreme cold can kill just as many skin cells as extreme heat. Cool water will stop the burning from spreading through your tissues and will act as a temporary painkiller.

Obsidian Knives for Surgery

Obsidian is a type of volcanic glass that has an extremely sharp edge when filed down. Some of the finest examples of blades made out of obsidian were discovered in Mesoamerica over 2,500 years ago. Dr. Don Crabtree re-discovered the ancient technology about twelve years ago, and along with other surgeons, believes there might be a place for obsidian blades in current medicine. Blades produced by Dr. Crabtree have been used in experimental microsurgery with excellent results.

The prismatic glass blade is infinitely sharper than a honed steel edge, and these blades can be produced in a wide variety of shapes and sizes. When used in experimental surgeries on animals, the blades yield comparable and even better healing than cuts made with traditional scalpels.

Blood Pressure

Blood pressure is really just that. It is the pressure at which blood moves around the body in the arteries.

The first known experiment to measure the exact pressure of blood was performed by Stephen Hales on December 1, 1733. He took a live horse, attached a tube to her left crural artery, then allowed her blood to rush through the tube and it rose to a height of 8'3".

He noted that "when it was at its full height, it would rise and fall at and after each pulse 2, 3, or 4 inches". The horse bled out, but he performed the experiment on a horse that was about to be put down.

The easiest and least invasive way to test the pressure is to momentarily stop the flow of blood and then slowly allow it to begin again. The pressure at which it begins to flow is the highest pressure the blood exerts on your artery walls.

Medical professionals do this by using a blood pressure meter known as a Sphygmomanometer. They encircle a limb, usually an arm, with a balloon-like device known as a blood pressure cuff. While pumping the cuff up, they use a stethoscope to listen for a heart beat past where the cuff is cutting off blood flow. When they no longer hear the heart beating, they slowly release the pressure while watching the pressure gauge.

When they start to hear the heart beat again, this is the top number of blood pressure, known as systolic pressure. They continue to release the pressure until they once again, no longer hear the heart beating, this is the bottom number of blood pressure, known as diastolic pressure. Together these numbers tell them two things: the pressure that is inside arteries <u>between heartbeats</u> (diastolic, the bottom number) and the pressure inside arteries <u>when the heart squeezes</u> (systolic, the top number).

Different disease processes like coronary artery disease can cause higher than normal blood pressure. Lower than normal blood pressures can be a sign of other disease processes, like shock caused by infection. The difference between top and bottom numbers, or a change in that difference, can also point to specific problems like too much fluid around the heart, not allowing it to work properly.

Combining this information with a person's heart rate can also tell numerous other things that could be happening. If you have been in a car accident and have a lower than normal blood pressure and higher than normal heart rate, you could be bleeding internally. If you were in another car accident and have an extremely high blood pressure and a low heart rate, you could have bleeding in your brain.

High blood pressure is caused by a combination of environmental factors and genes. High blood pressure is defined as any systolic pressure above 140 or diastolic higher than 90.

High blood pressure is not a disease itself, but indicates a risk factor for several other conditions like heart attack, stroke, and kidney failure. The most beneficial way to control blood pressure is naturally. This is because some medications that control blood pressure come with serious side effects. These side effects can sometimes be more harmful than the high blood pressure itself.

Things like lack of exercise and bad eating habits can cause a buildup of plaque inside your arteries. Excessive plaque on the interior walls of your arteries makes them smaller, known as "Atherosclerosis". When the pipes that transport fluid get smaller, the pressure that same volume of fluid exerts goes up. If the blood pressure gets too high, arteries have a greater chance of bursting.

Arteries get larger or smaller depending on the needs of the body. Excessive plaque makes this increasingly more difficult for a body to achieve.

A landmark study published in Nature in 2011 found 29 genetic variants that affected blood pressure. The authors found any one variant in a gene did not increase risk of hypertension, but people with multiple variants were much more likely to have high blood pressure.

Performing the Valsalva Maneuver

It is the act of exhaling forcibly while keeping the respiratory tract closed. You might have performed the Valsalva maneuver the last time you flew; it is easily done by pinching your nose shut, sealing your lips, and trying sharply to blow the air out of your lungs. This process builds pressure in various parts of the body, including the abdomen, which is why you might also engage in a version of the Valsalva maneuver on the toilet. The technique provides relief from the blocking sensation caused by high external air pressures in an aircraft cabin.

The Valsalva maneuver is a diagnostic tool for detecting certain kinds of cardiac abnormalities, as it changes venous and arterial pressure in ways that reliably affect the intensity of various heart murmurs. In some cases, it is also a medical intervention; it often halts episodes of tachycardia (abnormally fast heart rate).

Named after the 18th-century Italian anatomist Antonio Maria Valsalva, who offered the first formal description of the maneuver.

Gene Therapy Virus

In 2012 the European union authorized UniQure to use Glybera gene therapy for commercial use. The medicine sends a virus into your body, containing the correct genetic code. The therapy, developed by UniQure uses a virus to infect muscle cells with a working copy of the gene. Once the virus infects muscle cells, the correct code overwrites the bad DNA.

Glybera is used to treat lipoprotein lipase deficiency. One in a million people have damaged copies of a gene which is essential for breaking down fats. It means fat builds up in the blood leading to abdominal pain and potential life-threatening inflammation of the pancreas, pancreatitis.

A few years ago, three academic groups showed that AAV2, another adeno-associated virus, can correct a rare form of inherited blindness, by targeting a certain cell type within the retina.

Pills and Pencils

Pills go back thousands of years. They were often squished up bits of plant matter. During the early 1800s, attempts to produce pills with specific chemicals had many problems. Coatings would often fail to dissolve, and the moisture required in pill production could often deactivate ingredients.

In 1843, English artist William Brockedon was facing similar problems with graphite pencils. To get around this, he invented a machine which was able to press graphite powder into a solid lump and produce high-quality drawing tools.

A drug manufacturer saw that the device had potential for other uses, and Brockedon's invention was soon being used to create the very first powder-based tablets. This technology was adapted to mass manufacturing for medicines. Since then there have been many other ways of produce pills, but the original is still in use.

In 1875, William Upjohn, a University of Michigan student began experimenting with new pill formulas that would be more effective. He is the main reason pills are now such a convenient means of medication.

A tablet is a mixture of pharmacological substances pressed into a small cake or bar.

All tablets are pills, but all pills are not tablets.

A pill can be a capsule, which usually contains liquid, or a pellet, which usually is dry pressed. Pills can also be lozenges, which were traditionally diamond shaped and are usually sucked, rather than swallowed.

Here is the order of pills that act the quickest: Liquids, Liqui-gel caps, Chew or rapid-release tablets, Capsules, Hard tablets.

So, all tablets are pills, but all pills are not tablets. *If you find this hard to swallow, take two aspirin and see me next week.*

200 Types of Cancer

The reason is that there are over 200 different types of cells in the human body with each of these having the potential to become cancerous. Cancer can develop in any of the over 60 organs in the body. Cancers are named for the part of the body where it started and the type of cell that has become cancerous. All cancers start because abnormal cells grow out of control.

There are two general categories of cancer. Carcinomas are cancers that develop on the surface linings of the organs. Sarcomas are cancers that develop in the cells, and they affect solid tissues, such as

193

muscle and bone. They can also develop in the blood vessels. Cancer tumors can either be malignant or benign.

Normal healthy cells divide and die as they should. The average number of times normal healthy cells divide is known as the Hayflick Limit. It was named after Dr. Leonard Hayflick, who in 1965 noticed that cells divide a specific number of times before the division stops. The average was between 40-60. (There is one woman who had tissue in her body that could divide apparently forever: The Woman with Immortal Cells)

If you took every cell in your body, at the time you were born, and accounted for all the cells they would produce and multiplied that number by the average time it takes for those cells to die, you get what is known as the ultimate Hayflick limit or the maximum number of years you can theoretically live. This is how researchers come up with the theoretical life limit of 120 years.

Carcinomas are cancers that develop on the surface linings of the organs. Sarcomas are cancers that develop in the cells, and they affect solid tissues, such as muscle and bone.

For the first time since the government began collecting mortality data early in the last century, cancer death rates began to decline in 1993. It significantly declined from 1994 to 1998 with a non-significant decline from 1998 to 2001 and falling death rates from 2001 to 2008. In 2008, the death rate for all cancers was 175.67 per 100,000 people in the US. *Cancer is not contagious.*

Chemotherapy and Hair Loss

Chemotherapy, sometimes referred to as chemo is the use of medicines or drugs to treat cancer. There are more than 100 chemo drugs. Chemo may be used to: keep the cancer from spreading, slow the cancer's growth, kill cancer cells that may have spread to other parts of the body, relieve symptoms such as pain or blockages caused by cancer and, in some cases, cure cancer. Different types of chemotherapy work in different ways and have different side effects. It can be administered as a pill, liquid, shot, IV, or rubbed on the skin.

Most cells in the human body divide using a process called mitosis. When a cell reaches the end of its lifespan, it gets destroyed in a pre-programed process called apoptosis. Cells that divide more rapidly than apoptosis can regulate is simply too much mitosis. The result is excessive tissue, known as tumors. Tumors can be localized or spread through the lymphatic system or blood stream.

Many chemotherapy drugs are administered in combinations and work by interrupting mitosis and most cannot differentiate between abnormal cancer cells and normal healthy cells. Because of this, any cells that multiply rapidly can also be affected by chemotherapy.

Fast growing cells are found in hair follicles, lining of the mouth, stomach, and bone marrow. Since these fast growing sites are also affected by chemo, the result can be hair loss, decrease in production of white blood cells, and inflammation of the digestive tract, etc. Luckily, healthy cells, like hair follicles and the others usually repair themselves, so hair loss temporary. *Radiation can cause some of the same symptoms, but that story is for another day.*

Vitamin C Myth

It might be interesting to follow up on the persistent vitamin C myth of using it as a prevention and cure for the common cold. Some people have also claimed it to be a cure for cancer.

Hundreds of studies have now concluded that vitamin C does not treat the common cold. The results of many studies of various types, involving hundreds of thousands of people from around the world have all arrived at the same conclusion - vitamin C has no effect to prevent or cure colds or cancer.

The FDA, the American Academy of Pediatrics, the American Medical Association, the American Dietetic Association, the Center for Human Nutrition at the Johns Hopkins Bloomberg School of Public Health, and the Department of Health and Human Services do not recommend supplemental vitamin C for the prevention or treatment of colds. *Vitamin C does have other benefits and the studies did not say vitamin C is bad for you, it just does not provide the cancer and common cold remedies claimed.*

Health Insurance Statistics

The Census Bureau survey report on health insurance said there were about 311,116,000 people in the United States in 2012. Of these, 263,165,000 had some kind of health insurance coverage and 47,951,000 did not. Of the 263,165,000 who had health insurance coverage, 101,493,000 million obtained it from the government. That means almost 33% of Americans get health care from the government.

According to the survey, there were approximately 114,809,000 people who usually worked full-time in the United States in 2012. Percent of all people working in 2012 was less than in many decades past.

Eight Brain Myths Debunked

Many myths persist even after being thoroughly proven to be incorrect. Here are some myths that are incorrect, but still linger:

1. It has been scientifically proven that fatty acid supplements (omega-3 and omega-6) have a positive effect on academic achievement. *Wrong*

2. We only use 10% of our brain. *Wrong*

3. The brains of boys and girls develop at the same rate. *Wrong*

4. Individuals learn better when they receive information in their preferred learning style (auditory, visual, etc.). *Wrong*

5. Mental capacity is hereditary and cannot be changed by the environment or experience. *Wrong*

6. Brain training does not work. *Wrong*

7. Differences in hemispheric dominance (left brain, right brain) can help explain individual differences among learners. *Wrong*

8. Children are less attentive after consuming sugary drinks and/or snacks. *Wrong*

BMI and Life Expectancy

A comprehensive review published in 2013 in the 'Journal of the American Medical Association' examined the relationship of BMI (Body Mass Index) to death rates. The study researchers found that increasing levels of obesity were associated with progressively higher premature death rates.

Mildly obese people, however, did not have a significantly greater risk of death compared to those with a normal BMI. In fact, the finding that people classified as overweight, but not obese had a lower overall death rate compared to those with a normal BMI. Researchers are exploring possible reasons for this finding.

The 'International Journal of Obesity' published a study in 2012 comparing BMI and waist circumference as predictors of life expectancy. The authors reported that waist circumference is a better predictor of death from any cause than BMI.

The researchers also found that adults with a high waist circumference had an increased risk of death regardless of BMI.

Although neither BMI nor waist size can accurately foretell the life expectancy of any individual, waist circumference may be a better tool for estimating longevity. *In other words, they are saying "we cannot accurately tell life expectancy with either of these measurements, but it does help get us grants and headlines."*

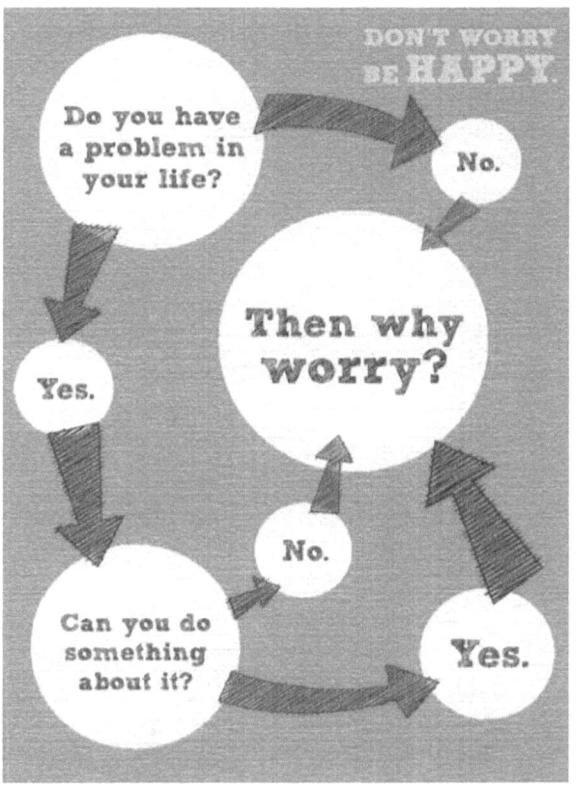

HAPPY FACTS

Happiness and a Happy Heart

Scientists have long known that people who are chronically angry, anxious or depressed have a higher risk of heart attacks. A new study shows, the opposite type of being upbeat and optimistic may help protect against heart disease.

Rather than focusing only on how to lessen heart risks, "it might also be useful to focus on how we might bolster the positive side of things," said a lead researcher from the Harvard School of Public Health.

They reviewed dozens of studies examining a positive outlook on heart health. A number of studies found the most optimistic people had half the risk of a first heart attack when compared to the least optimistic. People with a better sense of well-being tend to have healthier blood pressure, cholesterol, and weight, and are more likely to exercise, eat healthier, and get enough sleep.

Results cautioned that it will take more research to identify if a positive outlook makes people feel more like taking heart-healthy steps, or whether living healthier helps you feel more positive. So the researchers are still not sure if it is 'be happy be healthy' or 'be healthy be happy'. They do know stress associated with negative psychological traits can lead to damage of arteries and the heart.

Other research found that asking people to smile helps put them in a better mood. *Many of my books will make you smile and put you in a better mood. Pick up a few and we will both be happy and healthy. A bonus is that if you at least have a Happy Friday each week, you will be one seventh more healthy.*

Smile for Your Health

Researchers have found what we always knew. Smiling is good for you. A smile slows down your heart and reduces stress. These results follows research that proved the act of smiling can make you feel happier.

Other studies indicate even a polite smile may be beneficial. Frowning also may have a health effect. Preventing people from frowning, such as with the use of Botox can help alleviate depression, according to another study.

A study published in the journal Psychological Science found that people who smiled after engaging in stress-inducing tasks showed a greater reduction in heart rate than people who maintained a neutral facial expression. "We saw a steeper decline in heart rate and a faster physiological stress recovery when they were smiling, even though the participants were not aware they were making facial expressions," according to Sarah Pressman, co-author of the study and an assistant psychology professor at UC Irvine.

Pressman is currently researching how smiling affects certain stress hormones, such as cortisol, and oxytocin. "We've already seen it with heart rate; we are hoping to see it with these other stress levels in the body," she says.

Smiling Reduces Stress

Results of an interesting study to find out if smiling, even forced smiling can reduce stress. The Study is published in the journal Psychological Science.

Researchers used chopsticks to manipulate the facial muscles of their 169 participants into a neutral expression, a standard smile, or a Duchenne smile. A Duchenne smile engages the muscles around the mouth, raises the cheeks, and includes eyes.

In addition to the chopstick placement, some were explicitly instructed to smile. Then, they were subjected to a series of stress-inducing, multitasking activities, which they struggled to perform while continuing to hold the chopsticks in their mouths. The subjects' heart rates and self-reported stress levels were monitored throughout.

> Smiling is good for you. A smile slows down your heart and reduces stress.

The participants who were instructed to smile recovered from the stressful activities with lower heart rates than participants who held neutral expressions. Those with Duchenne smiles were the most relaxed of all, with the most positive affect. Those with forced smiles held only by the chopsticks also reported more positive feelings than those who didn't smile.

When a situation has you feeling stressed or flustered, even the most forced smiles can genuinely decrease your stress and make you happier.

Duchenne Smiles and Duchenne Laughter

While conducting research on the physiology of facial expressions in the mid-19th century, Guillaume-Benjamin-Amand Duchenne (de

Boulogne) identified two distinct types of smiles. The eponymous Duchenne smile involves contraction of both the zygomatic major muscle, which raises the corners of the mouth and the orbicularis oculi muscle, which raises the cheeks and forms crow's feet around the eyes.

A non-Duchenne, or politician smile involves only the zygomatic major muscle. Research with adults initially indicated that joy was indexed by generic smiling, involving just the raising of the lip corners by the zygomatic major. More recent research suggests that smiling in which the muscle around the eye contracts, raising the cheeks high (Duchenne smiling), is uniquely associated with positive emotion.

There are also two types of laughter, Duchenne and non-Duchenne. Duchenne laughter is the type of natural chuckle that people experience when they see or hear something funny, which is often contagious. This giggling involves the contractions of the orbicularis oculi muscle and adds more pain relief than non-Duchenne laughter, which is emotionless and context-driven. Duchenne laughter might be so effective because it involves muscle activity much like exercise, which releases endorphins. The capacity to sustain laughter for periods of several minutes at a time may exaggerate the opioid effects.

Laughter is Natural

Laughing is extremely difficult to control consciously. Most people cannot laugh on command.

Laughter almost always occurs during pauses at the end of phrases. It requires the coordination of many muscles throughout the body. A good hardy laugh is like a full body workout. It gives your diaphragm, abdominal, respiratory, facial, leg, and back muscles a workout.

If you want an easy way to trim a few pounds, watch a funny movie or share a good joke with friends. *If you need some new material, try some of my humor books.*

Here is another good way to burn calories. When you kiss someone for a minute, you both burn about 2.6 calories. According to that math, that is about 156 calories an hour. *I am available for testing the theory.*

Laughing Burns Calories

Laughing helps burn calories by increasing your heart rate by 10 to 20 percent. Your metabolism increases as well, meaning you will burn more calories at rest once you have stopped laughing. Find something hilarious which makes you laugh, watch a funny movie or TV show for 15 minutes and burn up to 50 calories.

Over the course of a laughter-filled year, the daily calories burnt from laughing result in a net loss of more than 4 pounds.

Laughter is the Best Medicine

Proverbs 17:22, "a merrie heart doth good like a medicine: but a broken spirit drieth the bones," has transformed into the popular saying, "Laughter is the best medicine."

A Laughter Study

A recent study found that groups that either watched or participated in comedy felt less pain than their peers, who watched a documentary. People who laughed more had an even higher pain threshold than those who only had a few giggles. Chuckling with others also increased laughter's positive impact. People are 30 times more likely to laugh in a group than alone.

Laughing triggers endorphins, neurotransmitters produced by the pituitary gland and hypothalamus, which spark a feeling of comfort similar to what occurs when someone takes an opiate. Love, excitement, spicy foods, orgasms, exercise, and pain all cause the brain to produce endorphins, which also provide an analgesic effect.

Clowns and Laughter

Being a clown is a noble profession. Clowns have proven to improve lung function in patients with chronic obstructive pulmonary disease. Genuine laughter for a whole day could burn 2,000 calories and lower the blood sugar in people with diabetics, a review published in the British Medical Journal found.

Laughter also enhanced fertility, Thirty six percent of would-be mothers who were entertained by a clown after in vitro fertilization and embryo transfer became pregnant compared with 20 percent in the control group. *OK, women, no jokes please.*

Belly Laughs and Giggles

Every time someone laughs around us, our brains must interpret what it means. German scientists have discovered it is more complex than we thought. A group of scientists from Tübingen, Germany have found a joyful belly laugh is interpreted by the brain in a completely different way from a scornful snicker or the giggle from someone being tickled.

In experiments designed to help patients with chronic anxiety disorders, they found that positive non-verbal communication from a joyful laugh was processed by a different part of the brain from a negative, scornful snicker.

Laughing is one of the oldest forms of non-verbal communication and could be key to helping patients with psychiatric disorders, who often are unable to correctly interpret non-verbal communication.

Humans have developed several different forms of laughter, each of which can have a complex series of meanings and intentions behind them. "Laughing is a very strong signal in social interaction. If you are laughed at with joy you feel accepted. If you are the victim of scornful laughter, you feel shut out of the group," said Dr. Dirk Wildgruber.

In their experiments, Wildgruber and his team played various types of recorded laughter and measured how the sounds were interpreted in the brain. They found that giggles generated when someone is being tickled stimulates areas of the brain responsible for interpreting complex acoustic signals. Happy or scornful laughter, on the other hand, stimulates completely separate brain regions usually tasked with guessing the intentions of others. From there, the laughter kick-starts connections with different parts of the brain depending on the tone - negative or positive.

The next step will be to look into how people with psychological disturbances react to different laughter signals to find out which areas of the brain could be artificially stimulated to help them, said Wildgruber.

Eleven Ways to be Happy

Spend money on other people. A study concluded that "the happiest people were the biggest givers, no matter what they earned."

Count your blessings. A University of Pennsylvania professor proved that people who wrote down three good things that happened to them every night were significantly happier than control group who did not.

Try something new. People who try new experiences are generally happier, research has shown.

Delay gratification. Anticipating happiness actually makes you happy. Studies have shown that it is human nature to forestall an enjoyable event.

Expose yourself to more blue. Researchers showed that exposing yourself to the color blue sent "self confidence soaring, cut stress, and boosts happiness."

Set goals for yourself. Psychologist Jonathan Freedman claims that people who set objectives for themselves are happier than those who do not.

Go to church. In a study, people who attended church regularly responded that they were happier and more satisfied with their lives than people who were not religious.

Sleep at least six hours every night. Six hours and 15 minutes a night of un-interrupted sleep makes for the happiest people, a British study found.

Make sure you have at least ten good friends. Adults who said they had 10 good friends were happier than those who could count five or less close friends.

Fake it 'til you make it. Several studies have shown that just the act of smiling can cause people to experience happy feelings.

Have a romantic relationship. People in relationships were generally found to be happier than other people, and spouses have the highest sense of well-being whether they are happily married or not, according to a study from Cornell University.

Seven Steps to Happiness

Think Less Feel More

Frown Less, Smile More

Talk Less, Listen More

Judge Less, Accept More

Watch Less, Do More

Complain Less, Appreciate More

Fear Less, Love More

Last Regrets

Seeking some more happy thoughts, I came across the following. It brings into focus that way too many people fail to cultivate relationships and be happy until it is too late. This is not meant to be morose, but rather as a heads up to celebrate, have fun, and laugh so you do not have these regrets.

A nurse, Bronnie Ware, on her blog, inspirationandchai relates some things shared by her patients, who were within the last few weeks and months of their life. The most common five regrets her patients related were:

1. I wish I'd had the courage to live a life true to myself, not the life others expected of me. *This was the most common regret.*

2. I wish I didn't work so hard. *Mostly men said this, but also women. They regretted missing so much time with family.*

3. I wish I had the courage to express my feelings. *They regretted not saying how they really felt, just to keep peace with others.*

4. I wish I had stayed in touch with my friends. *After family, they most regretted letting friendships lapse by not taking the time to stay in touch.*

5. I wish that I had let myself be happier. *Too many people forget that happiness is a choice and they waste time on old comfortable habits. They longed to laugh properly and have silliness in their life again.*

Calendar and Holiday Facts

INTERESTING HOLIDAYS

There are many national and international holidays and holy days, but there are many more unofficial holidays that are fun to celebrate.

The act of observing a holiday and cessation from work is called feriation. I use every excuse for feriation.

St. Agnes Eve

- The night of January 20 is "Saint Agnes' Eve", which is regarded as a time when a young woman dreams of her future husband.

Groundhog Day

- It is official. Pennsylvania's Punxsutawney Phil emerged from his lair to see his shadow yesterday. Thus we can expect six more weeks of winter.

The groundhog is also called a "woodchuck" and its scientific name is Marmota monax. Marmots are ground squirrels, living in burrows rather than trees. The marmots are related to tree squirrels, and all these animals are classed as rodents. A groundhog is one of the largest varieties of marmot and can weigh over 30 pounds just before going into hibernation.

Births usually occur during May. After four weeks, their eyes open and they begin to explore the outdoors. By August, they establish new burrows.

By the middle of October most groundhogs are hibernating and normally hibernate until about March. They can live up to about six years in the wild. Of course Punxsutawney Phil has been around since 1887.

Texas Independence Day

- The celebration of the adoption of the Texas Declaration of Independence on March 2, 1836. Settlers in Mexican Texas officially broke from Mexico, creating the Republic of Texas.

Uncle Sam Day

- March 13 is Uncle Sam Day. On this day in 1852, the New York *Lantern* newspaper published an Uncle Sam cartoon for the first time from Frank Henry Bellew. Through the years, the caricature changed with Uncle Sam becoming symbolic of the U.S. Example of this symbolism were U.S. Army posters that portrayed Uncle Sam pointing and saying, "I want you!"

He always wore red, white, and blue with a hat of stars and he had stripes down both pant legs. How he became known as Uncle Sam has been lost, but one story was about a dock worker wondering what the words "From U.S." meant on shipping crates. Someone said jokingly, "It is from your Uncle Sam."

National Potato Chip Day

- March 14 is National Potato Chip day. Flavors you might enjoy include: Lincolnshire sausage and brown sauce, sour cream and spring onion, and Birmingham chicken balti.

The brand of chips, which goes under the name Lay's in the United States, also produces many flavors: char-grilled steak, cheeseburger, steak and onion, smoky bacon, roast chicken, prawn cocktail, pickled onion, tomato ketchup, BBQ rib, Worcester sauce, cheddar cheese and bacon, sweet chili chicken, and flame grilled steak. Also, Cajun herb and spice, Chile limon, chipotle ranch, classic BLT, dill pickle, garden tomato and basil, sweet southern heat barbecue, tangy Carolina, Parmesan and Tuscan herb, southwestern ranch, creamy Mediterranean herb, spice rubbed BBQ, Maui onion, jalapeno, mesquite BBQ, and spicy cayenne and cheese.

Beer Chips company boasts potato chips made with beer. According to inventorspot.com, that same company is responsible for the Chip Shots: Margarita and Salt Potato Chips.

A company named Route 11 in Virginia produces some sea-inspired chips. An account is set up on Amazon where crab and chip lovers can purchase Chesapeake Crab Potato Chips.

National Doctor's Day

- March 30, 2012 is National Doctor's Day. The first observance of Doctor's Day was in 1933 observed in Winder, Georgia on the 91st anniversary of the first administration of anesthesia by Dr. Crawford W. Long in 1842. It was proclaimed a national day of celebration beginning in 1991 by President George H.W. Bush. This first observance included the mailing greeting cards and placing flowers on graves of deceased doctors. The red carnation is commonly used as the symbolic flower for National Doctor's Day.

Dr. Crawford W. Long performed the first operation while a patient was anesthetized by ether in 1842 as he removed a tumor from the neck of a boy.

This event has been celebrated as Doctors' Day since this day in 1933. The idea of setting aside a day to honor physicians was conceived by Eudora Brown Almond, wife of Dr. Charles B. Almond. Doctors throughout the United States celebrate in Dr. Crawford W. Long's honor and, in honor of ether as an anesthetic.

Easter

- The Easter Bunny, at least as we know it today, first appeared in 16th century writings in Germany. In the 1700s, Pennsylvania Dutch settlers brought the tradition of the Easter Bunny with them to the US. Their children believed that if they were good, the Easter Bunny would come and lay eggs and treats into nests the children made out of upturned hats and bonnets.

It is believed that the tradition of hiding Easter eggs was first started in Southern Germany. While the legend of the Easter Bunny laying eggs in the grass had been around for some time, the Germans decided to have children hunt for the eggs in hard to see places. *Happy Easter!*

Atlas Obscura Day

- It is celebrated April 28. Obscura Day is an international celebration of wondrous, curious, and esoteric places that is organized by Atlas Obscura, a website that catalogs bizarre and curious attractions around the world, both natural and manmade.

May 35th

- That date is used by some people in China to refer to June 4, which is the anniversary of the 1989 crackdown on student protesters at Beijing's Tiananmen Square. Other names include the Tiananmen Square massacre or the June Fourth Incident. Variations of the date June 4 are periodically banned from internet postings and search engines within China.

Donut Day

- The Salvation Army is behind the creation of this June 3 holiday. According to its website, "the first National Donut Day was celebrated in Chicago in 1938 to help raise needed funds during the Great Depression and commemorate the work of the "donut lassies" who helped make the donut what it is today by feeding the tasty confection to American soldiers during WWI." In modern times, companies like Entemann's are donating a portion of their donut profits to the Salvation Army. *Canadians eat more donuts per capita than any other country.*

Father's Day

- In Germany along the River Elbe, a special Father's Day tradition is upheld. It is the tradition of Christi Himmelfahrt. The fathers pull wagons full of alcohol through the streets to celebrate their day. They fill a hand wagon, large enough for a few coolers and maybe small keg with locally crafted hefeweizen, Gewürztraminer, and schnapps, then pass through the city into the forest, walking slowly until the sun has set and the wagon's contents have been drained. For luck, they also carry bratwurst, mustard, pretzels, Ritter chocolate, and a small hookah.

It is an important tradition to specific places within Germany and will often get out of control with drunken mayhem. Father's day always coincides with Ascension Thursday, a holiday when all the stores are closed. The men get their beer and later use their wagons to be dragged home after getting drunk. *Happy Father's Day to all the Germans and everyone else who knows how to party.*

Free Hug Day

- Did you get yours? The first Saturday in July is free hug day. It started by an Australian who realized the healing powers of a simple hug. He went to a shopping mall equipped with a "Free Hugs" sign and soon overcame leery passersby to give his free hugs exactly as advertised.

In 2006, the Australian band Sick Puppies made a video of his endeavor, and helped spread the movement by way of a 74 million times viewed video on YouTube.

International Bacon Day

- Bacon Day is an official observance held on the Saturday before Labor Day in the United States. (Labor Day is traditionally the first Monday of September). The first Annual Bacon Day was held about 2005. It is celebrated by having a bacon party and eating bacon in every way imaginable.

Did you know that bacon is a cut of meat taken from the sides, belly, or back of a pig, then cured, smoked, or both? Meat from other animals, such as cow, lamb, chicken, goat, or turkey, may also be cut, cured, or otherwise prepared to resemble bacon, and may even be referred to as 'bacon' also, although this is just wrong.

Wikipedia says "Bacon Day is the traditional day on which bacon lovers express bacon mania. This is typically exhibited during social gatherings during which participants create and consume creative dishes containing bacon, including breakfasts, lunches, dinners and desserts. All are welcome at a standard Bacon Day celebration, even vegetarians, with consumption of soy bacon or turkey bacon encouraged for inclusiveness."

Bacon Day is celebrated in the US, Australia, Canada, South Africa, Switzerland, the UK, and more.

Talk Like a Pirate Day

- The establishment of International Talk Like a Pirate Day took off in 2002 when Dave Barry mentioned us in his nationally syndicated newspaper column, and the date September 19th was based on someone's ex-wife's birthday. There is a Facebook page, Twitter account, and much more on the web.

Here are some origins of pirate words: A starboard is a steering paddle or rudder and in England, it was on the right side of the ship, hence starboard side.

The port side of a ship was originally called the larboard side, or loading side, but became verbally confusing, especially in bad weather or battles, so it was changed to port side.

Duffel is a sailor's personal belongings and the bag that carries them. It is named after the Flemish town of Duffel that produced the woolen cloth which the bags were made of.

Avast comes from the Dutch phrase 'houd vast' which meant 'hold fast' or 'stop'. Over time it became 'hou vast' and later 'avast'.

Poop deck originates from the French word for stern, la poupe. The poop deck is technically a stern deck, which in sailing ships was usually elevated as the roof of the stern cabin, also known as the 'poop cabin'. In sailing ships, an elevated position was ideal for both navigation and observation of the crew and sails.

Oktoberfest

- September is considered the beginning of Oktoberfest. The multi-week festival of beer, oompa music, and wurst always starts in late September. It is one of the most famous events in Germany and is the world's largest fair, with more than 5 million people attending every year.

The Oktoberfest is an important part of Bavarian culture and has been held since 1810. Now Oktoberfests are celebrated in cities around the world.

The holiday started as a royal wedding celebration for Crown Prince Ludwig. Beer must adhere to strict German Beer Purity laws (Reinheitsgebot) to be considered official Oktoberfest Beer.

World Smile Day

- The first Friday in October is World Smile Day®. Harvey Ball, a commercial artist from Worcester, Massachusetts created the smiley face in 1963. He worried the world lost sight of the meaning of his famous smiley face and thought that we all should devote one day each year to smiles and kind acts.

It began in 1999 and has continued every year around the world. Ball passed away in 2002, but 'Harvey Ball World Smile Foundation' was created to honor his name and memory. The Foundation continues as the official sponsor of World Smile Day® each year. Do an act of kindness and make someone smile today.

National Sausage Month

- October is National Sausage Month. In the UK it is celebrated in September. In addition, October 11 is National Sausage Pizza Day.

A sausage is a prepared food product usually made from ground meat, animal fat, salt, and spices, and sometimes other ingredients such as herbs and generally packed in a casing. Sausage making is a traditional food preservation technique originating with European cuisine. Traditionally, casings have been made of animal intestines, though they are now mostly synthetic. Some sausages are cooked during processing, and the casing may be removed at that time. Sausages may be preserved by curing, drying in cool air, or smoking. The distinct flavor of some sausages is due to fermentation during curing.

International Day for Failure

- October 13th is International Day for Failure. A new holiday intended for people to share stories of failure and learn from them. The goal of the people organizing the event is to have it be an internationally-recognized holiday by 2020.

The holiday was created in Finland in 2010. In 2012 it expanded to over 17 different countries, their goal is for it to be accepted worldwide by 2020. In 2011, their campaign got over 30 public figures in Finland to talk about their failures. They managed to reach 1/4 of the population with their media coverage. *It will be interesting to see if their failure campaign will be a success.*

World Toilet Day

- The United Nations General Assembly adopted a resolution to mark "World Toilet Day." The day will be celebrated November 19.

"The amusement and laughter likely to follow the designation of 19 November as 'World Toilet Day' would all be worthwhile if people's attention was drawn to the fact that 2.5 billion people lacked proper sanitation and 1.1 billion were forced to defecate in the open, the General Assembly heard today," a U.N. press release reads.

"Ending open defecation will lead to a 35 per cent reduction in diarrhea, which results in over 750,000 deaths of children under five years of age every year," Singapore's representative said. Apart from establishing World Toilet Day, the text also urged Member States and the United Nations system to encourage behavioral change, to introduce policies that would increase sanitation among the poor.

India's novel approach is to encourage families not to let their daughters marry if the potential husband does not have a toilet. The initiative from the government is called "No toilet, no bride". There are more temples than toilets in India, said Union Minister Jairam Ramesh.

The Indian state of Madhya Pradesh pays for a wedding and provides qualifying couples with housewarming gifts totaling 15,000 rupees (about $270) if they can prove the husband-to-be's house has a toilet.

Over 75 per cent of the 1.2 billion Indian population currently have a mobile phone subscription, but only 50 per cent of households have a toilet and only 11 per cent have one connected to the sewerage system, according to the 2011 Indian census. *I love the headline from the Washington Post, "In India, New Seat of Power for Women".*

More November Holidays

The day after Thanksgiving is National Day of Listening.

It is sponsored by oral history nonprofit StoryCorps. One year's National Day of Listening honors teachers. The organization asked everyone to participate by taking a few minutes to thank a teacher. Other ways to commemorate National Day of Listening is by recording interviews in veteran's hospitals, senior centers, homeless shelters, and other community centers.

November 13th brings us *'World Kindness Day'* founded in 1998 by an organization called the World Kindness Movement, this international holiday encourages everyone to look deep into their hearts past religion, race, and other differences to do something nice for their neighbors and/or humankind.

This followed on November 15th with *'Clean Out Your Refrigerator Day'*. It was probably started as a way to make room to stock up on Thanksgiving goodies. November 15th also shares the spotlight with 'I love to Write Day'. *I will refrain from writing about the things I find growing in my refrigerator.*

National Bacon Day

Only bacon gets a second day to celebrate. This one is unofficial and celebrated on December 30. *What a great way to end the year!*

Memorial Day

Memorial Day is a United States federal holiday which occurs every year on the final Monday of May. It is a day of remembering the men and women who died while serving in the US Armed Forces. Originally, it was known as Decoration Day to commemorate the Union and Confederate soldiers who died in the Civil War. Now it has been extended to honor all Americans who have died in all wars.

Taps

Taps is widely played on Memorial Day and this music is a variation of an earlier bugle call known as the Scott Tattoo, which was used in the US from 1835 until 1860 and was arranged in its present form by Union Army Brigadier General Daniel Butterfield a Medal of Honor recipient. His bugler, Oliver Wilcox Norton, was the first to sound the new call. It was officially recognized by the United States Army in 1874.

The first notes in any bugle call tells the troops in a particular command to pay attention to it, and then tells them what to do, such as to go forward, stop and lie down, or, in this case to go to sleep. Taps also concludes many military funerals.

The term 'Taps' originates from the Dutch term taptoe, meaning close the beer taps and send the troops back to camp.

"Military tattoo" comes from the same origin. The original meaning of military tattoo was a military drum performance, but subsequently came to mean army displays. Drummers were sent out into the towns at 9:30PM each evening to inform the soldiers that it was time to return to barracks. Tattoo, tap-too, and taptoo are derived from the Dutch taptoe and have the same meaning.

Taps Lyrics

Many do not know, but there are words to Taps, written by Horace Lorenzo Trim:
 Day is done, gone the sun
 From the lakes, from the hills, from the sky
 All is well, safely rest
 God is nigh.

 Fading light dims the sight
 And a star gems the sky, gleaming bright

From afar, drawing near
Falls the night.

Thanks and praise for our days
Neath the sun, neath the stars, neath the sky
As we go, this we know
God is nigh.

Il Silenzio

'The Silence' in English, is an Italian pop music instrumental piece written in 1965 by Nini Rosso and Guglielmo Brezza, its melody is an extension of the Italian Cavalry bugle call used by the Russian composer Tchaikovsky to open his Capriccio Italien. It is often mistaken for Taps.

Halloween

In parts of Mexico, rather than saying the Spanish equivalent of "trick or treat", "dulce o travesura" (literally "candy or mischief"), it is common to say ¿Me da mi calaverita? ("Can you give me my little skull?")

During Samuin, it was also traditional to leave a place and food at the table for deceased loved ones temporarily returned from the grave.

The word Halloween originally came from the Middle English 'Alholowmesse', meaning "All Saints' Day". The night before Alholowmesse was called "All Hallows Even (evening)" which was eventually shortened to "Hallowe'en" until it just became "Halloween" in the 20th century.

In North America about $3 billion is spent on Halloween costumes.

Haunted house attractions bring in about half a billion dollars annually.

Halloween candy sales average around $2 billion per year in the United States. Chocolate candy bars are consistently rated as the #1 treat to get, with the Snickers candy bar being most preferred. In addition, Reese's peanut butter cups and candy corn are among the most sold Halloween candy items.

Over 35 million Halloween cards, worth $100 million are given every year. Halloween is the second most commercially successful holiday world-wide after Christmas.

Recently "Trunk or Treat," where many people will gather in a parking lot with their trunks open and the children will walk from car to car to get their treats from the trunks. This is purported to be a safer way to do trick or treating than having kids go door to door.

Jack O' Lantern

This was originally one of the numerous names given to ignis fatuus (Medieval Latin for "foolish fire"), another of which is "Will O' the Wisps", basically the odd light that can occasionally be seen over marshes, swamps, etc.

When you see someone carrying a lantern in a distance at night you see is a man, but you can't make out who exactly it is, he is literally "man with a lantern", a.k.a. "Jack of the Lantern" or "Jack O' Lantern." This was also commonly used for a nickname for night watchmen.

"Jack O' Lantern" first popped up in the mid-17th century in East Anglia, UK and spread from there through parts of England, Ireland, and Scotland. The name likely originally derived from the practice of calling men generically "Dick, Jack, Tom, etc." In particular, men who were lower class, were often called generically "Jack" beginning around the 14th century in England.

How this name made the jump to referring to carved pumpkins with lights inside, has its origins in the Celtic practice of hollowing out and carving faces into turnips and other vegetables during Samuin (a festival where many of the traditions of Halloween come from). After carving the vegetables, they placed candles inside and put them in windows or carried the make-shift lanterns with them as they walked, to ward off evil spirits.

In Britain, pranksters would make these types of carved lanterns to scare people on the road or children would carry them around during Hallowmas while begging for soul cakes.

Halloween Fears

Boo! Samhainophobia is an intense and persistent fear of Halloween, and it can cause panic attacks for people who suffer from it. The word is derived from the old Celtic festival of Samhain, which marked the end of the Celtic year. They believed that the ghosts of the dead returned to the Earth on this day. Other Halloween related fears are wiccaphobia, fear of witches: phasmophobia, fear of ghosts; and coimetrophobia, fear of cemeteries.

Thanksgiving

There was not always a choice of dark meat or white meat after carving the turkey. These terms have nothing to do with the color of the meat as they were American euphemisms for the leg and breast of turkey and other fowl. In the Victorian times, the words 'leg, 'thigh', and 'breast' were considered embarrassing, so they awkwardly decided to call the leg "white meat" and the breast "black meat."

Did you know Benjamin Franklin wanted the turkey to be the national bird of the US, or that Abraham Lincoln issued a 'Thanksgiving Proclamation' on third October 1863 and officially set aside the last Thursday of November as the national day for Thanksgiving? He was persuaded by Sarah Josepha Hale, an American magazine editor to declare Thanksgiving a national holiday. She is also the author of the popular nursery rhyme "Mary Had a Little Lamb". (*see below for more about Sarah*)

Turkeys

In the 16th century, when North American turkeys were first introduced to Europe, there was another bird that was popularly imported throughout Europe, called a guinea fowl. This guinea fowl was imported from Madagascar via the Ottoman Empire. The merchant importers were known as "turkey merchants". The guinea fowl themselves eventually were popularly referred to as "turkey fowl", similar to how other product imported through the Ottoman Empire acquired their names, such as "turkey corn", "turkey wheat", etc.

The North American turkey was first introduced to Spain in the very early 16th century and later introduced to all of Europe. The North American turkey was thought by many to be a species of the type of guinea fowl that was imported from the Ottoman Empire and also were called a "turkey fowl" in English and later shortened to just turkey.

Turkey Pickings - A group of turkeys is technically called a "rafter", though they are often incorrectly referred to as a "gobble" or a "flock".

Due to the reputation of turkeys being thought of as stupid, the term turkey began being used as a slang, derogatory term meaning dumb or idiot in the early 20th century. Of course, domestic turkeys are stupid, but wild turkeys are not.

The phrase "Turkey Shoot" comes from the mid-20th century practice of tying turkeys behind logs, with only their heads exposed, and then holding a marksmanship competition, trying to shoot the turkey's head off.

Due to the white meat being the most popular part of a turkey, turkeys have been bred to have huge breasts. Because of this, modern domesticated turkeys are no longer typically able to mate, due to the breasts getting in the way of a male mounting the female. Most hatcheries use artificial insemination to fertilize the eggs of the domestic turkey.

Pilgrims and Thanksgiving

Pilgrims did not celebrate the first Thanksgiving in America. In fact, the particular Pilgrim event that is often cited as the first Thanksgiving was not even the Pilgrim's first Thanksgiving. They had several before at various times and none were celebrated annually. The days were merely a particular time when people had something significant to thank God for, so would set aside a day to do so.

Around the time the Pilgrims came to America in 1620, it was common in England and many parts of Europe to frequently set aside days for giving thanks to God. In the New World, where life was harsh in the beginning, there were numerous opportunities to hold such days of thanks, such as any time a particularly good crop would come in, when drought would end, when a particularly harsh winter was survived, when a group repelled an attack by Native Americans, when a supply ship arrived safely from Europe, etc. *Seems like they had many reasons to party.*

These celebrations remained fairly common up until the time when Thanksgiving became a national holiday. Most of these celebrations bore little resemblance to what we think of as Thanksgiving. The Pilgrims celebrations bore little resemblance to what is depicted now.

No one knows for sure who actually celebrated the first actual Thanksgiving in America. The most popular examples often referenced as the actual "firsts" include:

The day of thanksgiving celebrated in September 1565 by a group of Spaniards lead by Spanish explorer Pedro Menéndez de Avilé, in Saint Augustine, Florida. Pedro invited the Timucua tribe to dine with them on that Thanksgiving.

The group led by Spanish explorer Juan de Onate in 1598 in San Elizario, Texas held a Thanksgiving festival after successfully crossing 350 miles of Mexican desert.

The thirty-eight settlers who landed on James River by Jamestown in December 1619. Their charter required that the day of landing be set aside as a day of thanksgiving both on that first date and every year after.

The Pilgrim's Thanksgiving that took place sometime between September and October of 1621.

Thanksgiving Traditions Origin

The Pilgrim Thanksgiving that happened in the fall of 1621 is the most popular reference to the first Thanksgiving in the US. This is largely because of Sarah Josepha Hale, author of the nursery rhyme "Mary Had a Little Lamb" and one of the most influential women in American history.

She was particularly enamored with the Pilgrim event she had read about in a passage by William Bradford in 'Of Plymouth Plantation' as well as the particular Thanksgiving tradition which was somewhat common in New England at the time. She tirelessly campaigned for over 20 years to have Thanksgiving become a national holiday with a set date.

Through her highly circulated editorials, she was largely responsible for much of why we view the Pilgrim's 1621 Thanksgiving how we do and was also largely responsible for many of the traditions we now tend to attribute to that Thanksgiving, even though there are actually only two brief passages that record what happened during the Thanksgiving celebration in 1621.

Things like the tradition of eating turkey, mashed potatoes, stuffing, cranberry sauce, and pumpkin pie on Thanksgiving were all popularized by her while it is unlikely that the Pilgrims ate any of those things.

Leftovers From Thanksgiving

For those who still have an appetite, here is a bit of brain stuffing for the day.

In the US, about 280 million turkeys are sold for Thanksgiving celebrations.

Each year, the average American eats between 16 - 18 pounds of turkey.

Californians are the largest consumers of turkey in the United States.

Thanksgiving Day is celebrated on the fourth Thursday in November in the United States.

Although, Thanksgiving is widely considered an American holiday, it is also celebrated on the second Monday in October in Canada.

Black Friday is the Friday after Thanksgiving in the United States, where it is the beginning of the traditional Christmas shopping season.

More Fun Turkey Facts
The average weight of a turkey purchased at Thanksgiving is 15 pounds.

The heaviest turkey ever raised was 86 pounds, about the size of a large dog.

A 15 pound turkey usually has about 70 percent white meat and 30 percent dark meat.

The five most popular ways to serve leftover turkey is as a sandwich, in stew, chili, soup, casserole, and as a burger.

Turkey has more protein than chicken or beef.

Turkeys have about 3,500 feathers at maturity.

Male turkeys gobble. Hens do not. They make a clucking noise.

Commercially raised turkeys cannot fly.

Turkeys have heart attacks. The United States Air Force was doing test runs and breaking the sound barrier. Nearby turkeys dropped dead with heart attacks.

Turkeys have poor night vision.

It takes 75-80 pounds of feed to raise a 30 pound tom turkey.

A 16-week-old turkey is called a fryer. A five to seven month old turkey is called a young roaster.

Cornucopia

There are multiple stories about the cornucopia's origins. The first begins with Zeus, the greatest of all the Greek gods. Cronus, his father, wanted to kill Zeus, so his mother Rhea hid him in Crete to protect him. The king of Crete had several daughters who raised him, and their goat provided milk for the child. When Zeus grew older he broke off one of the goat's horns and gave it the magic power to fill up with whatever the owner of the horn desired. Zeus gave the horn to the king's daughters to thank them for caring for him. According to legend, whoever owned the horn would never go hungry.

An alternate story involves the goat giving Zeus one of her horns in reverence. Zeus repays her by placing her image in the sky. We know the image as the constellation Capricorn.

Another story in Greek mythology concerns Hercules' role in creating the cornucopia. A feud erupted between Hercules and the river-god Achelous. The two competed for the love of Dejanira, a young woman of breath-taking beauty. The two fought in a colossal wrestling match and Hercules began to get the better of Achelous.

Achelous, a shape-shifter, changed into a serpent and then into a bull in an effort to gain leverage against Hercules. Hercules broke off one of Achelous's horns, and when he did the river changed course. The water-nymphs came upon the horn in the river and treated the horn as a sacred object. They filled the horn with flowers and took care of it. Later Copia, the Goddess of Plenty, adopted the horn. Hercules married Dejanira and they had a family.

Mythological beings and deities illustrate a theme in classical paintings, and the cornucopia became a popular design element. Artists often painted the curved goat's horn filled with fruit and grain, and thus it came to symbolize wealth and plenty. Tyche, the goddess of riches and abundance, also became associated with the cornucopia. It also became the emblem for several other deities.

Modern design for cornucopias usually involves the use of it as a fall decoration. A favorite of florists, they often act as a vessel for containing bright, decorative flowers, fruits, gourds and many other decorative items that make a pretty table ensemble.

The cornucopia symbolizes riches and plenty in some folklore, art and mythology, so the decoration rightfully belongs on the table at which you plan to have a meal while enjoying the company of family and friends.

The cornucopia has a close association with Thanksgiving, but people considered it symbolic before the holiday existed. The word originated in 1508 and comes from the Latin cornu, meaning horn, and copia, meaning plenty. Thus some also call it the horn of plenty.

Christmas

Advent Calendar

The origins of this Christmas tradition come from the German Lutherans, during the beginning of the 19th century. The calendar started off simple, a written way to count down the days until Christmas. Eventually, lighting 24 candles became popular. Very early in the 20th century, Gerhard Lang was credited with printing the first Advent calendar. Several years later, he decided to add little doors that would open to reveal the date or a scripture. It wasn't until after WWII that the calendars began to be filled with candies and treats for the days before Christmas.

12 Days of Christmas

The end of Christmastime is the Epiphany, also Theophany, and the day that the three kings, Caspar (sometimes Gaspar), Melchior, and Balthazar showed up in Bethlehem after following the star. *I find it interesting while searching my family genealogy, all three names are found, although not recently.*

Noel

Did you know that "Noel" entered English in the late 14th century and is from the Old French noël or naël, which itself is from the Latin nātālis (diēs), and means "day of birth".

Mistletoe

The name comes from the fact mistletoe starts from bird droppings made from the red or white berries. It is a parasitic plant and roots to the branches of trees. Thus "mistle" or "missel", which meant "dung", and "toe", which came from the Anglo-Saxon "tan" meaning "twig." There are over 900 species of mistletoe and it grows on a wide variety of trees.

Ancient Greeks considered the plant an aphrodisiac and believed it aided in fertility. Norseman believed mistletoe was a plant of peace and when enemies met under the mistletoe they were obliged to stop fighting for at least a day. Eventually, this spawned a tradition to hang mistletoe over the doorway for peace and good luck. For the Norsemen the mistletoe caused the death of Baldur, the shining god of youth. The Druids believed that a sprig of mistletoe fastened above a doorway would ward off many things, such as witchcraft, disease, bad luck and fire. In addition, it would enhance the hospitality and fertility of the household. Hence the English Christmas custom of kissing under the mistletoe. *If you see me during the holidays, pretend I have mistletoe in my hair. I can always use another kiss and hug.*

It became associated with Christmas from the tradition of hanging mistletoe in one's home to bring good luck and peace to those within the house. It hung year round and was replaced each Christmas eve or at New Year.

During the 16th century in Britain, it became popular to create a ball of mistletoe hung as a Christmas decoration. Couples standing under the mistletoe were to kiss if the mistletoe ball still had berries. For each kiss, one berry would be taken from the ball. Once all the berries were gone, all the "luck" was drained out and it became bad luck to kiss beneath it.

Mistletoe leaves and young twigs are used by herbalists, and it is popular in Europe, especially in Germany, for treating circulatory and respiratory system problems.

Nativity

For many people, the word Nativity is only used this time of year as the birth of Christ and other religious connotations for Christmas. Lately the original definition is being used more often in statistical charting. According to a few online dictionaries, 'nativity' means:

1. Birth, especially the place, conditions, or circumstances of being born.

2. Nativity
   a. The birth of Jesus.

   b. A representation, such as a painting, of Jesus just after birth.

   c. Christmas.

Notice that 'Nativity' as capitalized has a religious connotation, while 'nativity' as non-capitalized is the number one definition. Many population and other economic charts use nativity in conjunction with ethnicity. It is a distinction, for instance 'Hispanic' as natural born or foreign born, when showing statistical differences.

Bottom line, before you wonder, there is no conspiracy theory; there is no anti-religious effort put forth. Statisticians are using the word in its original definition to more specifically segment populations by origin of birth.

Christmas Wise Men

According to the bible - 1. Three in number (the number is not mentioned).

2. Kings (they were "wise" men) – this probably comes from Psalm 71:11 (72:11 in protestant bibles): "And all kings of the earth shall adore him: all nations shall serve him."

3. Traveling on camels. Matthew 2:1–2 says: "When Jesus therefore was born in Bethlehem of Juda, in the days of king Herod, behold, there came wise men from the east to Jerusalem." It says a little later that they offered Him gifts of "gold, frankincense, and myrrh" – but that is about as specific as it gets. *Now we are all wiser for knowing this.*

Christmas Tradition, Caga tió

One of the more unusual bearers of Christmas presents, with a unique delivery method, is the Caga tió (pooping uncle or, pooping tree trunk). It is found in the Catalonia region and consists of a hollow log. Beginning at the Feast of the Immaculate Conception, the family "feeds" the tio and covers him with a warm blanket each night.

Then, at Christmas, the family gathers together, sings songs, and beats it with sticks, until it excretes presents of candy, nuts or figs. When the tio is finished pooping, it signals this by dropping salted herring, a head of garlic, an onion, or by "urinating", then the entire log is burned.

Holidays and Weight Gain

Postprandial weight gain is especially troublesome during the holidays. In the immediate short term any food and drink that you put into your body will make you exactly that much heavier. Eat a pound of chocolate and you add one pound to your mass, until your body starts to excrete the food or use it for energy.

That gain begins to decrease almost as soon as it begins. The time it takes for food to pass through the digestive tract varies widely. Overall, the journey of a meal takes between 20 and 56 hours. Once it is metabolized and excreted only excess calories converted to fat remain. If you ate a very salty meal, you tend to retain water, and a greater proportion of the weight temporarily remains. How much remains long term depends on the energy content of the food consumed as excess calories are converted into fat to be used for energy in the future.

In a recent study, a team of Israeli scientists tested different diets on almost 200 obese adults. One group consumed a greater proportion of their calories at breakfast and lost significantly more weight, on average, than the others in the study.

The bottom line is, the net weight gain associated with any one meal will be very small. However, a prolonged series of excess eating can accumulate to have a significant, long-term effect. A few overindulgent meals for the holidays are not a problem, the problem is the three overindulgent meals a day over a long period of time. *Just as it takes time to reduce weight, it takes time to gain lasting weight, so enjoy the Holidays.*

Gingerbread House

The Gingerbread house was first noted in the Grimm's Fairy tale, Hansel and Gretel, and followed in a German opera by the same title. After the show was first produced only days before Christmas, it became a holiday tradition in German Opera houses to build miniature replicas of the gingerbread house from the story. The tradition then spread to bakeries and, eventually, to homes.

Fascinating Reindeer Facts

Reindeer are the only mammals whose eyes are known to change color. The eyes are gold during the summer when the reindeer experience almost constant sunlight. During the darkness of winter their retinas become less reflective and their eyes appear blue.

They are also the only known mammals able to see in ultraviolet. During the Northern winter, when the sun barely rises above the horizon, snow reflects about 90 percent of UV. While that can cause snow blindness in humans, reindeer use it to their advantage.

Reindeer need their excellent eyesight when they run, because they can approach 50 miles per hour (80 km) at full run.

Calendar Facts

Leap Year - For those born on February 29, you finally get another birthday after having a few years with no presents.

Of course, if we ever adopt the new calendar proposed you will have a birthday every year. The Hanke-Henry Permanent Calendar has at least 30 days in every month and an extra week at the end of every five or six years. An interesting concept that has the same date on the same day every year. Seems too practical to ever be adopted, but it is a nice concept. You will probably be reading more about it soon and can see details here. http://henry.pha.jhu.edu/calendar.html

Samoa skipped Friday December 30 in 2011 and went from Thursday to Saturday so it could be moved to the other side of the international date line. It decided it was losing two business days a week with its favorite trading partners in Australia and New Zealand. American Samoa, an hour away by plane, will remain on the other side of the international dateline. *That will be some time travel. You can go there and celebrate two birthdays every year.*

A look back to 1912 - Here is a political quote from that year, "Former U.S. president Theodore Roosevelt wins all the Republican primaries, but party bosses beholden to Wall Street block his nomination by the convention."

Here are a few prices from 1912: Federal spending 690 million dollars, World Series tickets box seat $5 (bleacher seats 50 cents), Chevy six cylinder $2,150, gas 7 cents gallon, Loaf of bread 8 cents, Pound of coffee 15 cents, Dozen eggs 22 cents, Pound of butter 35 cents, Milk 12 cents quart, Ham 15 cents pound, Bacon 16 cents pound, Oreo cookies came to market in 1912

Alaska and Calendars - Speaking of days and dates, did you know that Alaska was the last state to adopt our current, Gregorian calendar? Many think our calendar has been around forever, but it is not that old.

In Alaska, the change took place when Friday, 6 October 1867 was followed again by Friday, 18 October after the US purchase of Alaska from Russia. Eleven days were skipped, and the day of the week was repeated on successive days, because the International Date Line was shifted from Alaska's eastern to western boundary along with the change to the Gregorian calendar.

In Russia the Gregorian calendar was accepted Wednesday, 31 January 1918, followed by Thursday, 14 February 1918, thus dropping 13 days from the calendar.

The last country of Eastern Orthodox Europe to adopt the Gregorian calendar was Greece on Thursday, 1 March 1923, which followed Wednesday, 15 February 1923. Korea adopted the Gregorian calendar on 1 January 1895. China finally agreed to use the Gregorian calendar 1 January 1929 (*Yes, only eighty six years ago*).

Many religious sects and countries still use other official calendars, but have unofficially adopted the Gregorian calendar for convenience of doing business. *Kind of makes one question the exact dates in many history books. . .*

Gregorian Calendar Exception - Most of the world uses the Gregorian Calendar. Even China also follows this calendar, although it also celebrates its own New Year.

North Korea uses the names of months we are familiar with, but the calendar year one begins in 1912 rather than two thousand years ago. That year, 1912 was the birth of former North Korea despot Kim Il-sung (grandfather of Kim Jong-un). Three years after Kim Il-sung's death, the nation promulgated the new Juche calendar after the state's official ideology of the same name.

It is a government allusion to the idea of Kim Il-sung as god. When Kim Il-sung died, his son and successor, Kim Jong-il redid the calendar to imply that his father was divine. In September 1998, the North Korean constitution deemed Kim Il-sung the "Eternal President of the Republic." *Nice to have a family tradition that changes the calendar for an entire nation.*

Calendar Trivia - The word calendar comes from the Latin word Kalendae which meant the first day of the month. The calendar currently used in most countries is the Gregorian Calendar and was proposed by the Catholic Church and introduced by Pope Gregory XIII in 1582 and adopted by several Catholic countries. Its predecessor was the Julian Calendar which had been introduced by Julius Caesar.

The reason for the introduction of the Gregorian calendar was because the old Julian calendar lost days, because there were too many Leap Years using the Julian Calendar.

Earth was thought to take roughly 365.25 days (365 days, 6 hours) to orbit the Sun, so an extra day was added every four years to compensate for the extra quarter of a day of an actual year. However, Earth actually takes just under 365 days and 6 hours to complete an orbit (365 days, 5 hours and 49 minutes), so adding an extra day every four years was too much. The solution was to skip some Leap Years.

Basically, every year divisible by 4 is a Leap Year. However, years divisible by 100 are not, but years divisible by 400 are. So, 1800 was not a Leap Year, nor was 1900, but 2000 was.

Although September, October, November and December are the 9th, 10th, 11th and 12th months of the year, the name September comes from the word "septem" which means 7, October comes from "octo" meaning 8, November from "novem" meaning 9, and December from "decem" meaning 10. The reason for this is in the ancient Roman calendar, there were 10 months in the year, so the names of the months reflected when they occurred in the year.

There are six other regular calendars: the Chinese calendar, the Hebrew Calendar, the Islamic Calendar, the Persian Calendar, the Ethiopian Calendar, and the Balinese Pawukon.

Although the months of the year have a different number of days in them (31 in January, 28/29 in February, 31 in March, 30 in April, 31 in May, 30 in June, 31 in July, 31 in August, 30 in September, 31 in October, 30 in November and 31 in December), the total number of days in 5 consecutive months which do not include February, always adds up to 153. For example, August (31) + September (30) + October (31) + November (30) + December (31) equals 153.

Date Great Britain and the American colonies accepted the Gregorian calendar was 1752.

Fun Facts

Every Day Billions - Here are billions of things that happen every day.

Over 5 Billion times: the +1 Google button is served.

Over 4 Billion views: YouTube video views.

Over 3.6 Billion dollars: dollar increase of the U.S. national debt.

Over 2.7 Billion likes: Facebook "likes" and comments.

Over 1.7 Billion drinks: servings of Coca-Cola or branded Coke products.

Over 1 Billion searches: Google searches.

1 Billion buyers: *Number of people who have not bought any of my books, but should.*

French Fry Calorie Fact - A single McDonald's French fry has 5 calories A single Pringle has twice as many calories, 10.

Parking Tip - Since most of us have smart phones and usually do not carry pencils, pens, or paper - take a picture of the nearest sign where you parked so when you return, it will be easy to find your vehicle.

Purse Germs - One of the most germ infested places many come into contact with is the bottom of a woman's purse. Many women fear the germs of public toilet seats, but do not think twice about placing their purses down on the floor of the stall.

They also set them on the floor while riding the bus, in the car, at a restaurant, in a bar, or on floor at the office. Then, when they get home and set that same purse bottom on the kitchen counter or the dining room table.

Nelson Laboratories tested a random selection of ladies' purses and found Pseudomonas, staphylococcus aureus, salmonella, and e-coli. Many of the handbags also had fecal contamination. *Something to think about.*

Numbers and Letters - If you spell out numbers individually, (one, two, three, etc.) you will need to reach a thousand before you find the letter A.

Toilet Talk - The film "Psycho" was the first movie to show a toilet flushing. The scene caused a huge number of complaints about indecency.

The Roman army didn't have toilet paper so they used a water soaked sponge on the end of a stick instead.

The toilet is flushed more times during the super bowl halftime than at any time during the year.

The average person spends three years of their life sitting on the toilet.

Over $100,000 US dollars was spent on a study to determine whether most people put their toilet paper on the holder with the flap in front or behind. The results showed that three out of four people have the flap in the front.

The first toilet cubicle in a row is the least used.

German Sex Meters - The German city of Bonn is calling its policy of levying a surcharge on streetwalking prostitutes via curb-side meters a success that would continue.

The municipal government said a "sex tax" covering levies on sauna clubs, erotic centers, and automated pay stations similar to parking meters that were rolled out in August 2011 had brought in around $326,000 the following year.

The former West German capital became the first city in Germany to introduce the meters for sex workers as a means of extending a general tax on prostitution beyond brothels to the streets of Bonn.

The meters were installed in an industrial area near the center of town used by prostitutes to solicit clients, with each sex worker paying €6 per night worked, regardless of how many customers they have. Those repeatedly caught without a ticket can be fined.

Closet Organizing - Some tips I recently saw on the web that seem to make sense for cluttered closets. Use shower curtain hooks in your closet to hang those things you want to keep off the floor, like purses, gift bags, and other small things that do not fit on a hanger. You can use pants hangers for flat things like wrapping paper and other flat items. A pegboard attached to the inside of your closet door can be used to hang everything from jewelry to watches, and umbrellas.

Those plastic travel soap dishes with watertight covers are great for organizing jewelry, vitamins, or other small items when traveling.

Try those little magnets to hang stuff on the inside of your medicine cabinet, such as tweezers to keep them off the shelf and close at hand when you need them.

Party Tip - Use a colander in your ice bucket or a large bowl to put ice in. The water will drop out the bottom and your guests can get at the ice without the mess.

China and US Facts - China produced 19.8 percent of all the goods consumed in the world during 2011 while the United States only produced 19.4 percent.

The U.S. trade deficit with China in 2010 was 27 times larger than it was back in 1990.

World Newspapers - Here is a site that you can go to and choose the paper from your hometown and read it as if you had it delivered. http://www.newseum.org/todaysfrontpages/ Was at the site one day and found that the 'Top Ten' papers each had a picture and article about the new basketball favorite Jeremy Lin. Not surprising, he even made it to the front page of the Daily News in Taipei and Chongging Times in China.

If you read six or eight papers, you will be amazed that many articles are almost word-for-word, regardless of city or state as they are mostly taken from the top three news sources. *Too bad we are losing independent thoughts from the media. Luckily the Internet, with all its diversity has stepped in to fill the void.*

Baseball Clothing Rules - Basketball and hockey coaches wear business suits on the sidelines. Football coaches wear team-branded shirts and jackets and khakis. Baseball managers are the only ones who wear the same outfit as their players.

It goes back to the earliest days of the game, when the person known as the manager was the business manager, the guy who kept the books in order and the road trips on schedule.

The person we call the manager today, who arranges the roster and decides when to pull a pitcher, was known as the captain. He was usually also on the team as a player. There were also a few captains who did not play for the team and stuck to making decisions in the dugout, and they usually wore suits. With the passing of time, it became less common for the captain to play and on most teams they had strictly managerial roles. *The rules do not state whether a manager should wear a uniform or not.*

Another Use for Old Jeans - Here is a tip to give a bit more life to your safety razor. Place old jeans on a hard flat surface; then run your safety razor up the pant legs about 10-15 times quickly; then repeat running it down the pant legs. No need to press hard, just a little pressure.

Point the top of the razor in the direction you are rubbing so you do not shave the pants or try to cut them.

The threads on the jeans will fix any tiny bends in the blades and sharpen the blades. For an already dull blade, you can sharpen it by doing 50-100 swipes both ways.

Crooked Forest - The Crooked Forest is a grove of oddly shaped pine trees located outside the village of Nowe Czarnowo, in western Poland. The forest contains about 400 pine trees that grow with a 90 degree bend at the base of their trunks. All of the trees are bent northward and surrounded by a larger forest of straight-growing pine trees. The crooked trees were planted around 1930 when the area was inside the German province of Pomerania.

It is thought that the trees were formed with a human tool, but the method and motive for creating the grove is not currently known. It also appears that the trees were allowed to grow for seven to ten years before being held down and warped by a device.

The exact reason why the Germans would want to make crooked trees is unknown, but many people have speculated that they were going to be harvested for bent-wood furniture, the ribs of boat hulls, or yokes for ox-drawn plows.

Swiffer Fixer - If you use a swiffer, you can save a bundle by using old kitchen towels instead of buying the Swiffer throw away sheets. You can wash and reuse the towels at no additional cost. Micro-weave towels work great.

Using Epsom Salts - Epsom salts are rich in magnesium, which plants need in order to grow well, particularly roses and tomatoes. You can mix 1 cup of Epsom salts with 1 gallon of water and water your plants. Try not to get it on the leaves if you water during the day. You can also sprinkle some of the salt into the soil. Palm trees especially need magnesium. I sprinkle it on the ground about eight inches around the whole trunk in March, July, and September.

Traffic Light Color Facts - The color scheme comes from a system used by the railroad industry since the 1830s. Railroad companies developed a lighted means to let train engineers know when to stop or go, with different lighted colors representing different actions. They chose red as the color for stop, because red had for centuries been used to indicate danger. For the other colors, they originally chose white as the color for go and green as the color for caution.

The choice of a white light for go caused an incident in 1914 when a red lens fell out of its holder leaving the white light behind it exposed. This ended with a train running a "stop" signal and crashing into another train. The railroad decided to change it so the green light meant go and a yellow caution was chosen, because the color is so distinct from the other two colors used.

In 1920 in Detroit Michigan, a policeman named William L. Potts invented the four-way, three-color traffic signal using all three of the colors used in the railroad system. Thus, Detroit became the first to use the red, green, and yellow lights to control road traffic.

During the late 1920s, several automated and manual variations were tried, but in 1935, the Federal Highway Administration created "The Manual on Uniform Traffic Control Devices." This document set uniform standards for all traffic signals and road signs. The current change to LED lights greatly reduces the amount of electricity needed and the bulbs last for years, saving a bundle on replacement costs.

Feed When They are Hungry - Here is another example of stupid research headlines. It says if you feed your baby when he or she is hungry, he or she will be smarter. I suppose that means as opposed to letting them scream until it is dinnertime.

According to a study published March 18, 2012, babies who are fed on demand perform better academically than those who are fed on a schedule. Using data from more than 10,000 children, researchers found that demand-fed babies scored four to five points higher on IQ tests at age eight. Demand-feeding also was associated with higher scores in school tests at ages five, seven, eleven and fourteen, according to the study published in the European Journal of Public Health.

And now the disclaimer - However, the researchers, from the University of Essex and the University of Oxford, urged caution in interpreting the findings. "At this stage, we must be very cautious about claiming a causal link between feeding patterns and IQ ... more research is needed to understand the processes involved." *So, the bottom line is that we should be cautious about believing the results.*

Guinness and Bar Bets - Guinness World Records was invented by the beer company to sell in bars and to settle bar bets. In 1951, the managing director of Guinness Brewery was on a bird-hunting trip in Ireland, hunting the golden plover. After failing to shoot even one, he declared that the bird must be the fastest in Europe. His friends said no, but they had no reliable source to turn to for bird speed. So he decided the public needed an official book of records that could be used to settle bar bets.

Some time later, he hired the Norris and Ross McWhirter fact-finding agency to put together a definitive book of facts. The result was a 198-page book published in 1955 with the Guinness name on the cover that was handed out in bars as a giveaway to increase the sales of Guinness. The Guinness Book of Records was in such demand that Guinness immediately reprinted another 50,000 copies (44.7 tons) and started selling them.

In case you were wondering, according to the book, Britain's fastest game bird is the Red Grouse which, in still air, has recorded burst speeds up to 58-63 mph over very short distances. It is doubtful that the Golden Plover can exceed 55 mph, even in an emergency.

Seven Facts from the Seventies - The World Trade Center twin towers were opened in 1973.

Eleven members of the Israeli Olympic team were taken hostage and killed in Munich by the Palestinian group Black September.

President Nixon resigned in 1974.

Three Mile Island meltdown happened in 1979 and was the worst accident in US nuclear power plant history.

During the oil crisis in 1979, license plates ending in odd numbers could buy gas on odd number days and even number plates on even days.

Lyme disease is named after the town of Lyme, Connecticut, where several cases were identified in 1975.

The IRS regulated alcohol, tobacco, and firearms, until the ATF became its own bureau in 1972.

Ig Nobel Awards 2011 - *MATHEMATICS PRIZE*: Dorothy Martin of the USA (who predicted the world would end in 1954), Pat Robertson of the USA (who predicted the world would end in 1982), Elizabeth Clare Prophet of the USA (who predicted the world would end in 1990), Lee Jang Rim of KOREA (who predicted the world would end in 1992), Credonia Mwerinde of UGANDA (who predicted the world would end in 1999), and Harold Camping of the USA (who predicted the world would end on September 6, 1994 and later predicted that the world would end on October 21, 2011) - for teaching the world to be careful when making mathematical assumptions.

PEACE PRIZE: Arturas Zuokas, the mayor of Vilnius, Lithuania, for demonstrating that the problem of illegally parked luxury cars can be solved by running them over with an armored tank.

Sounds of the Past - Here are a few things we will likely not hear again. A gas station driveway bell, a flash cube flashing from a camera, a rotary dial sound from a phone, a coffee percolator perking, film moving through a film projector, and scratches from a well used 33 and a third or 45 rpm record.

Interesting Number - If you divide 87912 by 4 the result is the same number backward, 21978.

Listerine - Walmart pulled Listerine off shelves in 1989 after a woman claimed it burned her mouth. After testing, they restocked it. Turns out that's just how Listerine tastes. *I could have told them that.*

Just Words - Green Eggs and Ham contains just fifty words. Doctor Seuss' publisher, Bennett Cerf bet him fifty dollars he could not write a book using just fifty words. Cerf lost.

The US Constitution has 4,543 words, including signatures. Abraham Lincoln's Gettysburg Address contained 271 words. The US Tax Code has more than 4,000,000 words, but is constantly being updated.

The Cool Botijo - The botijo generally has a wide, spherical belly with two openings on top - a wide opening to pour water in the jug and a smaller drinking spout - as well as one or two handles to carry it. Traditionally, people drink the water directly from the botijo by holding it up and tilting it so that the water pours from the drinking spout.

Botijo etiquette demands that the lips do not touch the drinking spout, as the water container is usually shared among several people. The large opening is covered with a cork or a cloth after filling the jug, in order to keep insects out. Botijos come in different sizes, but on average it contains about 3 liters of water, with larger ones holding up to 7 liters, enough to supply a small group of people with drinking water for a full day.

After the botijo is filled with water, it is preferably placed outside in the shade, although it also works when placed in the sun or indoors. The technology is based on evaporative cooling, the same process that keeps the human body cool by sweating. Because the ceramic jug is not completely water-tight, a small amount of the stored water filters through the pores of the clay and evaporates once it comes in contact with the outside, dry environment. Evaporation requires thermal energy, which is partly extracted from the water inside the jug, cooling it down. One study showed that, under optimal conditions, a cooling of up to 15 degrees Celsius can be obtained.

Glazed botijos often sold as tourist souvenirs do not cool water as it cannot evaporate through the glaze.

The botijo is a mobile refrigeration device, for which there exists no modern counterpart.

The famous "I am stuck on Band-Aid..." jingle was written by Barry Manilow.

The Charleston - The Charleston was one of the biggest dance crazes of all time It was popularized in a song of the same name in the 1923 Broadway show Runnin' Wild.

The choreography for the show was most likely original, but the style came from the Juba dance moves that originated among slaves on plantations and in southern cities like Charleston, South Carolina, where the name comes from.

Bye Bye Light Bulbs - As we said goodbye to 2013, we also said goodbye to more incandescent light bulb types. On Jan. 1, 2014, the most popular incandescent light bulbs, 40W and 60W were no more. They joined the already gone 75W and 100W incandescent bulbs as their domestic manufacture and import has been legislated away as part of the final phase-out stage of the Energy Independence and Security Act of 2007.

By 2020, a second tier of restrictions will become effective, which requires all general-purpose bulbs to produce at least 45 lumens per watt. Exemptions from the Act include reflector flood, 3-way, candelabra, colored, and other specialty bulbs.

An estimated 30 percent of informed consumers have raided the aisles of local stores, grabbing all of the 40W and 60W bulbs that they could get their hands on to delay the inevitable - and save big bucks in the process. Maybe by the time their final stash is gone the newer bulb prices will have come down from the stratosphere.

Another icon of the late 19th and early 20th centuries likely to become extinct soon is the landline telephone. This will not need to be legislated out; new technology has rendered them mostly unnecessary, even though the new technology has yet to achieve the clarity and dependability of the landline instruments. The number of home landlines in the US is dropping at a rate of 700,000 per month and currently just five percent of people depend solely on copper phone lines.

Toilet Tales - In 2009, cosmonaut Gennady Padalka complained to a Russian newspaper that he wasn't allowed to use the bathroom on the American side of the Space Station.

As it turned out, Padalka actually blamed the closed bathroom door on the Russian government, which had started charging NASA for resources used by American astronauts in 2003.

The United States reciprocated by asking the Russians to keep out of its facilities, including the toilet, which NASA paid $250 million to develop. Padalka told the newspaper that the bathroom shutout was having a negative effect on morale.

Castle Stairs Fact - Castles were always built with a spiraling staircase that turned clockwise. This design served a practical purpose, because incoming bad guys would ascend the stairs and have a huge disadvantage with their sword arm. Since most people are right-handed, the advantage was to the castle occupants descending the stairs had their sword-arm free to attack.

Secret Camera Symbol - Most cameras have this strange symbol imprinted somewhere on the case. If you read the camera's manual, you know what it is, but if you didn't, that circle with a line drawn through it marks exactly where the sensor of the camera is located.

It is called the 'film plane mark' and is helpful for people who take macro shots. Knowing exactly where the sensor plane (or film plane or focal plane) is inside the camera's body let's photographers know the exact distance between their subject and the film plane.

Fuel Gauge Arrow - Have you ever noticed a little arrow on your gas gauge? Did you know the symbol pointing left means the gas filler cap is on the left side of the car and vice versa. This little arrow is on nearly every car sold in the US during the past few years.

The vast majority of new cars have this arrow. In older, arrow-less cars, the hose part of the gas-pump symbol sometimes indicates the side of the car that has the filler cap. *Handy to know when renting or borrowing cars.*

Lawyers Get Automated - Being a lawyer isn't perhaps as much fun as it seems in the movies. It involves weeks of reading boring documents. Now a recent court ruling suggests that computers can take over part of their job for them. A US judge has approved the use of 'predictive coding' software which can sift through millions of documents and spit out only those the lawyer might need for use in a case.

Thomas Gricks, the lawyer who was pushing for the use of predictive coding, wanted to use the software to sift through two million emails in a case defending aircraft-hangar operator Landow Aviation against private-jet owners seeking compensation after a roof collapse in 2010.

He estimated that the email would take twenty thousand person hours to sift though, in the process costing two million dollars. Now, the software will provide just a couple of thousand relevant documents, cutting the time investment to two weeks, and slashing the cost by 98 percent.

In a recent study, pitting lawyers against the software over the course of 800,000 Enron emails, the software came out on top. In fact, it even managed to spot relevant details that the humans didn't. *Something tells me they still will not reduce their rates.*

Mooning History - Some sources have cited mooning, or baring one's butt at another as an insult that stretches back to the Romans, but the gesture as we know it today seems to have started in the Middle Ages.

Wikipedia claims that the first known instance of mooning was recorded by the famous Roman-Jewish historian Josephus in the 1st century A.D. According to Josephus' account in The Wars of the Jews, a Roman soldier bared his rear to an audience of Jews celebrating Passover, and incited a riot that killed upwards of thirty thousand. A closer examination of Josephus' account shows that the soldier was not mooning the crowd, but rather farting in their general direction. Josephus puts it more delicately, "One of the soldiers, raising his robe, stooped in an indecent attitude, so as to turn his backside to the Jews, and made a noise in keeping with his posture."

One of the earliest known instances of mooning happened during the Fourth Crusade around 1203, when Western Europeans attempted to take Constantinople. As the crusaders' ships pulled away after the failed attack, the Byzantines hooted and hollered and "showed their bare buttocks in derision to the fleeing foe." Another account tells of the Italian nobleman and troubadour Alberico da Romano, who was so indignant at losing his favorite falcon during a hunt that he "dropped his trousers and exposed his rear to the Lord as a sign of abuse and reviling."

Though it was a worldwide phenomenon by the 19th century, mooning did not get its name until the 1960s. The Oxford English Dictionary dates moon and mooning to student slang of the 1960s, when the gesture became increasingly popular at American universities. The term derives from the use of moon or moons as slang for the bare buttocks.

Presidential Height Index - Did you know that in the past 27 US presidential elections, the shorter candidate has won only six times? Handlers for Jimmy Carter (5' 9") went to great lengths to prevent him from standing next to the taller Gerald Ford (6'). It worked, Carter won.

The tallest President elected to office was Abraham Lincoln at 6' 4" and George Washington was 6' 2". Eighteen presidents have been 6 foot or taller. James Madison was the shortest at 5' 4".

Mitt Romney is 6'2" and Barack Obama is 6'1".

Michigan is the only state that has a statute prohibiting height discrimination. *(Maybe because Jimmy Hoffa was 5' 5")*.

YouTube Free Movies - Have you seen any free movies or TV shows on YouTube? If you have a big monitor or can hook your PC to your TV, as you can with most flat screens, this is a cheap alternative to pay-for-view.

Is It Cheaper - When offered the possibility of 33% off a product or the same product with 33% more quantity, which would you choose? The Economist sums up the results of a study published in the Journal of Marketing, which reveals that most consumers view these options as essentially the same proposition, but they are not. The discount is by far the better deal. The Economist says, most shoppers do not realize that a "50% increase in quantity is the same as a 33% discount in price."

In one part of the study, the University of Minnesota's Carlson School of Management asked undergraduate students to evaluate two deals on loose coffee beans, one with 33% more beans for free and the other at 33% off the price. The students viewed the offers as equal.

The initial price is $10 for 10 oz. of coffee beans or $1 per oz. An extra 33% more free beans would bring the total up to 13.3 oz. for $10. That $10 divided by 13.3 oz. give us a unit price of $0.75 per oz. With a 33% discount off the initial offer, though, the proposition becomes $6.67 for 10 oz., for a unit price of $0.67 per oz.

In another marketing experiment involving hand lotion in an actual store, researchers sold 73% more when it came in a bonus pack than when it was priced at a discount with the same exact unit price. *Caveat Emptor and go for the discount.*

CRWTH - The crwth (Prounouced Crooth) is also called a **crowd** and is an archaic stringed musical instrument, associated particularly with Welsh music, once widely-played in Europe. It is played like a violin and has six strings tuned e e' a' a b' b" and a flat bridge and fingerboard. It has begun to make a mini comeback in folk music circles.

Olympic 3D - While the 2008 Olympics were the first to be broadcast entirely in HD, the 2012 Olympics were the first to broadcast in HD as well as 3D. The games were first televised in Berlin in 1936 and played on big screens around the city. Then came the first games to enter households in 1948 in London, followed by the first internationally televised games during the 1960 Olympics in Rome.

Free Museum Maps - Visitors at the Smithsonian Institution can use an Android smartphone to find their way through 17 museums, the National Zoo in Washington, and locations in northern Virginia and New York City.

The interior maps totaling 2.7 million square feet can be accessed by visitors with Google Maps for Android. They include maps of the National Air and Space Museum, National Museum of American History, and National Museum of Natural History, which draw millions of visitors.

Maps also have been completed for the National Portrait Gallery and six other art museums.

Aluminum Foil Tip - Check each end of the foil box and you will find small tabs. Press in the tabs and they hold the roll in place while you pull out the foil.

Bird Poop - Today I learned why bird poop is usually white vs. other animal and human poop. Birds do not urinate. While their kidneys extract nitrogenous waste it is not expelled in the urea as ours (and many other animals) does. It is excreted in the form of uric acid, which has low solubility and, when combined with other waste comes out like white paste. Other colors from various fruits, etc., do not change as they pass through the system, so they come out the color of the fruit ingested. Some vegans seem to pass green due to the excess green vegetables and iron in the body.

In order to fly efficiently, birds, especially smaller birds need to eliminate waste often. A small budgie may excrete 40 to 50 times in a day, whereas a much larger macaw may only go 15 or 20 times.

Since birds only have one opening, it is used for sex, waste elimination, and dropping eggs.

The word poop comes from the Middle English word poupen or or latin puppis, and it originally meant fart. It acquired its current meaning around 1900.

Flush Tax - You pee, you poo, you pay. A while back, the Maryland Legislature took a step towards protecting the Chesapeake Bay and its tributaries when it passed what has become known as the 'flush tax'.

The bill established the Chesapeake and Atlantic Coastal Bays Restoration Fund to be supported by a $2.50 a month fee on sewer bills and an equivalent $30 annual fee on septic system owners. These funds are collected by the County and turned over to the State which distributes the funds to utilities to upgrade waste-water treatment plants to reduce nitrogen discharge which causes algae blooms that harm other aquatic life.

The revenues from septic tank users are used to upgrade or replace failing septic systems and to provide financial assistance to farmers to help plant cover crops to prevent nutrient runoff from agricultural land. This is the government equivalent of the pay toilet. *The government has now completed the cycle where what we eat and drink is taxed when it goes in and now it is taxed when it comes out.*

Smallest Park in the World - The smallest park in the world is Mill Ends Park in Portland, Oregon. It is 452 square inches or barely two feet across. The nearby Forest Park is 60 million times as big.

Mill Ends started in 1948, when Oregon Journal journalist Dick Fagan noticed a forgotten hole outside his office on Front Street. He planted flowers and began to write a weekly column about goings-on there.

When Fagan died in 1969, Portland took up the tradition and dedicated Mill Ends as an official city park in 1976. Sometimes it has a swimming pool for butterflies with diving board, a miniature Ferris wheel, and statues. It hosts snail races, weddings, and regular rose plantings.

A Long Rhode Island - Speaking of small, it is the smallest US state with the longest name. The official name, used on all state documents, is "Rhode Island and Providence Plantations."

Why Crustaceans Turn Red - Crabs, lobsters, crayfish, shrimp, and some other crustaceans turn red/orange when cooked from their typical blue-green to grayish color.

The exoskeletons of such creatures are made up of several pigments, one of which is a carotenoid called astaxanthin, which provides it's reddish coloring (astaxanthin is the same carotenoid that gives salmon its color). At normal temperatures and when alive the astaxanthin pigments are hidden, because they are covered with other protein chains that give their shells the bluish-gray or brownish-green color we see.

Exposure to heat destroys this protein coating, while the carotenoid pigment remains stable. So when you cook a crab or lobster or other crustaceans, the heat breaks down all the pigments except for astaxanthin, causing the bright red color we see in cooked lobsters, crabs, and crayfish, or the reddish-orange color of cooked shrimp.

Only the albino crab and lobster do not turn red when cooked because they have no pigmentation.

A one pound lobster is about seven to eight years old, and a eight pounder may be 20 to 50 years old. Lobsters are capable of living over 100 years.

Traffic Sign Tip - To check for left and right exits along freeways, check the exit number sign. If the exit number is on the left, the exit is on the left. If the exit number is on the right, the exit is on the right.

Facts about Plants and Oxygen - Plants do not turn carbon dioxide into oxygen. The way this happens is a complex process called photosynthesis. Plants convert carbon dioxide into carbohydrate precursors and water as fuel for the plant. This does not require any light. Oxygen is a byproduct of photosynthesis where the plant uses light and converts it to potential energy.

Hollywood Walk of Fame - It is not just for people. Some other famous characters with stars include Mickey Mouse, Bugs Bunny, Donald Duck, Winnie the Pooh, Tinker Bell, and more, including Shrek. Dubious achievement to be able to say, "Yes I am right up there with Mickey Mouse."

Titanic Numbers - It cost seven million dollars to build the Titanic and 200 million dollars to make a film about it. The ship sank and the movie is still floating.

Ponzo Illusion - Have you ever wondered why the Moon looks bigger on the horizon? It is an illusion, known as the Ponzo Illusion. What is happening is actually something your brain does all the time.

Think about what happens when you see one of your friends on the horizon. Although they appear to be very small, your brain does not actually interpret them as being that tiny. This is what happens when we look at the moon. Your brain inflates the size of the Moon to make it appear larger than it really is. Next time you are looking at an over-sized moon, block everything else out with your hands and watch it appear to shrink.

Ten Tiger Facts - Most tigers have more than 100 stripes, and no two tigers have the same stripes.

The roar of a tiger can be heard from over a mile away.

There are nine subspecies of tiger: the Bengal tiger, the Indochinese tiger, the Malayan tiger, the Sumatran tiger, the Siberian tiger, and the South China tiger. Three subspecies are extinct.

The Siberian tiger is the biggest of the nine subspecies and can reach an average head and body length of 75-90 inches. They can weigh up to 660 pounds.

A tiger marks its territory by spraying trees and bushes (contained inside the territory) with its urine, and also leaves deep scratches on tree trunks.

One averaged sized tiger can eat up to 60 pounds of meat at a single time.

A tiger's canine teeth can grow up to three inches long, easily capable of crunching through the spine of any creature on Earth.

A tiger can go as long as a week without a meal.

A tiger's saliva is antiseptic, and is handy when a tiger cleans its wounds.

If you were to shave all the fur off a tiger's skin, the stripes would still remain.

Happy Birthday to You - AOL Time Warner owned the copyright of "Happy birthday to You" and was to do so until 2030 when the extended copyright was to expire. For this reason movies often use different songs, which are not in copyright or are owned by the studio for birthday scenes. AOL Time Warner earned over $2 million per year from royalties for the song.

Update - During September, 2015, a judge ruled that Warner/Chappell never had the right to charge for the use of the "Happy Birthday To You" song. Warner had been enforcing a copyright since 1988, when it bought Birch Tree Group, the successor to Clayton F. Summy Co., which claimed the original disputed copyright.

Judge George H. King ruled that a copyright filed by the Summy Co. in 1935 granted only the rights to specific piano arrangements of the music, not the actual song.

S.O.S Scrub Pads - S.O.S brand scrub pads stands for "Save Our Saucepans". The name was originally thought up by the wife of the creator of the S.O.S pad, Ed Cox.

In 1917, Cox was an aluminum pot salesman and when he introduced himself to potential new customers, he would give them a little steel wool pad that he had encrusted with soap as a gift. Eventually, these pads became more popular than the pans he was trying to sell so he began selling the pads.

The last period in "S.O.S" was left off because "S.O.S." could not be trademarked due to the SOS distress signal often being written as "S.O.S.".

Shape of the Earth - When thinking of geo stuff, it is interesting to note that the earth is not round. Most people know this, but did you know you weigh more or less depending on where you live?

The Earth's shape is classified as an oblate spheroid or ellipsoid. The polar diameter of the Earth is about 26.7 miles (43 km) shorter than its equatorial diameter causing a difference of about 0.3%.

This very slightly oblate shape affects the weight of an object according to its position on the Earth's surface. A 20-lb bag of sand would weigh less at the equator than at the North Pole. This is because the further an object gets from the center of the Earth, the less it weighs. *Maybe I might move to the equator.*

Bugs Feel No Pain - Bugs may be a pain to us, but they feel no pain. Pain is officially defined as, "An unpleasant sensory and emotional experience associated with actual or potential tissue damage." It is experienced differently by each person and organism. Because of this it is extremely difficult to describe just how an animal experiences pain.

To study how an animal experiences pain, argument-by-analogy is applied. This means if an animal reacts in a similar way to how we would, we believe it is experiencing pain. An example might be if a dog is pricked with a pin and runs away, as a human would.

Insects have no capacity to feel pain. Nociceptors are what carry the feeling of pain to the brain. These are essential to experience pain, yet insects and crustaceans have never been found to have any nociceptors. This means most of these animals are unable to feel any sort of pain. Most insects do not possess nociceptors.

Down Under Trivia - The official Royal New Zealand Air Force logo is the kiwi, a flightless bird.

Australia's tallest mountain and most populous city were named for people who never visited the country. Mount Kosciuszko was named after Polish military hero Tadeusz Kosciuszko, because of its resemblance to a prehistoric mound in Kraków, and Sydney was named for British politician Thomas Townshend, Lord Sydney.

Bubble Wrap - It was invented by two engineers Al Fielding and Swiss inventor Marc Chavannes in 1957. They were trying to create a textured wallpaper. They started out by sealing two shower curtains together in such a way that it would capture air bubbles which would make the textured appearance for their wallpaper. The wallpaper idea didn't sell. They tried to find another use for their product and tried to use it as greenhouse insulation. That idea was not popular either.

Three years later Frederick W. Bowers, a marketer at Sealed Air, which makes Bubble Wrap, came up with the perfect use for the product. IBM announced their new 1401 computer and Bowers got the idea that Bubble Wrap could be used as a packaging material to protect the computer while it was being shipped. He then pitched the idea to IBM and it began purchasing Bubble Wrap to protect their 1401 and other fragile products.

About $400 million worth of Bubble Wrap is sold annually. *Bubble Wrap can be used as a cheap burglar alarm by placing it on the floor in front of a door.*

Michigan Map Names - University of Michigan alum go to great lengths to taunt their sports rivals. One particularly astute grad, state highway commission chairman Peter Fletcher memorialized his on Michigan's official state map in 1978.

He asked a cartographer to add two towns to nearby Ohio. Thus the fictitious towns of Goblu and Beatosu were created. The map can be seen on the official michigan.gov web site. It noted that after the hoax was discovered, new maps were issued, minus the bogus towns. A few collector item maps remain in the public and copies are also available in the official Michigan archives.

Fletcher noted in a 2008 interview that he placed the fake towns in Ohio, safely outside Michigan state lines. "We have no legal liability for anything taking place in that intellectual swamp south of Monroe," he said. He added that he had never forgiven Ohio for the Toledo War of 1835.

Semi-Automatic Defined - In a semi-automatic firearm, whether it is a pistol, rifle, or shotgun, when the round is fired, the expanding gas from the cartridge launches the projectile and then opens the chamber, ejecting the spent cartridge and, if available, using a spring system to slide the next cartridge into place ready for the next trigger pull.

The gun will not fire the next round and most guns are designed to prevent this from happening. This means one trigger pull for each shot, like the old six-shooters.

More Tiger Facts - The final Bali tiger is thought to have been seen back in 1937, the last-remaining Caspian tiger was found in the 1950s, and the Javan tiger went extinct sometime in the 1980s.

Between 1998 and 2000, nearly twenty percent of the Sumatran tiger population was killed. The South China subspecies is also listed among the ten most endangered animals in the world. The Siberian tiger has recently been discovered as genetically identical with the extinct Caspian variety, meaning that human intervention over the past century is the only reason we thought they were different.

Oil Imports - The five countries that supply the most oil to the US (during 2011), in order, were Canada 133.8 million tonnes (sic), South America 111.2, Saudi Arabia 95.5, Nigeria Africa 68.3, and Mexico 59.8. *Taken from a series of 36 maps that explain the world.*

Aztec Facts - The Westerners who came up with the name Aztecs likely took it from one of the original places that the Aztecs lived around the twelfth century, called Aztlan, which was in the Northern part of Mexico. However, the Aztecs themselves actually referred to themselves as Mexica, which is where the name for the country of Mexico originally came from.

The Aztecs had their own language called N'ahuatl. The alphabet for this language was a form of picture writing. Knowledge about how to write things down was very specialized and was mostly performed by learned scribes and priests who had training.

Records were kept on paper made of bark or deer skin. The writing was usually performed using charcoal and then colored with vegetables and other substances. They kept tax records, historical records, records of religious sacrifices and other ceremonies, and even poetry. Sometimes they put their writings together in a makeshift book that they called a codice.

Aztec men were allowed to have more than one wife. However, there were certain strict rules governing these relationships. The first wife the man took was considered his principal wife, and was the only one he went through marriage ceremonies with. The other wives were secondary, but still recognized in the official records. While the first wife was considered the most important, the man was still expected to treat all of his wives with equal respect.

The man was the head of the household, but women still had power in the relationship and were well treated in Aztec society. Extra wives contributed to the wealth of the family and were considered a mark of great status and afforded a high position in the culture. The Aztecs allowed divorce in some situations, but adultery by either party was punishable by death.

While the Aztecs put strong emphasis on parents teaching their children properly, they also had mandatory public schooling for all children. Those of a noble class had different schools to attend and schools were also separated by gender.

Boys of nobility would be sent to the Calmecac School where they learned from the priests about history, astronomy, art, and how to govern and lead. Boys of lower caste were sent to the Cuicacalli School, which was much more focused on preparing them for possible service in the military as warriors.

Girls were sent to separate schools and much more of their education was focused at home where they were taught domestic duties such as cooking and weaving.

Forty Six States of America - Although it is a technicality, there are actually just forty six states. Virginia, Kentucky, Pennsylvania, and Massachusetts are all officially Commonwealths. This grants them no special constitutional powers; they simply chose the word to describe themselves at the end of the war of independence. Virginia, named after the 'Virgin' Queen Elizabeth I, was one of the original 13 states (hence the 13 stripes on the flag) and the first of the states to declare itself a Commonwealth, in 1776. Pennsylvania and Massachusetts followed shortly after, and Kentucky, which was formally a county of Virginia, became a Commonwealth in 1792.

Tin Foil - Almost no one uses real tin foil these days. The stuff we all call tin foil is actually aluminum foil. Originally foil was made of tin, but it gave a tin flavor to whatever it touched. It was also heavier than modern aluminum foil.

Aluminum foil began to surpass tin foil after World War II, but it had been available since 1910 when it was first produced by "Dr. Lauber, Neher & Cie." a Swiss company. Its first use in the US was as a wrapper on Life Savers candy in 1913.

Tin foil was also used to fill cavities in teeth before the 20th century.

Coincidences - A deck contains 52 cards, 12 court cards, 4 suits, and 13 ranks.

A year contains 52 weeks, 12 months, and 4 seasons of 13 weeks.

The given name of Prince Edward, Earl of Wessex, is Edward Anthony Richard Louis. - His initials are E.A.R.L.

Origin of Umbrellas - As the old song says, "Though April showers may bring the rain. . ." It sent me looking for facts about the umbrella. Jonas Hanway appears to be the first person who had the courage to hold an umbrella over his head while walking along the streets of London during the mid-1700s.

Apparently people in Paris used umbrellas in hot weather to defend them from the sun and save them from the snow and the rain. Someone wrote that Jonas was in delicate health and used the umbrella to protect his face and wig. During that time only dainty beings, then called "Macaronis," would carry an umbrella.

Bringing it forward a few years gets us to another song, Yankee Doodle. It began as a pre-Revolutionary War song, originally sung by British military officers to mock the disheveled, disorganized colonial Yankees.

"Yankee Doodle went to town riding on a pony;
"He stuck a feather in his hat and called it macaroni."

The Macaroni wig was an extreme fashion in the mid-1700s and became contemporary slang. The Macaronis adopted feminine mannerisms, and the men were deemed effeminate. In the song, the British were insinuating that the colonists were not very masculine.

Macaroni and cheese has been around since the 15th century, but became widely popular in the late 1700s and does not seem to have any relation to the wig style or derision. In the United States, July 14 is "National Macaroni and Cheese Day.

One current variation on the recipe is the state fair staple, deep fried mac and cheese. Some folks now cover it with bacon. *Isn't it amazing how we can get from umbrellas to bacon in a few short paragraphs!*

Not So Sandy Deserts - Believe it or not, most of the Earth's deserts are not composed entirely of sand. About 85% of them, are rocks and gravel. The largest, the Sahara, fills about 1/3 of Africa and is still growing. It would nearly fill the continental United States.

Renminbi and Sterling - Now that Australia joins a host of nations that are bypassing the US Dollar as the world's "reserve currency" and trading currency directly with China, I thought it might be interesting to remove some confusion about the name of the Chinese currency.

Renminbi is the name of China's currency, but yuan is the denomination of bills. It is equivalent to Britain's currency, which is sterling with its pound as denomination of bills. The number of renminbi per dollar or sterling per dollar is incorrect. Renminbi and Sterling are the currency, but not a unit of the currency. Prices and exchanges are measured in yuan and pounds, not Renminbi or Sterling.

The primary unit of renminbi is the yuan. One yuan is subdivided into 10 jiao , which is subdivided into 10 fen. Renminbi banknotes are available in denominations from 1 jiao to 100 yuan and coins have denominations from 1 fen to 1 yuan.

During the past few years - China and Japan economies bypassed the dollar and engaged in direct currency trade, China and Russia dropped the dollar for direct trade, China and Iran bypassed the dollar, India and Japan bypassed the dollar, Iran and Russia replaced the dollar with rial and ruble in trade, India and Iran transact directly in rupees, Brazil bypasses dollar for direct China currency, Australia and China bypassed the dollar for direct currency trade.

Eight Geography Quickies -

- Scranton, Pa., was formerly called Skunk's Misery.
- No point in Great Britain is more than 75 miles from the sea.
- On a map North East, Pennsylvania, is in northwest Pennsylvania and Northwest, Virginia, is in southeast Virginia.
- There is one spot on earth from which, within an hour's driving time, you can visit Athens, Belfast, Belgrade, Bremen, China, Denmark, Dresden, Frankfort, Limerick, Lisbon, Madrid, Mexico, Naples, Norway, Oxford, Palermo, Paris, Peru, Poland or Vienna. The spot is in the county of Sagadahoc, Maine, US. It is surrounded by towns bearing these names.
- No building in Washington, D.C., is taller than the Washington Monument. The city enacted a height restriction in 1899 to protect Thomas Jefferson's vision of an "American Paris" with "low and convenient" buildings on "light and airy" streets.
- Weirton, W.Va., is the only town in the United States that borders two different states on opposite sides. It borders Ohio directly on the west and Pennsylvania on the east.

- Canada's coastline is six times as long as Australia's.
- Vatican City occupies about 4,736,120 square feet. The Pentagon, by comparison, has a total floor area of 6,636,360 square feet.

Idaho and Iowa - Idaho is possibly the only state named due to a hoax. Lobbyist George Willing suggested the name "Idaho" for the new territory claiming it meant 'Gem of the Mountains' in a Native American language. It was later revealed Willing made up the name and the original Idaho territory was re-named Colorado because of it. Eventually the controversy was forgotten, and modern-day Idaho was given the made-up name when the Idaho Territory was formally created in 1863.

Des Moines, Iowa has an even more interesting origin. Two stories persist, the first that it was given the name La Rivière des Moines, literally meaning 'River of the Monks', by early French explorers. The second is that Peoria Indians told the first white settlers their rival tribe living in that area was named the Moingoana, which became the root of Des Moines.

Indiana University researchers studied the extinct Miami-Illinois language and discovered that Moingoana, translated literally, meant 'shit faces' and agrees with the commonly held notion that the 'Moines' in Des Moines is a French derivation of Moingoana. *Since neither can be proven, I'll go with the second.*

Six Uses for Nail Polish - Apply clear nail polish to a frayed screen to seal the hole.

Apply bright colored nail polish to mark levels (inside or outside) on buckets and containers.

Apply clear nail polish to screws, nuts and bolts to prevent rusting, especially outside.

Mark the perfect shower temperature on the handle. It is waterproof.

Apply clear nail polish to secure screws, repair small wood fractures, or re-set jewelry stones.

Use a drop of clear nail polish on eye glass screws to stop them from coming loose.

Air Traffic Control Tower Windows - Air traffic control towers always have windows that slope toward the tower at the base. Many people assume that they are designed that way to prevent the sun's reflection or glare from blinding incoming pilots.

The benefit is not for those outside the tower, but those inside it. Ordinarily, we see reflections in glass from computer screens, TVs, or car windows. Air traffic controllers must not have any distracting reflections as they monitor flights. By tilting the glass away, any errant light from inside the tower, such as video screens, lights, etc. are reflected up onto the ceiling, which is painted black.

Turquoise McDonald's - Only one McDonald's in the world has turquoise arches. Officials in Sedona, Arizona, thought yellow would clash with the natural red rock. The first color McDonald's offered was turquoise and the city accepted.

Russian Service - While many of our Western food flavors originate in French cuisine, the style of service we are all most used to, individual plates pre-filled and served, is called Russian service, and it originated from the table of the Czar.

In French cuisine it was traditional for all food to be prepared in advance and displayed in huge amounts on side tables. It was an extremely lavish affair, but the end result of this was that much food was wasted and was not always hot.

Russian service, prepared with the expertise of the chef in the kitchen, caught on very fast and was so convenient that it is now the primary way we dish our meals at home.

How Many People Can Fit on Earth - Many more people can be accommodated on our planet than headlines would have us believe. For starters, there are now seven billion people on earth.

The island of Japan has about 143,000 square miles of area. One square mile has 27.9 million square feet. Japan has a total of about 4 trillion square feet, enough to give each person of the earth 670 square feet.

For comparison, if we used the American average of 8,000 square feet to four people, the entire population of the planet would fit into a space as the size of Texas and Nevada combined. That would leave the rest of the world's land for food production, entertainment, and vacations. *These calculations do not include the oceans.*

Grandfather Clocks - The name for the free standing tall clocks is actually newer than you might think. In 1875, an American songwriter named Henry Clay Work was visiting England. While there, he checked in to the George Hotel in North Yorkshire.

In the hotel's lobby was a large pendulum clock. The clock had stopped many years prior and just sat in the lobby as decoration.

He was told a long made-up story how the clock stopped when the previous owner of the inn passed away. Work went home and penned a song about the clock. The song was called "My Grandfather's Clock", released in 1876.

What Fall Colors Mean - As the days turn longer, less sunlight means less oxygen and glucose for plants and leaves and ultimately less chlorophyll, which hides the reds, yellows and oranges. Different materials cause different colors in leaves. Red comes from glucose, brown from waste, and purple from anthocyanin. Yellow is always present in leaves, but during spring and summer, the green overpowers it.

The timetable for leaf transformation runs from September through early November. Typically, the first to see breathtaking fall foliage are the Rockies, Upper Midwest, and New England. From there leaves begin to change further south into the Ohio Valley, Pacific Northwest, and Middle Atlantic toward mid and late October.

The first frost and time of leaf change typically go hand in hand. Within a week or so of the first frost, expect quick leaf transformation. Other factors such as the amount of water during the summer and early fall impact the full potential of color. More water means better color.

Safety Glass Origin - In 1903 Edouard Benedictus, a French scientist, dropped glass flask and it did not shatter.

The pieces of glass were broken, but they stayed in place and maintained the shape of the container. Upon investigation Benedictus found the flask had originally contained a solution of cellulose nitrate, a liquid plastic that had evaporated.

This was the first type of safety glass developed, a product which is now frequently used in car windshields, safety goggles, doors, stairs, bank protection shields, and more.

State Rocks - Many people do not know there are many states that have a state rock. Here are states that do.

Serpentine, California
Geode, Iowa
Bauxite, Arkansas
Slate, Vermont
Thunder egg, Oregon
Red granite, Wisconsin
Agate, Kentucky, Nebraska
Limestone, Tennessee
Petoskey stone, Michigan
Cumberlandite, Rhode Island
Barite rose, Oklahoma
Mozarkite, Missouri
Roxbury puddingstone, Massachusetts
Marble, Alabama, Colorado, Vermont
Coal, Utah, West Virginia
Sandstone, Nevada
Granite, New Hampshire, North Carolina, Vermont

First-Down Line - Thought it might be interesting to review the technology behind the lines that TV adds to the field for down markers. Before the game begins, technicians make a digital 3-D model of the field, which is not flat. It is subtly curved with a crown in the middle to help water flow away. Each field is unique.

Technicians also put together two separate color palettes before each game. One palette contains the colors for the field's turf to automatically be converted into yellow, blue, or whatever color is used) when the line is drawn onto the field. All other colors, such as player and official uniforms, shoes, the ball, etc., go into the other palette. Colors that appear on this second palette are never converted. If a player's foot is situated on the line, everything around it will turn yellow, but not his foot.

Each camera used for the game contains sensors that record its location, tilt, pan, zoom and transmit this data to the graphics computers. These sensors allow the computers to process exactly where each camera is within the 3-D model, along with the perspective of each camera so the lines can be added to the picture. One version requires a four-man crew and costs about $25,000 per game to project the lines onto the field.

Poor Americans - In American today, those classified as poor*:
99% have electricity, flushing toilets, and refrigerator
95% have a television
88% have mobile phones
70% have car and air conditioning
from TiE Entrepreneurial Summit 2012

How Some Measurements Were Named - Can You Fathom a bushel and a peck? *Fathom* is derived from the Old English word faeom or the Old Saxon word fathmos, meaning the length of the outstretched arms. It was eventually standardized to the length of two yards. Although international nautical charts have converted to meters, the United States still measures depth with fathoms.

Bushel comes from the old French words boissel and boisseau and is a measure of dry goods equal to about eight gallons (or four pecks). Today, it is most commonly used to measure things by their weight, and that weight varies depending on the commodity measured. Typical goods sold by the bushel and their weights include oats (32lb), corn (56lb), wheat (60lb), and soybeans (60lb).

Peck is likely derived from the Old French, pek or picot, and is also a measure of dry goods or commodities. Some retailers, farmers at markets and roadside stands still sell fruits and vegetables by the peck. A peck is equal to about two gallons.

A *cord* is traced back to the 1600s when wood was sold in bundles tied with a cord. Today, a cord of firewood must take up 128 cubic feet, traditionally in a stack 8′ x 4′ x 4′. The size of a cord of wood is typically regulated, either by a state or national government.

Knot comes from the word of the same spelling meaning intertwined ropes. To measure speed, a long rope had knots tied regularly, about every 50 feet, and a log tied to the end. The log was dropped into the water and a sandglass upended at the same time to time how many knots per time unit. Eventually, the speed of one knot became standardized at one nautical mile (6,076 feet vs. land mile 5,280 feet) per hour.

Mach (pronounced mock) was named after Ernst Mach in 1937. Mach numbers represent the ratio of the speed of an object moving through a fluid, gas, or atmosphere and the local speed of sound. When space shuttles re-entered the atmosphere, they initially traveled at a speed greater than Mach 25.

An *inch* was originally the width of a man's thumb at the base of the nail. After 1066, 1 inch was equal to 3 *barleycorn*, dry and round, placed end to end, lengthwise.

A *foot* was the length of a human foot. A *yard* was the distance from the tip of the nose to that of the middle finger on an outstretched arm.

One thousand paces of a Roman Legion was a *mile*. A *furlong* was originally the length of one furrow in a common field, a bit over 200 feet long. In the 9th century, it was standardized to be the same as a Roman stadium, one eighth of a Roman mile.

Fugitive Glue - If you ever received a credit card, it was likely stuck to a piece of paper with some icky glue that you can rub off. The name of the glue is Fugitive Glue.

It is a low tack adhesive, which means that it is easy to remove. It leaves a minimal residue on the paper and card. The glue is used for marketing materials, as well as for mailing credit cards. The beauty is that fugitive glue tends to lose most of its stickiness after the first application and cannot be reused. *Hmmm, interesting name for credit card use.*

Global Warming, Global Cooling - It appears to me that long term climatologists may be suffering from the same afflictions as local weather celebrities, "It may be warmer tomorrow unless it gets cooler".

The web has an interesting article from 1975 decrying the various governments for not getting ready for the impending global cooling. The chart is interesting because it is markedly different from global warming charts for the same period. Change the word 'cooling' to 'warming' and we have the same dystopian rhetoric used in any number of articles from recent years. . . until this year. Seems some may be changing their minds again.

George Washington's Teeth - George Washington suffered from poor dental health and spent his life in frequent mouth pain. He used a variety of tooth cleaners, dental medicines, and dentures. Dr. John Baker fabricated a partial denture with ivory that was wired to Washington's remaining real teeth. When Washington was inaugurated President in 1789, only one real tooth remained in his mouth.

Dr. Greenwood fashioned a set of dentures of hippopotamus ivory and gold wire springs and brass screws holding human teeth. Greenwood left a hole to accommodate Washington's single tooth. When Washington lost this final tooth, he gave it to Greenwood who saved it in a special case.

Nothing Festival - The annual Teluride, CO Nothing Festival is held in mid-July. Here are the exciting (tongue-in-cheek) activities for the locals in addition to eating and drinking too much.

Sunrises and sunsets as normal.

Gravity continues to be in effect.

The earth's rotation will be increased to add a few thrills.

The laws of physics will be on display.

Duct Tape Seminar: How to defeat weapons of mass destruction for under $10.

How we use old Volkswagens.

Sense of humor search. *Am sure a fun time is had by all.*

Air Force One - Air Force One is not a single plane. There are a number of planes that are outfitted the same way and they are housed at Andrews Air Force Base, Maryland. The second official presidential plane used, in 1945 was named the 'Sacred Cow', although presidents had used other special planes since 1933.

In March 2012, President Obama took the British Prime Minister David Cameron to a basketball game in Ohio aboard Air Force One.

The planes are only designated as Air Force One when the president is on board.

A second plane that was once used as Air Force One and Air Force Two (vice president) were put up for auction sale in 2013 for an opening bid of $50,000, which was never received.

The original Air force One was up for sale since 1998 and finally sold in 2015. It is planned to be restored and put on display in a museum.

AstroTurf Facts - It was originally named "ChemGrass" before being used by the Houston Astros baseball team in the Astrodome.

Contrary to popular belief, AstroTurf was not first used or invented for the Houston Astros. It was originally invented in 1964, two years before the Astros would use it, by Donald L. Elbert, James M. Faria, and Robert T. Wright, working for Monsanto Company.

In 1965, the Houston Astros attempted to use a special type of natural grass on the indoor field, but the semi-transparent ceiling panels did not let in enough sunlight and the grass died within a few months. This resulted in the Astros organization having to paint the dirt field green, to make it appear more like a normal baseball field.

By the start of the 1966 season, the Astros decided to go with ChemGrass. Due to a limited supply, they were only able to get the infield covered for the first half of the season and the outfield was still painted green dirt. Shortly after the All-Star break, the entire field was covered in ChemGrass and this artificial surface received national attention for the first time.

Soon after, other sporting teams began using ChemGrass up for outdoor stadiums, particularly those in colder climates. The product was renamed AstroTurf by John A. Wortmann, an employee of Monsanto. By 1987, AstroTurf had become so popular that Monsanto made it an independent subsidiary, named AstroTurf Industries, Inc.

AstroTurf eventually became unpopular in outdoor fields, despite the cost benefit, mostly due to the extra wear on player's bodies. It was typically installed over cement and provided little cushioning compared to real grass and dirt. Currently, over 160 million square feet of AstroTurf is used on sporting fields and home use worldwide.

AstroTurf eventually lent its name to the political and business term 'AstroTurfing', where a business or political group will attempt to create an artificial 'movement' to sway public opinion about a topic by making people think 'regular' people are behind the movement.

The US government hired a software company in 2011 to develop special AstroTurfing software, partly by using Facebook, Twitter, and by social engineering that would help the government sway public opinion on various topics. The software would scan for online articles written by people with opposing views to what the Administration wanted people to think. It would then create fake accounts and post made up, discrediting information about the authors.

Flying the Philippines Flag Fact - The flag of the Philippines has three stars, the Sun, and two stripes. One stripe is blue and the other is red.

Which stripe is on top is dependent on whether the nation is at war. As stated by law, "the flag, if flown from a flagpole, shall have its blue field on top in time of peace and the red field on top in time of war."

Four Unusual Cemeteries - The largest man made reef in the world three miles off the coast of Key Biscayne, the *Neptune Memorial Reef*, is also an underwater mausoleum. The graveyard is 40 feet below the surface of the water, allowing divers swim among statues and sea life to visit deceased family members. Divers go down with ashes mixed with cement and place the mixture in a selected location. The cost for placement is $2,600 to $4,000, and there are 1,200 spots in the initial development.

In the lagoons of Venice Italy, *San Michele island* has been occupied only by the dead since the early 1800s. Two other structures on the island are the Church of San Michele, built in 1469, and the Cappella Emiliana, built in 1543. Because space is limited on the island, Venetians who are interred on San Michele have ten years of peace before their remains are exhumed and moved to an ossuary. Igor Stravinsky and Ezra pound are interred there.

The *Hallstatt, Austria Ossuary*, or Beinhaus (Bone House), is filled with about 700 painted skulls and 500 undecorated skulls. The ossuary dates back to the 17th century and is notable for the decorations painted on many of the skulls.

The *Calico, California Ghost Town Cemetery* is the town's original burial site with headstones dating back to 1882. Today, only those who have a long relationship with Calico are given the honor of being buried alongside the 19th-century miners, but space is limited

----

Dalai Lama, Winter Home - In case you were wondering where the Buddhist holy Dalai Lama spent his winters until he went into exile in 1959, this is it. Since then, he has been living in India and has referred to himself as a Marxist. He has received a Nobel Peace Prize.

The Potala Palace in Tibet was built in the 7th century.

Tibetans address the Dalai Lama as Gyalwa Rinpoche ("Precious Victor"), Kundun ("Presence"), Yishin Norbu ("Wish fulfilling Gem")

among others, and His Holiness by Westerners. The 14th Dalai Lama (since 1950) retired March 14, 2011.

All Dalai Lamas are a reincarnation of the previous one. High Lamas have a vision by a dream or if the Dalai Lama was cremated, they will often monitor the direction of the smoke as an indication of the direction of the rebirth. Once the High Lamas have found the home and the boy they believe to be the reincarnation, the boy undergoes a series of tests to affirm the rebirth. They present a number of artifacts, only some of which belonged to the previous Dalai Lama, and if the boy chooses the items which belonged to the previous Dalai Lama. This is seen as a sign, in conjunction with all of the other indications, that the boy is the reincarnation.

Tenzin Gyatso (religious name), who was born born Lhamo Dondrub on July 6, 1935 has stated that he will not be reborn in the People's Republic of China and has also suggested he may not be reborn at all, suggesting the function of the Dalai Lama may be outdated. He said, "Naturally my next life is entirely up to me. No one else, and also this is not a political matter."

World Record for World Records - Keith (Ashrita Furman) Record-Winning Age: 51 Award Date: June 6, 2006 Fastest Time for a Male to Hoola Hoop 10km.

Furman also holds the record for "most records held at one time by an individual" 160 as of 2012.

He has set records on seven continents and in more than 30 different countries
Since 1979, Furman has set 450 official Guinness Records, including juggling on a pogo stick the furthest distance (4 miles 30 feet) and quickest time for a mile-long piggy back (12 minutes, 47 seconds). He converted an indoor rower with wheels and brakes and rowed 1,500 miles (2,400 km) in 16 days in Bali in 1991. *When not breaking records, he manages a health food store in Queens, New York.*

Runner up is Suresh Joachim Arulanantham, a Canadian film actor and multiple-Guinness World Record holder who has broken 60 world records set in several countries in attempts to benefit underprivileged children around the world.

Paper Bag Numbers - The number on the bag indicates its capacity. Smaller units, called bags or grocers, have numbers from 1/2 to 25, signifying the approximate weight in pounds of sugar or flour the bag can hold.

Larger varieties, known as sacks, are sized by fractions of a barrel, e.g., 1/6, the size most commonly found in supermarkets.

Seven Kitchen Tips - Microwave garlic cloves for 15 seconds and the skins slip off.

When working with dough, coat hands with olive oil to prevent sticking.

Wrap celery in aluminum foil and put it in the refrigerator to keep for weeks.

Let raw potatoes stand in cold water for at least half an hour before frying to improve the crispness of french-fried potatoes.

Microwave lemons, limes, or oranges for 15 seconds in the microwave before squeezing them and you get twice as much juice.

After you drain pasta, while it's still hot, grate some fresh Parmesan on top, so the sauce has more to stick to before tossing it with your sauce.

Boy Scouts and Astronauts - Eleven of the twelve men who walked on the moon were Boy Scouts. Boy Scouts and astronauts require similar qualities. They are dependable, responsible, attentive to detail, and respectful. It makes sense that two thirds of all current and former astronauts were also Boy Scouts.

Since 1959, there have been 312 pilots and scientists selected to be astronauts, at least 207 were involved with scouts, as Eagle Scouts, Cub Scouts, Life Scouts, etc. Of the 24 men who traveled to the moon, 20 of them were scouts. All three members of the Apollo 13 mission were scouts. NASA supports both Boy Scouts and Girl Scouts as potential leaders.

Mountain Goats are Not - Mountain goats, found only in North America, are an even-toed ungulate of the family Bovidae that includes antelopes, gazelles, and cattle. It is the only species in the genus Oreamnos. The name *Oreamnos* is derived from the Greek term *oros*, "mountain," or, *oreas* "mountain nymph". They are sometimes referred to as goat-antelopes.

They have woolly coats, cloven feet, and horns, but not the same kind as true goats. The fur is thicker and shaggier than that of a domesticated farm goat. Their hooves are specially built for climbing and descending mountain slopes A rubbery padding covers the bottom of their hooves and their horns are long and pointy.

They spend most of their time grazing and their diet includes grasses, herbs, sedges, ferns, mosses, lichens, and twigs and leaves from the low-growing shrubs in their high-altitude habitat.

Henry VIII Wives - He actually had just two wives, not six. Henry's fourth marriage to Anne was annulled, as the marriage was never consummated, also Anne was betrothed to Francis, Duke of Lorraine. At the time 'betrothal' would bar the individual from marriage. That leaves 5 wives. Henry's second marriage to Anne Boleyn was declared illegal by the pope, because the king was still married to his first wife, Catherine of Aragon. That brings it to four. Henry, as the head of the church of England, declared himself that his first marriage was invalid on the grounds that a man cannot sleep with his brother's widow. Now down to three. He did the same with his fifth wife, Catherine Howard, leaving just two wives.

Farrington B Font - The squared-off numbers on almost every credit card were invented in a bar at the Waldorf-Astoria. David H. Shepard, who invented the first optical character recognition device (in his attic), and the first voice recognition system, also created the Farrington B numeric font to try to combat the smudging and smearing that would inevitably occur at gas pumps, one of the first places optical character recognition would be used.

These days, credit card companies could use any font for the account number, because the information is gathered from the magnetic strip on the back. Farrington B is still commonly used as tradition. Shepard passed away in 2007.

Daylight Saving - Benjamin Franklin is often credited with the idea of daylight saving, but he only mentioned it in jest in a satirical essay.

The idea was never seriously pushed until 1895 when George Vernon Hudson, presented the idea as a way for people to have more daylight and consequently more leisure time after work. While there was interest in Hudson's idea, it still did not catch on until 1916 when Germany adopted DST as a method to save fuel during World War I.

Others, including the US and Great Britain, used DST during World War I and II, yet reverted to standard time during peace years. It wasn't until about 40 some years ago, during the energy crisis of the 1970s that Daylight Saving Time was made permanent in many areas.

Much has been argued for and against Daylight Saving benefits. *I side with the majority who think it is a waste of time and energy to change clocks twice a year. Likely more time is wasted discussing the matter than any real or imagined benefits from it.*

Quotes from '1984' - George Orwell penned these prescient sobering quotes in his book, released in 1948.

"He who controls the past controls the future. He who controls the present controls the past."
"If you want a picture of the future, imagine a boot stamping on a human face—for ever."
"Big Brother is Watching You."
"Doublethink means the power of holding two contradictory beliefs in one's mind simultaneously, and accepting both of them."
"Until they became conscious they will never rebel, and until after they have rebelled they cannot become conscious."
"The choice for mankind lies between freedom and happiness and for the great bulk of mankind, happiness is better."
"The Party seeks power entirely for its own sake. We are not interested in the good of others; we are interested solely in power, pure power."
"Power is in tearing human minds to pieces and putting them together again in new shapes of your own choosing."
"Power is not a means; it is an end. One does not establish a dictatorship in order to safeguard a revolution; one makes the revolution in order to establish the dictatorship."

Twelve Famous Firsts - Thomas Jefferson, 1801 - First US president to be inaugurated in Washington, D.C.

Sam Patch, 1829 - First known person to survive the jump off of Niagara Falls.

Edward Smith, 1831 - First indicted bank robber in the US. He was sentenced to five years hard labor on the rock pile at Sing Sing Prison.

William Henry Harrison, 1841 - First US president to die in office. At 32 days, he also had the shortest term in office.

Elizabeth Blackwell, 1849 - First woman to receive medical degree in US. (from the Medical Institution of Geneva, N.Y.)

Jefferson Long, 1870 - First African American elected to US House of Representatives, Georgia.

Victoria Woodhall, 1872 - First woman to run for President of the US.

Grover Cleveland, 1886 - First President married inside the White House.

William Kemmler, 1890 - First criminal to be executed by electrocution (in Auburn N.Y. Prison)

Annie Moore, 1892 - First immigrant to pass through Ellis Island. She was 15 years old and from County Cork, Ireland.

Queen Isabella of Spain, 1893 - First woman to appear on a US postage stamp.

John J. McDermott, 1897 - First annual Boston Marathon winner - the first of its type in the US. *(Winning time was 2:55:10 vs. 2015 winning time of 2:09:17.*

Church Tax - Did you know a church tax is imposed on members of many religious congregations in Austria, Denmark, Finland, Germany, Iceland, Italy, Sweden, some parts of Switzerland and several other countries? The Roman Catholic Church, Church of Denmark, Evangelical Lutheran Church of Finland and the Finnish Orthodox Church, Protestant, Church of Iceland, Jewish Communities, Baptist, Buddhist, Hindu, etc. are all included in the tax collection from their respective members.

The tax was introduced by Hitler in Austria. Oxymoronically, after World War II, the tax was retained in order to keep the Church independent of political powers. Typically the tax is usually between .5% and 2.5%. Some countries even pay the salaries and retirement benefits of clergy, as well as upkeep for the buildings and grounds.

Recently many members have been going to their city halls to opt out of religious groups, which has significant ramifications for declining taxes.

Toilet Tips - After analyzing 51 public restrooms, experts found that the stall closest to the restroom door consistently had the lowest bacteria levels (and the most toilet paper). The first stall probably sees less traffic because it's near the door and people want privacy. When you are finished, stand before you flush. When toilets are flushed, a fine mist of water containing contagious bacteria sprays up. You can catch intestinal bugs and hepatitis from it.

Relieve yourself and relieve some stress at the same time. Before you go to bed, put some small strips of flushable paper and a pencil in the bathroom. In the following morning, take a seat and write down the names of all the people or situations in your life causing you angst. When finished with your business, throw the paper in the bowl and flush. You will be amazed at how great this makes you feel.

American Brands or Not - Do you know which of these ten brands are American owned? Lucky Strike, Budweiser, Vaseline, Good Humor, Hellman's (mayonnaise), Purina, French's (condiments), Frigidaire, Popsicle, 7-Eleven

Answer - None

Lucky Strike, England
Budweiser, Belgium
Vaseline, England
Good Humor, England
Hellman's, England
Purina, Switzerland
French's England
Frigidaire, Sweden
Popsicle, England,
7-Eleven, Japan

Kind of looks like England is buying the US back, one brand at a time. It has made its strike to take our good humor and other things to just rub it in and on us. At least we have Krafted a way with some Mondelēz to get back some sweets by taking over Cadbury a few years ago.

Boston Tea Party - December 16, 1773, American patriots, protesting the British tax on tea, dumped 342 chests of tea into Boston harbor. The act is known as the "Boston Tea Party." It was a nonviolent political protest by the Sons of Liberty in Boston. They were disguised as Indians and destroyed the entire supply of tea sent by the East India Company in defiance of the American boycott of tea carrying a tax the Americans had not authorized.

Origin of Birthstones - In the Bible, when Moses went to Egypt, his brother Aaron stayed behind in their birth town. When Moses asked the King of Egypt to set his people free, it was Aaron who sold the idea to their kinsfolk.

Aaron became a high priest. His ceremonial breastplate held four rows of three stones each. Exodus 28:17-20 states, "There were twelve stones, one for each of the names of the sons of Israel, each engraved like a seal with the name of one of the twelve tribes." These 12 stones also symbolized the 12 months of the year and the 12 signs of the zodiac.

Biblical scholars have a difficult time translating exactly what these stones are. The King James Bible lists the stones as: (Row 1) sardius, topaz, carbuncle; (Row 2) emerald, sapphire, diamond; (Row 3) ligure, agate, amethyst; (Row 4) beryl, onyx, jasper. The New American Standard Bible lists them as: (Row 1) ruby, topaz, emerald; (Row 2) turquoise, sapphire, diamond; (Row 3) jacinth, agate, amethyst; (Row 4) beryl, onyx, jasper.

The gems have changed a few times and different countries use different stones.

It was in 15th-century Poland that wearing these birthstones gained popularity. In contrast to today's custom of wearing your birthstone throughout the year, the early proponents owned a full set of 12 and wore each month's stone, regardless of birthday. The Gemological Institute of America says the custom began in Germany in the 1560s.

Seven Un-American Brands - Firestone tires was bought out in 1988 by Bridgestone, a Japanese rubber conglomerate based in Tokyo.

Dial soap was bought in 2004 by by Henkel KGaA, of Germany.

Shell Oil Company is the US-based affiliate of Royal Dutch Shell from Netherlands.

Holiday Inn is now owned by British InterContinental Hotels Group PLC.

The **Chrysler building** in New York is now owned by the Abu Dhabi Investment Council.

Budweiser is now owned by Belgian company InBev.

GM, Walmart, Symantec, Kodak, and McDonald's now get the majority of sales outside of the US. In fact, 47.8% of total sales from all the S&P companies were made outside of the US.

Seven Bits of Trivia - The 3 Musketeers bar was originally split into three pieces with three different flavors: vanilla, chocolate, and strawberry. When the other flavors became harder to come by during World War II, Mars decided to go all chocolate.

Carly Simon's dad is the Simon of Simon and Schuster. He co-founded the company.

Reno is farther west than Los Angeles.

Only female mosquitoes will bite you.

"Jay" used to be slang for "foolish person." So when a pedestrian ignored street signs, he was referred to as a "jaywalker."

The only number whose letters are in alphabetical order is 40 (forty).

The word "PEZ" comes from the German word for peppermint, PfeffErminZ.

Hummingbirds are the only birds that can fly backward.

Five Weaponology Facts - The Chinese invented gunpowder, but they were not the first to develop firearms.

Sam Colt invented the revolving pistol; therefore, all revolvers are correctly called pistols.

Revolvers cannot be silenced, due to all the noisy gasses which escape the cylinder gap at the rear of the barrel.

A 12 gauge rifled slug does not spin, even though there are grooves on its bearing surface. A slug actually travels like a dart.

A bullet fired from the 7.62 x 51mm NATO cartridge (also called the .308 Winchester) is still supersonic at 1,000 yards.

Facts About Plastic Bags - Plastic grocery bags may harm the planet. Paper grocery bags deplete the forests. Reusable grocery bags may contain lead and also cause illness from germs and cross contamination.

Los Angeles became the largest US city to ban the use of plastic grocery bags, along with four dozen other California municipalities. Every county in Hawaii also prohibits them. Austin, TX does them one better and passed one of the broadest bag laws in the nation, agreeing to ban disposable paper and plastic bags starting in March 2013 in favor of reusable bags.

Reusable grocery bags carry E. coli germs along with a variety of other bacteria and some bags contain seven times the lead limit of many states. According to one study, Grocery shoppers must us their reusable bags 131 times to see the environmental benefits touted by global warming zealots. To be safe, reusable bags need to be washed and preferably bleached to prevent cross contamination, especially bags that transport meat, fish, fresh vegetables, or fruit.

Another source of potentially dangerous infectious comes from the checker scanning foods over the same surface of the scanner that everyone else's food passes over.

Many people reuse plastic bags for garbage, pet cleanup, transporting wet clothing, etc., so not using them causes these people to buy plastic garbage bags, which helps defeat the purpose of bag bans.

Lower priced reusable bags found in stores are either plastic themselves or made from 100% non-woven polypropylene. In 2010, a study found that over half are contaminated with bacteria, some even with E. coli, because 97 percent of shoppers say they never wash their totes.

People are encouraged to wash counters and cabinets where bags are stored and never let them rest on the floor, because they pick up germs from food packaging, shopping carts, car trunks, etc. Some suggest putting reusable bags in a microwave for a minute or two after each use to sanitize them. An average family of four would need to keep at least a dozen or more bags for a normal shopping trip.

Follow-up regarding Austin Texas - In 2015, the city asked the Austin Resource Recovery group to investigate its effectiveness. Their June 10 report states that while the ban was successful in lowering the amount of single-use plastic bags made from high-density polyethylene in city landfills, it was actually worse for the environment overall.

It also reported that the ordinance increases costs for both consumers and retailers. Consumers are spending more money purchasing reusable bags and some businesses are losing customers due to the ordinance. Customers are going outside the city limits to buy groceries. The Dallas City Council voted to repeal its plastic bag ordinance after a group of bag manufactures filed a lawsuit. Then-Texas Attorney General Greg Abbott (now Governor) argued that state law prohibits local governments from enacting such ordinances.

A June 2014 report by the Reason Foundation also found that "for the main environmental effects of concern, i.e. non-renewable energy consumption, water consumption and greenhouse gas emissions, HDPE [high-density polyethylene] plastic bags are superior to the alternative options currently available.

"Advocates of restrictions on plastic bags frequently assert that their preferred option is for people to use reusable bags. When the impact of washing such bags is taken into account, the environmental effect of such bags is likely worse than HDPE plastic bags—especially in places such as California where fresh water is relatively scarce."

Top Ten Movie Lines - According to the American Film Institute, here they are:
1 - Frankly, my dear, I don't give a damn. (GONE WITH THE WIND)
2 - I'm going to make him an offer he can't refuse. (THE GODFATHER)
3 - You don't understand! I coulda had class. I coulda been a contender. I could've been somebody, instead of a bum, which is what I am. (ON THE WATERFRONT)
4 - Toto, I've got a feeling we're not in Kansas anymore. (THE WIZARD OF OZ)
5 - Here's looking at you, kid. (CASABLANCA)
6 - Go ahead, make my day. (SUDDEN IMPACT)
7 - All right, Mr. DeMille, I'm ready for my close-up. (SUNSET BLVD.)
8 - May the Force be with you. (STAR WARS)
9 - Fasten your seatbelts. It's going to be a bumpy night. (ALL ABOUT EVE)
10 - You talking to me? (TAXI DRIVER)

Laurel and Hardy came in 60th with the famous line delivered by Ollie in many of their movies, "Well, here's another nice mess you've gotten me into!"

Ant Facts - Spring is when the ants come out. Worker ants are foraging for food, looking after the colony's young, and defending their home for unwanted intruders. One nest in South America has had up to 700,000 members.

Ants are clean insects. Some worker ants are given the job of taking the rubbish from the nest and putting it outside in a special rubbish dump. Each colony of ants has its own smell. In this way, intruders can be recognized.

Black Ants and Wood Ants have no sting, but they can squirt a spray of formic acid. Some birds put ants in their feathers because ants squirt the formic acid which gets rid of parasites.

The Slave-Maker Ant raids the nests of other ants and steals their pupae. When these new ants hatch, they work as slaves within the colony. Worker ants keep eggs and larvae in different groups according to ages.

Ants undergo complete metamorphosis from egg, to larva, to pupa, to adult. Each ant colony begins with, and centers around the queen, whose sole purpose is to reproduce. Although the queen may copulate with several males during her brief mating period, she never mates again. She stores sperm in an internal pouch, where sperm remain immobile until she opens a valve that allows them to enter her reproductive tract to fertilize the eggs.

The queen ant lives a significantly longer life than her workers. A queen of the species Lasius niger in Europe lived for 29 years in captivity. Queen ants lay the eggs that grow into worker ants. A leafcutter ant queen in South America lived for 14 years and bred over 150 million worker ants in her lifetime.

The queen controls the sex of her offspring. Fertilized eggs produce females, either wingless workers seldom capable of reproduction, or reproductive virgin queens, which are produced only when there are sufficient workers to allow for the expansion of the colony.

Unfertilized eggs develop into winged males who do no work, and exist solely to fertilize a virgin queen. The queen produces myriads of workers by secreting a chemical that retards wing growth and ovary development in the female larvae.

After mating, queen ants and male ants lose their wings. The queen scurries off in search of a site to start her new nest. If she survives, she digs a nest, lays eggs, and single-handedly raises her first brood that consists entirely of workers.

Four Little Known Business Facts - Fifty percent of Domino's Pizza was once traded for a used VW Beetle.

The owner of Fedex once gambled his last five thousand dollars to win 32 thousand in Vegas to save the company.

SOS in SOS pads stands for 'save our saucepans' and was thought up by the owner's wife.

Ben and Jerry's was originally going to be a bagel company.

Who Owns What Auto Brands - During the 1990s Volkswagen acquired Lamborghini, Bentley, and Bugatti. VW also owns Audi, Ducati Motorcycles, MAN (Uzbekistan), Scania, Porsche, SEAT (Spain), and Skoda (Czech) brands, as well as 19.9% of Suzuki. All together, Volkswagen owns 340 subsidiary companies, with 550,000 employees. Interesting to know that Porsche produced the first VW Beetle. *Seems VW transformed itself from beetle to elephant.*

Other interesting brand owners:
BMW owns: BMW, Mini, and Rolls Royce.

Fiat owns: Fiat, Alfa Romeo, Chrysler, Dodge, Ferrari, Jeep, Lancia, Maserati, and Ram.

Hyundai owns: Hyundai, Kia. (It is pronounced Hun-Day, like Sunday)

Tata Motors (India) owns: Tata, Jaguar, and Land Rover.

Renault owns Nissan, which owns Infiniti.

Toyota owns: Lexus, Scion, Daihatsu, Hino Motors, Isuzu, and a stake in Fuji Industries (Subaru's parent).

Geely owns Volvo (Chinese Zhejiang Geely Holding Group).

Why Number 2 Pencils - Pencil makers manufacture No. 1, 2, 2½, 3, and 4 pencils, and sometimes other intermediate numbers. The higher the number, the harder the lead and lighter the markings. Number 1 pencils produce darker markings, which are sometimes preferred by people working in publishing.

The current style of production is profiled after pencils developed in 1794 by Nicolas-Jacques Conté. Before Conté, pencil hardness varied from location to location and maker to maker. Earliest pencils were made by filling a wood shaft with raw graphite.

Conté's method involved mixing powdered graphite with finely ground clay, shaped into a long cylinder and then baked in an oven. The proportion of clay versus graphite added to a mixture determines the hardness of the lead. Although the method is usually the same, the way companies categorize and label pencils isn't.

Today, many US companies use a numbering system for general-purpose writing pencils that specifies how hard the lead is. For graphic and artist pencils and for companies outside the US, systems use a combination of numbers and letters known as the HB Graphite Scale.

Testing centers prefer Number 2 pencils, because their machines use the electrical conductivity of the lead to read the pencil marks. Early scanning-and-scoring machines could not detect marks made by harder pencils, so No. 3 and No. 4 pencils usually resulted in erroneous results and softer pencils like No. 1 smudge. Because of this and general wide acceptance, No. 2 pencils became the industry standard.

Olympic Award Facts - For the London Games, the gold medals are roughly 93% silver, 6% copper and 1% gold. The silver medals are 92% silver and 8% copper. The bronze medals are 97% copper, 2.5% zinc and 0.5% tin.

Gold medals made from solid gold were introduced at the 1904 St. Louis Games, and four years later in London, the medals began to be awarded to the top three placing athletes in the gold-silver-bronze order we are familiar with today. The 1912 Stockholm Games were the last time solid gold medals were awarded.

These days, the IOC charter only requires that the first place medals be silver gilt, containing "silver of at least 925-1000 grade and gilded with at least 6g of pure gold." The second place silver medals must contain silver of a similar grade. Beyond that, the specific composition of the medals, and their design, is determined by the host city's organizing committee.

When the first modern Olympic games organized by the International Olympic Committee were held in 1896 in Athens, winners got a silver medal and an olive branch, and runners-up received a bronze medal and a laurel branch. Ancient Greek competitors were given an olive branch from a wild olive tree that grew at Olympia along with some money upon returning home.

Top Ten Toys of all Time - There is minimal agreement on the top toys of all time among many adults. Some are obviously biased, such as the first poll which includes Star Wars Figures. They have not been in existence long enough to even be considered by others.

Poll 1	Poll 2	Poll 3
1. Hula Hoop	1. Bike	1. G.I. Joe
2. **Barbie**	2. **LEGO**	2. Transformers
3. **LEGO**	3. Teddy Bear	3. **LEGO**
4. G.I. Joe	4. Crayons	4. **Barbie**
5. Mr. Potato Head	5. Slinky	5. View-Master
6. Monopoly	6. Ball	6. Bike
7. Star Wars figures	7. Etch A Sketch	7. Cabbage Patch Kids
8. Yo-Yo	8. Yo-Yo	8. Crayons
9. Slinky	9. **Barbie**	9. Play-doh
10. Wiffle ball, bat	10. Hula Hoop	10. Monopoly

The only 2 toys included on all three lists, in order are LEGO (introduced in 1947) and Barbie (introduced 1959).

I tend to agree with the following list according to another source, which lists the best 5 toys of all time. They are: Stick, Cardboard Box, String, Cardboard Tube, and Dirt. I would also add rocks, water, and snow. All have withstood the real test of time, are played with around the world, provide for endless enjoyment, and evoke magnificent flights of imagination.

ALCOHOL AND DRINKING

Most Expensive Beer in the World - Nail Brewing's Antarctic Nail Ale, Price: $800-$1815/500ml This high priced wonder beer was concocted by Nail Brewing in Perth, Australia. All profits go to the Sea Shepherd Conservation Society, the Whale Wars people.

The Sea Shepherds landed a helicopter on an Antarctic iceberg, dug up some ice, melted it in Tasmania, and flew it to Perth for brewing. Only 30 bottles were made, and the first bottle sold for $800 at auction.

Another extremely expensive beer is made by Pabst. Hard to imagine, but at $44 per bottle, Chinese Pabst Blue Ribbon costs about 40 times more than what is sold in the US. PBR 1844 is made from German caramel malts, is aged in uncharred American whiskey barrels, and comes in a fancy glass bottle. Master brewer Alan Kornhauser designed the ale to compete with higher end wines and brandies. It is not sold outside of China.

Belfast Sparkling Cider - This drink found in many Chinese restaurants in the San Francisco Bay Area, dates back to the Gold Rush of 1849. According to the story, gold prospectors and sailors would frequent San Francisco's bar scene in search of a good time.

The sailors treated the bar girls to what they thought was French champagne, but which was actually Belfast Sparkling Cider, a lightly sweetened drink introduced to the region by Irish refugees who immigrated to the US during the potato famine.

Ship captains apparently paid the bar girls to play along and watched their sailors become intoxicated to the point that it wasn't a struggle to get them back to sea.

According to the San Jose Mercury News, it can be found in almost every large Chinese restaurant in San Francisco and to retailers throughout Chinatown. Belfast is especially popular in the month of the Chinese New Year.

Alcohol and Drinking - The next time you're inclined to enjoy an extra glass of wine, consider that it may be a reflection of your intelligence. That is one of the findings from data from the National Child Development Study in the United Kingdom and the National Longitudinal Study of Adolescent Health in the United States. Childhood intelligence, measured before the age of 16, was categorized in five cognitive classes, ranging from "very dull," "dull," "normal," "bright" and "very bright."

The Americans were revisited seven years later. The British youths, on the other hand, were followed in their 20s, 30s, and 40s. Researchers measured their drinking habits as the participants became older.

More intelligent children in both studies grew up to drink alcohol more frequently and in greater quantities than less intelligent children. In the Brits' case, "very bright" children grew up to consume nearly eight-tenths of a standard deviation more alcohol than their "very dull" cohorts.

Researchers controlled for demographic variables, such as marital status, parents' education, earnings, childhood social class and more, that may have also affected adult drinking. The findings held true that smarter kids were drinking more as adults.

Psychology Today takes an evolutionary approach. It argues that drinkable alcohol is a relatively novel invention of 10,000 years ago. Our ancestors had previously received their alcohol kick through eating rotten fruits, so more intelligent humans may be more likely to choose modern alcoholic beverages.

Although increased alcohol consumption could be a reflection of exceptional brainpower, drinking more will certainly not make you any more intelligent than you already are. *I'll drink to that.*

Tequila - The clear white liquor with the unique taste that people either love or hate, tequila is thought to have been first produced around the second half of the 16th century in Mexico. It is made from the blue agave plant that grows so abundantly around the city of Tequila in the state of Jalisco.

Tequila is said to have been a result of the Spaniards running out of their own brandy. Upon hearing the Aztecs had once used the blue agave plant to produce an alcoholic drink (known as octli or pulque), the conquistadors set about distilling the plant to produce a drink they could use to replace their beloved brandy.

Mexican law dictates that tequila can only be produced in this and a few other very select areas if it is to carry the name of tequila. Over 300 million agave plants are harvested each year for the production of tequila.

It is distilled after fermentation and the end product is usually 38% to 40% alcohol. That brings it in at 76% to 80% proof.

Booze - The first references to the word "booze" meaning "alcoholic drink" in English appeared around the 14th century, though it was originally spelled 'bouse'. The spelling, as it is today, didn't appear until around the 17th century.

The word 'booze' appears to have Germanic origins, though which specific word it came from is still a little bit of a mystery. The three main words often cited are more or less all cousins of each other and are very similar in meaning and spelling. One of the words came from the Old High German 'bausen', which meant "bulge or billow". This was a cousin of the Dutch word 'búsen', which meant "to drink excessively" or "to get drunk". The Old Dutch language also has a similar word 'buise', which translates to "drinking vessel".

It is thought that the word "bouse" in English, which later became "booze", has its origins in one or more of those three words, with most scholars leaning towards it coming from the Dutch word 'búsen'.

The origin of the word "booze" does not come from E. C. Booz, a 19th century distiller in the United States.

Archeological evidence suggest that the earliest known purposefully fermented drink, beer, was made around 10,000 BC.

Native American tribes had numerous forms of alcoholic beverages they brewed, long before the 'white man' came to the Americas.

The Greek followers of Dionysus believed intoxication brought them closer to their god. *Some current imbibers still believe this.*

Wine Colors - Red wine and white wine do not come from red and white grapes. The color in wine comes from the inclusion of the grape skins. White wines are made from just the pulp.

Zinfandel is a variety of red grape. Red zinfandel and other red wines are made from it as well as white zinfandel and rosé (by using mostly pulp and not skins).

Beer Spread - Chocolate beer spread has hit the shelves at Selfridges stores in the UK as the result of a collaboration between an Italian chocolate maker and beer brewer. The result is a sweet and beer-perfumed jelly with an intense scent and a full-bodied taste, perfect for spreading on a slice of warm toast.

"Beer lovers rejoice, you can now enjoy your favorite tipple with cheeses and bread with Omid dark ale spreadable beer," explains the Selfridges sales pitch. 'The beer spread provides a unique accompaniment for hors d'oeuvres and cheeses... or as a stuffing or garnish for tarts and cakes.' *I think I need some of that.*

Seventeen Beer Facts - Here are a few beer facts that can be used to impress relatives, friends, and fellow boozers.

After he won the Nobel Prize, Niels Bohr was given a perpetual supply of beer piped into his house. (He lived next to a brewery).

The Code of Hammurabi decreed that bartenders who watered down beer would be executed.

At the Annual Wife Carrying World Championships (in Finland), the first prize is the wife's weight in beer.

The builders of the Great Pyramid of Giza were paid with a daily ration of beer.

The top five US states for beer consumption per capita: 1. North Dakota, 2. New Hampshire, 3. Montana, 4. South Dakota, 5. Wisconsin.

Germany is home to a beer pipeline. Taps in Veltsin-Arena are connected by a 5km (3 mile) tube of beer.

A Buddhist temple in the Thai countryside was built with over a million recycled beer bottles. >>>>

Thomas Jefferson wrote parts of the Declaration of Independence in a Philadelphia tavern.

George Washington insisted his continental army be permitted a quart of beer as part of their daily rations.

At spas in Europe, you can literally bathe in beer as a physical and mental therapeutic treatment.

In the 1990s, the Beer Lovers Party ran candidates in Belarus and Russia.

J.K. Rowling, of Harry Potter fame invented Quidditch in a pub.

Beer soup was a common breakfast in medieval Europe.

Beer helped Joseph Priestly discover oxygen. He noticed gases rising from the big vats of beer at a brewery and asked to do some experiments.

At the start of Bavarian Beer Week in Germany, an open-air beer fountain dispenses free beer to the public.

In the 1980s, a beer-drinking goat was elected mayor of Lajitas, TX.

The moon has a crater named Beer.

More Expensive Beers - For those still celebrating, here are a few beers to pick up or impress friends.

1. Sapporo's Space Barley, Price: $110/six-pack - The barley was actually grown about the International Space Station.

2. Crown Ambassador Reserve, Price: $90/750ml - It is aged in French oak barrels for 12 months and packaged in a champagne bottle.

3. Tutankhamun Ale, Price: $75/500ml - Developed from residue found in Queen Nefertiti's Royal Brewery. *No longer available.*

4. Brewdog's Sink the Bismarck, Price: $80/375ml - Also one of the worlds strongest at 41% abv and extremely bitter.

5. Samuel Adams' Utopias, Price: $150/700ml - America's most expensive by the second largest brewer in the US. It is actually banned in 13 states due to its high alcohol content at 27%.

6. Schorschbräu's Schorschbock 57, Price: $275/330ml - Only 36 bottles made and claims to be the world's strongest with 57.5% abv.

7. Carlsberg's Jacobsen Vintage, Price: $400/375ml - Limited to 600 bottles per year from 2008 to 2010.

8. Brewdog's The End of History, Price: $765/330ml - Only 12 bottles (or less) still exist and is 55% abv.

I do not usually drink beer, but if I did a few of these would be on my list.

INVENTIONS BY WOMEN

Josephine Cochrane invented the dishwasher. She was angry that hired domestic help continually broke and chipped her fine china. Cochrane's dishwasher used high water pressure aimed at a wire rack of dishes, she received a patent for it in 1886. During this era, most houses didn't have the technology of a hot water system to run such a machine, but Cochrane persisted and sold her idea to hotels and restaurants. Eventually dishwashers moved into households as more and more women entered the workplace.

Admiral Dr. Grace Murray Hopper was stationed at Harvard after WWII, where she worked on the development of the IBM-Harvard Mark 1, the first large-scale computer in the US. Dr. Hopper invented the compiler, which translates written language into computer code. She coined the term "bug" for a computer problem, and co-developed COBOL, the first user-friendly business computer software program. As a woman inventor, she won numerous awards, including the National Medal of Technology in 1991. Dr. Hopper received honorary degrees from 30 universities.

Mary Anderson noticed a problem with cars of her time and in 1903 she invented windshield wipers. It was the ingenious squeegee on a spindle attached to a handle inside the car. To clear the windshield, the driver would pull down on a handle. Ten years after she patented the device, another woman, Charlotte Bridgwood first patented the automatic windshield wiper in 1917, called the 'Storm Windshield Cleaner'. *The reason we call it a windshield is because that is what it actually does, shields us from wind.*

In 1949, *Marion Donovan*'s first successful invention called "Boaters" was a waterproof baby diaper cover that prevented diaper rash. She also created the disposable diapers, Pampers in 1961.

Hedy Lamarr the actress, patented a secret communications system in 1941. The system manipulated radio frequencies with an unbreakable code to prevent classified messages from being intercepted by enemies. The device was meant to be used against the Nazis in WWII, but in actuality it came into use 20 years later. Lamarr was raised in Austria, grew to despise the Nazis and eventually escaped to London and then to the United States.

Alice H. Parker filed the first U.S. patent for the precursor to a central heating system in 1919. The system was able to regulate the temperature of a building and carry heat from room to room. The drawings included for the patent show a heating furnace powered by gas. An entire house required several heating units, each controlled by individual hot air ducts. The ducts directed heat to different parts of a building structure.

Mary Phelps Jacob was awarded a US patent in 1914 for a brassiere that supported the breasts up from the shoulders and separated them into two individual shapes. People had experimented with making brassieres before, but it was the idea of separating the breasts, that made her design unique.

Prior to brassieres, women's undergarments were uncomfortable, containing whalebones and steel rods. They virtually squeezed the wearer into shape. Jacobs' design was soft, light, and conforming to the wearer's anatomy. During WWI her bra design became popular when the U.S. government requested that women stop purchasing corsets in order to conserve metal.

Patsy Sherman's role in the invention of Scotchgard™ was a happy mistake. As a research chemist with 3M in 1953, a lab mishap with fluorochemicals lead her to a new discovery. An assistant accidentally dropped a bottle of synthetic latex that Sherman had made, it splashed onto the assistant's white canvas tennis shoes. The substance did not change the look of the shoes, it could not be washed away by any solvents, and it repelled water, oil, and other liquids.

Tabitha Babbitt created the circular saw in 1813. It was circular so that the teeth would continue cutting, unlike the straight saws that only cut on the pull and not the push motion. Her other building innovations, like machine-cut nails instead of individually hand-crafted nails. As a Massachusetts Shaker community member, she helped create tool innovations for furniture making. She lived a simple Shaker life and never applied for patents.

The inventor of "Mistake-Out," "Liquid Paper," or "White-Out" was *Betty Nesmith Graham*. Graham got an idea she had seen done by sign painters, which was to add another layer of paint to cover-up mistakes. She used a kitchen blender to mix-up her first batch of substance to cover-up over mistakes made on paper at work in a Dallas, TX bank.

After much experimenting and then being fired for spending so much time distributing her product as a trial, she received a patent in 1958. In 1979, six months before her death she sold Liquid Paper to the Gillette Corporation for USD $47.5 million. (She was also the mother of musician and producer Michael Nesmith of The Monkees)

Sarah E. Goode was granted a US patent in 1885 for the invention of the foldaway bed. The bed could be folded into a cabinet while it was not in use. It made an attractive piece of furniture that could also be used as a roll top desk or a stationary shelf. The idea for her invention came out of necessity of the times.

Most people she knew lived in small homes or studios and these residents had a minimum amount of habitable space. Many of her customers complained of not having enough room to store things much less to add furniture. Versions of her original bed design are still made today.

Dr. Maria Telkes was a biophysicist who invented the first home solar heating system. She grew up in Hungary and moved to the US in 1925. She became an American citizen after receiving her Doctorate in physical chemistry. Telkes' other solar-powered inventions included a distilling system for life rafts and a solar oven.

Ruth Handler, along with co-founding the renowned toy company Mattel, she also designed the doll that would become an American cultural icon.

While watching her daughter play with paper dolls, Ruth noticed that she and her friends used the dolls to act out the future rather than the present. She set out to invent a grown-up, three-dimensional doll that girls could use to act out their dreams. The female inventor named her new Barbie doll invention after the nickname of her daughter Barbara. Later on, a male counterpart doll would be named after her son, Ken.

After premiering at the Toy Fair in 1959, Barbie became an instant sensation. The success of the doll propelled Mattel to become a publicly owned company that soon made Fortune's list of the 500 largest U.S. industrial companies. Handler served as the company's president for several of its most successful years.

Stephanie Kwolek invented Kevlar, a tough durable material now used to make bulletproof vests. For years she worked on the process at DuPont and in 1963, she got the rod-like molecules in fibers to line up in one direction. This made the material stronger than others, where molecules were arranged in bundles. In fact, the new material was as strong as steel.

Kwolek's technology also went on to be used for making suspension bridge cables, helmets, brake pads, skis, and camping gear.

Patricia Bath, MD patented in 1988, a new method of removing cataracts. The medical laser instrument made the procedure more accurate and is termed the cataract Laserphacoprobe. As a laser scientist and inventor, she has 5 patents on the laser cataract surgery device.

Rachel Zimmerman's Blissymbol Printer is a software program invented by the Canadian 12-year-old in the mid-1980s. The printer enables those with severe physical disabilities, like cerebral palsy to communicate. The user records their thoughts by touching symbols on a page or board through the use of a special touch pad, the printer then translates the symbols into a written language.

Zimmerman's system started as a project for a school science fair, but ended up competing and winning a silver medal in a nationwide contest and received the YTV Television Youth Achievement Award.

Sally Fox invented Foxfibre cotton during the 1980s, naturally colored cotton could be directly spun on a machine. Before her development, coloring cotton was a long and laborious process that businesses instead chose to take white cotton, bleach it, dye it and spin it on a machine. This produced the colored fabrics people wanted, but also created pollution through the bleaching and dying processes.

While working as a pollinator for a cotton breeder looking to develop more pest-resistant plants, Fox began breeding brown and green cotton by picking out the best seeds that produced the longest fibers and replanting them year after year. Seven years of hand selecting for fiber length and spinning quality produced two varieties protected by Plant Variety Protection Certificates and a United Nations Environmental Program. She improved traditional pest-resistant self-colored cotton to accommodate the modern milling process.

By the early 1990s, she produced naturally colored cotton for major companies like Levi's, Espirit, Land's End and L.L. Bean. Fox is now evaluating the practice of coating sheep to protect their wool from excessive vegetable matter.

Margaret Knight created a machine to cut, fold, and glue square bottoms to paper bags and gained a patent for it in 1871, but not without a lawsuit against a fellow who stole her idea. She had the drawings to prove the invention was hers and she won the case. Knight's career with inventions started at age 12, when she developed a stop-motion device that immediately brought industrial machines to a halt if something was caught in them. Over the course of her lifetime, she was awarded more than 26 patents.

GEOGRAPHY FACTS

Greenland and Australia - Australia is a continent and also the largest island. Greenland is the second largest island, but not a continent.

There are several accepted factors that classify continents. These factors include tectonic independence from other continents, unique flora and fauna, cultural uniqueness, and local belief in continental status.

Australia rests on its own tectonic plate called the Australian Plate. It has its own unique flora and fauna, with native animals unlike any others in the world. Its inhabitants consider themselves to live on both an island and a continent.

Greenland rests on the North American tectonic plate along with Canada, the United States, and Mexico. It has a number of unique species of plants, but its animals, like reindeer, polar bears, and arctic foxes, can also be found elsewhere. Greenland has its own culture, but considered part of the larger North American arctic culture. Its inhabitants consider themselves islanders.

Australia is part of Britain's Commonwealth and Greenland is officially part of Denmark.

Australia is about 3 million square miles and the sixth largest country in the world. Greenland is about 834 thousand square miles and the twelfth largest country in the world.

Eighty percent of Greenland is covered by ice. Eighteen percent of Australia is covered by deserts.

84% of Greenlanders live in urban areas and 89% of Australians live in urban areas.

Greenland's one major city is its capital, Nuuk. Inhabitants of both live mostly along the coast.

Greenland's population is 89% Inuit and 11% Danish. Australia's population is 92% white, 7% Asian, and 1% Aboriginal.

There are almost 6 migrants leaving Greenland per 1,000 people. In Australia, there are almost 6 migrants entering the country per 1,000 people.

Russia's Caucasus - The area is responsible for people being called Caucasian. It all began in the late 1700s when German anthropologist Johann Friedrich Blumenbach divided Homo sapiens into five distinct 'varieties' based on their physical characteristics. There was the Mongolian or yellow variety, the red American variety, the brown Malayan variety, the black Ethiopian variety, and the white Caucasian variety.

Caucasians are some or all of the populations of Europe, North Africa, the Horn of Africa, Western Asia/Middle East, Asia Minor, and Central Asia. The name stems from the Caucasus Mountain Range, where the people who most resembled his definition came from. He did not specifically say they were just white. He described the characteristics as color white, cheeks rosy, hair brown or chestnut-colored, head subglobular, face oval straight, its parts moderately defined, forehead smooth, nose narrow slightly hooked, and mouth small.

The term 'Caucasian race' was coined by German philosopher Christoph Meiners in 1785. In Meiners' racial classification, there were only two racial divisions, Caucasians and Mongolians.

Currently, Caucasian lacks any real scientific meaning, but is commonly used, especially on TV cop shows, as a blanket term, for white/European people. Caucasoid is the new term anthropologists use.

The US court, in Ozawa v. United States declared skin color was irrelevant in determining whether or not a person could be classified as 'white' and instead emphasized ancestry. The United States National Library of Medicine discontinued using Caucasian in favor of the geographical term "European", which traditionally only applied to a subset of Caucasoids.

Bottom line - the terms used for race, 'variety', ethnicity, and other characteristics of humans is not currently universally agreed to. I tend to agree with Shakespeare view, "Beauty is in the eye of the beholder".

Canada Facts - Canada is the world's second-largest country by total area, and its common border with the United States is the world's longest land border. It has ten provinces and three territories located in the northern part of North America. It extends from the Atlantic to the Pacific, northward into the Arctic Ocean (just south of Greenland), and borders on the south with The US. Its capital is Ottawa and its population of about 35 million is about one tenth the size of the US population. *The top five largest countries in order are: Russia, Canada, China, United States, and Brazil.*

The current Canadian flag is fifty years old. On December 15, 1964 the Canadian Parliament voted to accept the current maple leaf design. The official flag was hoisted for the first time February 15, 1965. Two years later, Canada celebrated its 100th anniversary and used the occasion to promote the new flag.

The maple leaf design by George Stanley and John Matheson is based on the flag of the Royal Military College of Canada. February 15 is now celebrated annually as National Flag of Canada Day.

Canada is a federal state governed as a parliamentary democracy and a constitutional monarchy, with Queen Elizabeth II as its head of state. However, Canada has complete sovereignty as an independent country and the Queen's role as monarch of Canada is separate from her role as the British monarch or the monarch of any of the other Commonwealth realms.

The Canada Act of 1982, among other provisions formally ended the British parliament having power to pass laws extending to Canada at its own request.

In 1958, a US high school student, Bob Heft designed the current US flag for a class project and received a B- grade. He also designed a flag with 51 stars, just in case. The current United States flag has been used since July 4, 1960.

Driest and Wettest - Parts of Antarctica have had no rain for two million years, so it is considered the driest place on earth.

A desert is technically defined as a place that receives less than 254 mm (10 inches) of rain a year. The Sahara desert gets just 25 mm (1 inch) of rain a year.

Antarctica's average annual rainfall is about the same, but 2 per cent of it, known as the Dry Valleys, is free of ice and snow and it never rains there.

Antarctica can also claim to be the wettest; since seventy per cent of the world's fresh water is found there in the form of ice.

The next-driest place in the world is the Atacama Desert in Chile. In some areas, no rain has fallen there for 400 years and its average annual rainfall is 0.1 mm (0.004 inches).

Size of England and UK - England makes up about half the total area of the UK. It is also about the size of the state of Alabama. You could fit about three of the entire United Kingdom in the state of Texas.

Drain the Mediterranean - During the 1920s, Herman Sorgel, a German architect, proposed creating a dam across the Strait of Gibraltar, turning the area into a massive hydroelectric plant, creating enormous amounts of renewable energy.

A natural byproduct of the dam would be to drain much of the Mediterranean Sea by restricting the flow of water into it. The idea was to create much new land for Germany to grow into. They called the project Alantropa.

During the early 1900s, many German leaders were espousing a political science theory called Lebensraum, literally "space of life." Lebensraum advocates argued that overpopulation required a solution, and that solution should simply be to acquire more space. While the easiest and most straightforward way to spread is to take over the land of others, there could be another way, to create new land. Doing so would require a public works project larger than anything the world has ever seen, like draining the Mediterranean Sea.

Sorgel's top objective was to stem the flow of water into the Mediterranean and over time, the water level would drop, creating more inhabitable land in both Southern Europe and Northern Africa. Low-lying lands would emerge basically everywhere, as hundreds of square miles of habitable space would be reclaimed from the sea. Europe and Northern Africa would, effectively, merge.

The Atlantropa Project's support was strongest toward the end of the 1920s and into the 1930s, but waned as Hitler rose to power and in 1942, the Nazis banned Sorgel from publishing his plans further. Atlantropa sunk.

Tokyo - It is one of the 47 prefectures of Japan and is the capital of Japan, the center of the Greater Tokyo Area, and the largest metropolitan area in the world. It is the seat of the Japanese government and the Imperial Palace, and the home of the Japanese Imperial Family.

Tokyo is often thought of as a city, but is commonly referred to as a metropolitan prefecture. The prefecture is part of the world's most populous metropolitan area with over 35 million people and the world's largest urban agglomeration economy. *Canada has a fewer people than the Tokyo island metropolitan area.*

Debunking Myths

Aluminum Foil Myth

The old myth was that aluminum foil and cookware is linked to Alzheimer's Disease and it has been around since the 1980s.

This myth has its roots in research from the 1960s and 1970s that showed elevated levels of aluminum in the brains of Alzheimer's patients. For years people were warned off of aluminum pots and pans, and even aluminum foil to store food.

Since those studies a great deal of research has been done into what possible connections aluminum may have with Alzheimer's Disease, and failed to show any substantive link or connection between aluminum and risk for Alzheimer's Disease.

Most experts now believe any aluminum absorbed by the body is processed by the kidneys, urinated out, and it does not pose a threat for Alzheimer's Disease.

Bat Myths

Bats eyes are very functional. Bats' retinas have an abundance of rods (a prerequisite for night vision) and also two types of cones: the ordinary, that serves them well in daylight conditions, and UV-sensitive that gives them night vision. Bats use, but do not depend exclusively on their sonar. Some bats can see better than others, but none are blind. Some varieties of bats can see color and others can only see black and white.

Bats groom themselves by meticulously licking and scratching themselves and each other for hours. Bats are the only mammals that can fly. An average bat lives about thirty years.

Out of the 900 species of bats, there are only three vampire bats in the entire world and they are generally found in South America. The remaining species of bats over the world feed off of fruit, nectar, pollen, and insects.

Energy Drink Facts and Myths

A friend of mine, Jeff Flanagan wondered what is in energy drinks that makes them work and are they safe. That sent me scouring my personal stash and the web for answers. The following excludes the larger volume drinks, such as Monster, Red Bull, etc., and offerings from Pepsi, Coke, and others. Those all have their own host of reasons to avoid, but that is for another discussion.

Most of the two ounce shot energy drinks contain varying amounts of taurine, caffeine, sucralose (splenda), niacin, vitamin B12, B6, folic acid, sodium, acai fruit extract, guarana, and many other ingredients that are almost impossible to spell or pronounce. Others have green tea, L-carnitine, ginseng, yohimbine, and all contain water and natural and artificial ingredients (*whatever that means*). Most have zero calories listed. Many have warning not to take more than one every four or six hours (likely in self defense from the FDA).

Many are described as an energy shot to enhance concentration and improve performance. They do not specify what performance. A number of them are designed specifically for hangover relief, and a few for diet suppression. The only difference I could find in these ingredients was more vitamin B12 (in one type 10,000% of the daily value). Some of the names are 'pure energy, 5-hour energy', 'eternal energy, 'extra energy', 'Extra strength energy', 'java-mite', 'XX Energy', 'high energy', 'hangover recovery, 'diet aid', etc.

The majority of the dozen I checked come in little white two ounce bottles covered with shrink wrap covers. Interesting that so many have the identical bottle (with the exception of the bottom indents) and wrapper type regardless of manufacturer. Could find no common denominator other than that. Prices ranged from as low as $.88 to $3.98 for the same size. Also interesting to note that one of the most popular and most expensive, 5 hour energy has the least liquid at 1.93 ounces.

Most sites agreed the biggest reason for the jolt is the large amount of caffeine, about as much as two cups of coffee in a small two ounce dose. Studies show they are no better as a pickup than coffee, although they are concentrated in less liquid as well as more convenient and quicker to drink. Annual revenue for energy drinks is about US 13 billion dollars.

Bottom line, the caffeine is the kicker, the vitamins go out in the urine, the other ingredients are for flavor, preservatives, and color. None have proven to be bad for us, probably due to the trace amounts contained. None are good for children for the same reasons as coffee.

In spite of a few rantings by the usual fear mongers, these have yet to be proven unsafe, with the exception of occasional jitters common to those who do not well tolerate caffeine. *In my case, they seem to work as advertised and do not provide any physically noticeable high or low.*

Velcro Myth

Some say that Velcro was invented by NASA for the space program. Not true, Velcro was already commercially available before being used by NASA. It did receive a huge boost in popularity after being used by NASA on parts of astronaut's space suits as well as used to allow astronaut's to store things along the walls of their space craft. Because of this, similar to Tang, it is a common misconception that Velcro was invented by or for NASA.

High-Fructose Corn Syrup (HFCS) and Obesity Myth

HFCS entered the American food supply in the 1970s and the rates of obesity began to rise about the same time. Consequently, many blame HFCS.

However, the calories in HFCS are no different from those in refined white sugar. The makeup of HFCS (55 percent fructose and 45 percent glucose) is close to that of white sugar (50 percent fructose and 50 percent glucose) and our bodies digest HFCS and sugar in very similar ways. Nutritionally speaking, the two are virtually identical.

Interesting Fact: Coca Cola produced in Mexico is still made with sugar (as opposed to corn syrup in the US), and many people claim to be able to taste the difference, but after numerous tests, results vary widely in their conclusions.

Wood Cutting Board Myth

Never Use Wooden Cutting Boards with Meat comes from the thought that using a wooden cutting board will result in tiny scratches and cuts from your knife, and if you use that cutting board with meat, especially raw meat, all those meat juices will settle into the tiny cuts in the board and cause germs. The solution proposed is to use plastic cutting boards, which can be dishwashed and sanitized, and therefore must be safer.

There is much research that disputes this myth. One of the most famous studies was conducted by Dean O. Cliver, Ph.D of the UC-Davis Food Safety Laboratory. His research points out that there is no significant antibacterial benefit from using a plastic cutting board over a wood one. He notes that even if you apply bacteria to a wooden cutting board, its natural properties cause the bacteria to pass through the top layer of the wood and settle inside, where they are very difficult to bring out unless you split the board open.

Although the bacteria that disappeared from the wood surfaces are found alive inside the wood for some time, they do not multiply and gradually die. They can be detected only by splitting or gouging the wood or by forcing water completely through from one surface to the other. If a sharp knife is used to cut into the work surfaces after used, plastic or wood has been contaminated with bacteria and cleaned manually, more bacteria are recovered from a used plastic surface than from a used wood surface.

Dr. Cliver's study tested 10 different hardwoods and 4 different plastic polymers. It found, if you want a plastic cutting board, anti-bacterial property is no reason to buy one. If you want a wooden cutting board, bacterial infection should not scare you away.

Bottom line: It is more important that you properly clean and disinfect whatever board you buy, regardless of what it is made of. Cutting boards touted as being coated or made with anti-microbial chemicals or materials are mostly not.

Cracking Another Egg Myth

The nutritional value of the egg and its yolk has been debated by nutritionists for years. Years ago, the egg received a bad reputation with regard to cardiovascular health, as one large egg contains approximately 187 milligrams of cholesterol. However, most research has shown that cholesterol found in foods is not fully to blame for increased LDL cholesterol in the body.

"Eggs are an animal product, and they do contain cholesterol, but actually, cholesterol in foods does not affect our blood cholesterol as much as saturated fat does. Cholesterol in food, in general you do want to avoid, but it is not necessarily the main culprit of high cholesterol." Lisa Cimperman, registered dietician for UH Case Medical Center.

Compared to other animal products, the average egg actually contains relatively low amounts of saturated fats – approximately 1.6 grams per egg yolk. Additionally, various studies from the Harvard School of Public Health and the British Nutrition Foundation have found that eggs have clinically insignificant effects on blood cholesterol, and are not associated with an increased risk of cardiovascular disease.

Many consumers are still concerned over the yolk's fatty content, so rather than eat the full egg; they often eat just the egg's albumin, the egg white. However, some dieticians argue it is important to consume both the egg's fat and protein, as the combination can have positive health benefits for blood sugar.

"You want the fat, because it not only satiates you, but also slows the absorption of your food, so you stay fuller longer, and it won't increase blood sugar. A lot of people have toast with just egg whites, but it's giving them a quicker rise in their blood sugar, but if you have the yolk with it or a different form of fat like avocado, your blood sugar won't rise as quickly, because it takes longer to break the food down." Laura Cipullo registered dietician. Egg yolks are a good source of vitamin A and iron, along with a host of other nutrients. Eggs are also good sources of B vitamin, thiamine, and selenium. *Eggs also pair very well with bacon.*

Folding Paper Myth

The statement, "you can't fold a piece of paper in half more than 7 times has been around for a long time." Many still believe it.

However, in 2002 a US high school student Britney Gallivan bought a large roll of toilet paper on the internet and along with her family took it to the local mall, where they toiled for seven hours and folded it into 12 folds. She also folded a piece of thin gold leaf more than 7 times with the use of tweezers.

De-oxygenated Blood Turns Blue Myth

The common misconception that blood which lacks oxygen turns blue probably comes from the fact that veins appear blue and blood in the veins is typically heading back to the lungs, hence depleted of oxygen.

People who perpetuate this myth often claim that the reason we never see blood in its blue form is that the instant we get cut, the blood is exposed to oxygen and instantly turns red. However, when you get blood drawn from your veins that isn't exposed to air, it is dark red.

When blood is deprived of oxygen it actually just turns dark red. When it is oxygenated, it turns a brighter red. The red color primarily comes from the hemoglobin, which contains four heme groups. These heme group's interactions with various molecules end up giving it the dark red or light red color we see. The hemoglobin itself is a protein that binds with oxygen to be distributed throughout the body in blood.

Veins are very close to the surface of skin. This location under the skin is largely why veins appear blue despite the fact that the blood is dark red. This is from the way light diffuses in the skin. Veins appear blue from the way subcutaneous fat absorbs low-frequency light. This permits only high frequency blue and violet wavelengths to penetrate through the skin to the vein, with the other wavelengths getting filtered off from the pigmentation of your skin.

If a person has darker or lighter skin the veins tend to appear green or brown. People with extremely light skin, such as an albino, will typically have veins that show up as dark purple or red, more closely resembling the actual color of the blood running through the veins.

Antibiotics and Drinking Myth

With the advent of antibiotics to treat sexually transmitted diseases came a word of advice: don't drink while taking the pills. The reason given - it will stop the medication working. This is not true.

Most antibiotics are not hindered in any way by the consumption of alcohol, though it may cause a stomach upset depending on the type. In fact, only five of the more than one hundred types of antibiotics really do have adverse effects when taken with alcohol.

The real reason for telling people not to drink is that people suffering from STDs would most likely be the type to have casual sex when drunk. Stopping drinking for a short period of time would often help to prevent them from spreading their illness before others caught it.

Less than five of the more than one hundred types of antibiotics do have adverse effects when taken with alcohol. *Obviously, moderation in all things is the key.*

Mice and Cheese Myth

Mice do not really like cheese and they will even actively shy away from certain types of cheese.

According to Dr. David Holmes of Manchester Metropolitan University who recently did a study on whether mice liked cheese or not, while hungry mice will pretty much eat anything (even cardboard), most types of mice strongly prefer grains, fruits, and sweet things. Certain types of mice will also eat insects and other small animals.

Basically, they like to eat what they have been accustomed to eating since before humans started making cheese around 10,000 years ago.

Many mice also like peanut butter and sweet chocolate. *Unrelated, but interesting to know that mouse urine glows under florescent light.*

Eight Glasses of Water Myth

Drinking eight glasses of water a day is believed by about three fourths of adults with no reliable clinical evidence to support it.

One study on this myth was conducted in 2002 by Heinz Valtin, a Dartmouth Medical School physician and kidney specialist, who researched the subject. He believed that the statement supporting the eight glasses belief is taken from the Food and Nutrition Board of the National Research Council. It grossly misrepresented the facts by removing facts from the original context. The sentence that followed it stated, "most of this quantity is contained in prepared foods," which was left out and led to the false interpretation that the requirement needed to be fulfilled by drinking water alone.

After 45 years of studying the biological system that keeps the water in our bodies in balance, Valtin concluded that drinking such large amounts of water is absolutely not needed. He pointed out a number of published experiments that attest to the capability of the human body for maintaining proper water balance from sources other than directly drinking water which may include drinks such as tea, coffee, and soft drinks, as well as prepared foods.

Most foods have some water content. For example, apples: 85%, bean sprouts: 92%, boiled chicken: 71%, raw cucumbers: 96%, lettuce: 96%, potatoes: 85%, roast turkey: 62%, etc.

The bottom line is that the body lets us know when we need more water by making us feel thirsty. People who have specific health concerns, such as kidney stones or urinary tract infections require drinking large amounts of water. Other reasons for drinking water, such as before meals to curb an appetite is its own benefit.

Further scientific evidence also debunks the myth that by the time you feel thirsty, you are already dehydrated. A number of scientific studies have confirmed there is no support for this. Thirst hits long before we are near risk for dehydration and most folks thirst mechanism kicks in when the osmolality of the blood plasma is less than 2%, and dehydration begins at osmolalities of 5% and higher. *I'll drink to that.*

Dissolving Tooth Myth

Here is another common myth debunked. The most popular Coke myth is that if you were to leave a tooth in a cup of coke overnight by morning the tooth would be completely dissolved. Like most of the other legends involving Coke, this has been proven totally untrue.

Shampoo Myth

Hair products, like shampoo and conditioner are mostly useless and cannot physically change your hair. The hair that is visible on the human body is dead hair and live hair is beneath the surface of the skin. Nothing you add to the visible hair can actually make it healthier. Also, no hair products can repair split ends.

Some hair products may add the artificial appearance of shine or color and for most, that is sufficient.

Junk Food Diet Myth

Junk food is commonly associated with a coffee break and this junk food diet works. Nutritionist Mark Haub went on a junk food diet to determine if he could eat almost nothing but junk food and still lose weight. His theory was that weight loss is primarily tied to calorie intake, rather than what type of food you eat. He stuck to an 1,800 calorie per day diet of mostly Twinkies, Donuts, Doritos, Oreos, and sugary cereals. He also drank a protein shake and took a multivitamin.

During the two months of his diet, his body mass index dropped from 28.8 to 24.9 and he lost 27 pounds, dropping from 201 pounds to 174 pounds.

In addition to his weight loss, bad cholesterol levels dropped 20% over his normal healthy diet and his good cholesterol levels increased by 20%. He even dropped 39% on his bad fat levels, including triglycerides. *This does debunk a number of other "fad" diet claims and proves it is calorie volume that counts when trying to lose weight.*

German Chocolate Cake Isn't

German chocolate cake is actually named for Sam German, the American who invented a dark baking chocolate when he worked for the American Baker's Chocolate Company in 1852.

However, Germany has been instrumental in the advancement of many desserts, with contributions that include lebkuchen or spicy gingerbread, apple strudel, stollen, which is similar to fruitcake, and of course, the Berliner, which we call the jelly doughnut. Christmas has many more German specialties, not the least of which are rum ball cookies.

Exploding Phone Myth

We might as well dispel another popular myth that has been hanging around since at least 1999. The myth says that explosions in gas stations have been caused by cellphone use.

Emails were purported to have been sent by Shell Oil and others, but this was proven false.

There never has been a documented case of a cellphone causing an explosion at a gas station, no one has been able to prove that it is even possible in scientific testing. The American Petroleum Institute said, "We can find no evidence of someone using a cellphone causing any kind of accident, no matter how small, at a gas station anywhere in the world." Mythbusters TV program even tried and could not find a way to make it happen.

Police and firefighters often assume a connection between the two could be valid, but have never followed up with proof. The city of Cicero, Illinois (with no evidence to back it up) has made the use of cellphones at gas stations illegal. *So, is it possible, but it has never happened yet with almost seven billion cellphones in use.*

Warm Beer Myth

The myth says if cold beer gets warm, cooling it again will make it stale. This myth was started by marketing people. Beer experiences substantial fluctuations in temperature during shipping. Although excessive heat will ruin beer, the notion that beer can only be refrigerated once is a complete myth.

Diamonds are Formed from Coal Myth

According to evolutionists and geologists, diamonds were formed about 1 to 3 billion years ago, much earlier than any known record of Earth's first land plants. Coal is formed from the dead remains of vegetation, such as trees and plants. The formation of coal takes millions of years and can be traced back 300 to 400 million years, but not a billion years.

Coal is an amorphous form of carbon and at the most can change its chemical composition and transform into its nearly purest form which is Graphite, but not diamond. The conversion of coal into diamond is almost impossible due to its impurities and the fact that coal is rarely found at depths greater than two miles which is not conducive to the formation of diamonds. In addition, coal seams are sedimentary rocks that usually occur as horizontal or nearly horizontal rock units. The source rocks of diamonds are vertical pipes filled with igneous rocks.

Natural diamonds require depths of 87 to 120 miles in the Earth's mantle, very high temperatures, and resulting pressure that exists at those depths to form. Unlike other gems which are formed by a combination of elements, diamonds are made up of one single element, Carbon. Carbon-containing minerals present in the Earth at those depths, crystallize to form diamonds, because of the immense pressure together with the heat from molten magma.

The diamond crystals, along with other minerals are transported to the earth's surface during deep-source volcanic eruptions in the magma. This is quite a rare occurrence as diamonds are formed at depths usually 3 to 4 times deeper than normal volcanoes originate.

Diamonds color is influenced by impurities and can be blue (boron), yellow (nitrogen), brown (lattice defects), green (radiation exposure), purple, pink, orange, red, and grades of those colors. Red diamonds are the rarest and most exotic diamonds and the most expensive.

When this magma cools, it forms igneous rocks known as kimberlites and lamproites, used as an indicator by geologists that diamonds may be found in the area. The Kimberlites form narrow pipe shaped fissures which are also referred to as diamond pipes. Many of the pipes are also rich sources of garnets. The most prominent kimberlites are located in South and Central Africa, which contribute almost half of the natural diamonds mined in the World. Over 500 kimberlite deposits have also been found in Northern Canada.

Africa, Russia, Australia, and Canada are the largest diamond producing countries. *Diamonds are not in short supply and are a terrible investment, because there is no aftermarket.*

Dog Years Myth

Most of us have heard one dog year is equal to seven human years. This bogus fact is usually worked out so that a dog life is equal to a human life in total years, but the numbers do not add up. The average human life expectancy is 78, while the average dog life expectancy in dog years would equal around 90 years.

Furthermore, different dog breeds have dramatically different life expectancies, ranging from a short 6 years to 13 or more years. In general, the smaller the dog, the longer its life expectancy. *Well, I'll be doggoned.*

Touching Birds and Eggs Myth

Many of us have heard that handling a baby bird or bird egg will cause the parent birds to reject it.

Most birds have a very poor sense of smell, so they are unable to notice human scent on baby birds (even a skunk's spray does not seem to bother many types of birds). In most cases, even if the nest is destroyed by wind or other means, you could create a new one and put all the nestlings back in it and the parents would not care that their baby birds were in a different nest when they come back; so long as the new nest is near where the old one was so they can find it.

Ducks and Hoopoe will often poop on their own eggs with particularly smelly discharge to discourage predators from eating them.

Ostriches Bury Their Heads Myth

This is one of those myths that is accepted as fact without question. People generally believe this is something the birds do when danger is near.

Ostriches do run if they feel that danger is approaching, but they also have a powerful kick to defend themselves. Ostriches may hold their heads low in an attempt to be harder to see, but they do not actually bury their heads.

Tongue Myth

The tongue does not have zones specializing in specific tastes. It turns out this myth started when Harvard Psychologist Edwin G. Boring mistranslated a German paper written in 1901 titled "Zur Psychophysik des Geschmackssinnes." The tongue paper, written by German Scientist D.P. Hanig, outlined Hanig's research on the four known basic tastes. He put together a group of subjects and tested the main tastes on each of them on various parts of their tongues until he figured he had a good map put together on where they tasted various tastes the most.

This myth endured until the 1970's when scientists tested tongue maps and debunked Hanig's paper.

Poinsettia Poison Myth

Myths and rumors about the toxicity of the poinsettia plant are common late in the year, when the popular red-leaved plants take center stage in holiday decorations. While the genus (Euphorbia) to which the poinsettia plant belongs does contain some highly toxic plants, the popular poinsettia itself is not toxic. Some sources attribute the rumor about the dangers of poinsettia leaves to a case of poisoning in 1919 that led to the death of a two year-old child. At the time, the cause of the poisoning was incorrectly determined to be a poinsettia leaf.

Contact with the sap of a poinsettia plant may cause a mild, itchy rash. If this happens, wash the affected area with soap and water and apply a cool compress to ease itching. Eating the leaves or stems of a poinsettia plant may cause a mild stomachache, vomiting, or diarrhea, but severe signs and symptoms are unlikely.

A 50 pound child would need to eat about 500-600 leaves or about 20 ounces of the bitter tasting leaves of a poinsettia plant before any medical action would be necessary.

Rapture Myth

The "Rapture" is not in the Bible. Despite being believed by a large number of protestants (many of whom also believe only that which is in the Bible can be true) it was actually invented in the 1600s by Cotton Mather, otherwise famous for murdering women by hanging them during the Salem witch trials.

The term in the Bible commonly mistranslated to the word "rapture" comes from the Greek ἁρπάζω (harpazo) which actually means "caught up" or "taken away" and it refers to one person only, Philip.

Three Kings Myths

The feast of The Three Kings, or Epiphany is January 6. The famous "three kings" from the Biblical birth of Christ narrative were not:

Three in number - the number is not mentioned.

Kings – Likely from Psalm 71:11 (72:11 in protestant bibles): "And all kings of the earth shall adore him: all nations shall serve him."

Traveling on camels - Matthew 2:1–2 says: "When Jesus therefore was born in Bethlehem of Juda, in the days of king Herod, behold, there came wise men from the east to Jerusalem." It says a little later that they offered Him gifts of "gold, frankincense, and myrrh." Since there were three gifts, the number of wise men has been assumed to be three. In the East, the number is twelve.

Historical references depict the three variously as scholars, or noblemen, or kings. *Incidentally, Magi is the origin of the word magic.*

Candy Cane Myths and Facts

The myth is the white base color of the candy cane symbolizes Jesus' purity; the red stripes symbolize Jesus' blood when he died on the cross; and the J shape was chosen to represent the J in Jesus. These and all other religious connotations have been debunked or not able to be proven as fact.

The facts - Candy canes started as white sugar sticks with no hook as early as the 1600s. There is no reference to calling them candy 'canes' until the mid to late 1600s. No fact as to why the sticks were changed into canes, although many believe it was so the candy could be hung on a Christmas tree.

The red stripe was not added until the early 1900s. No one knows who invented the stripes, but Christmas cards prior to the year 1900 showed only all-white candy canes. Christmas cards after 1900 showed illustrations of striped candy canes.

The bottom line is that we do not know who started making them, why, or who added the hook, but most people love candy canes and that is a fact.

Myth: Earth is Close to Overpopulation

This is a myth has been around since the 18th century, but the world is a really big place with plenty of space.

Let's look at how much land it really takes to hold 6 billion people. To give you an idea, consider the small nation of Japan, which has about 143,000 square miles of land. One square mile has 27.9 million square feet. Japan has a total of about 4 trillion square feet, enough to give each person on earth 670 square feet. If we housed people in families of four in simple two-level buildings (8 people per building, one family of four per level), each building could be on a lot of over 5300 square feet.

Using the American average of 8,000 square feet to house four people, the entire population of the planet would fit into a space the size of Texas and Nevada combined or less than the state of Alaska. That leaves a bunch of unused space for growing crops, sailing, and going on vacations. *Incidentally, Tokyo has more people living there than the total population of Canada.*

Snake Charm Myth

Snakes do not hear and react to music. Snake charmers play their flute and snakes appear to sway to the music, charmed by the soothing notes. Snakes can feel vibrations, but while the sway appears to be from the music, they are actually responding to the movements made by the snake charmer and not the sound of the flute.

Seven Common Quotes Debunked

Wrong - Money is the root of all evil.
Correct - "For the love of money is the root of all evil."

Wrong - Nice guys finish last.
Correct - "Why, they're the nicest guys in the world! And where are they? In seventh place!"

Wrong - Play it again, Sam.
Correct - "Play it once Sam. . . play it, Sam."

Wrong - Theirs not to reason why, theirs but to do or die.
Correct - "Theirs not to reason why, theirs but to do <u>and</u> die."

Wrong - Hell hath no fury like a woman scorned.
Correct - "Heav'n has no rage, like love to hatred turn'd/Nor hell a fury, like a woman scorn'd."

Wrong - Houston, we have a problem.
Correct - "Houston, we've had a problem"

Wrong - Mirror, mirror on the wall, who's the fairest of them all?
Correct - "Magic Mirror, on the wall, who is the fairest of them all?"

They Never Said That

Sherlock Holmes Never Said, "Elementary, My Dear Watson."
Captain Kirk never said, "Beam me up Scotty."
Darth Vader never said, "Luke, I am your father".

They said things that were similar, but they never actually said those exact words.

Famous Last Words

"I should never have switched from Scotch to Martinis." Humphrey Bogart

"Dammit. Don't you dare ask God to help me." Joan Crawford to her housekeeper who began to pray aloud.

"Hey, fellas! How about this for a headline for tomorrow's paper? 'French Fries'!" James French, a convicted murderer sentenced to the electric chair to members of the press who were to witness his execution.

Epitaphs - To end on a happy note, here are the epitaphs of my heroes.

Stan Laurel
A master of comedy
His genius in the art of humor
Brought gladness
To the world he loved.

Oliver Hardy
A genius of comedy
His talent brought joy and
Laughter to all the world.

and

Mel Blanc
"That's All Folks!"
The Man of a Thousand Voices

Index

INDEX

www.ingramcontent.com/pod-product-compliance
Lightning Source LLC
Chambersburg PA
CBHW030420290526
45786CB00001B/65